REPARENTING
THE
INNER CHILD

ALSO BY DR NICOLE LePERA

How to Do the Work
How to Be the Love You Seek
How to Meet Your Self

REPARENTING THE INNER CHILD

THE NEW SCIENCE OF OUR OLDEST WOUNDS AND HOW TO HEAL THEM

DR NICOLE LePERA

First published in the United States of America in 2026 by Flatiron Books
First published in Great Britain in 2026 by Orion Spring,
an imprint of The Orion Publishing Group Ltd
Carmelite House, 50 Victoria Embankment
London EC4Y 0DZ

An Hachette UK Company

The authorised representative in the EEA is Hachette Ireland, 8 Castlecourt Centre, Dublin 15, D15 XTP3, Ireland (email: info@hbgi.ie)

1 3 5 7 9 10 8 6 4 2

Copyright © JuniorTine Productions 2026

The moral right of Dr Nicole LePera to be identified as the author of this work has been asserted in accordance with the Copyright, Designs and Patents Act of 1988.

All rights reserved. No part of this publication may be reproduced, stored in a retrieval system, or transmitted in any form or by any means, electronic, mechanical, photocopying, recording, or otherwise, without the prior permission of both the copyright owner and the above publisher of this book.

A CIP catalogue record for this book is available from the British Library.

Shame Spiral illustration courtesy of the author

Designed by Leah Carlson-Stanisic

ISBN (Hardback) 978 1 3987 2543 0
ISBN (Export Trade Paperback) 978 1 3987 2544 7
ISBN (Ebook) 978 1 3987 2546 1
ISBN (Audio) 978 1 3987 2547 8

Printed and bound in Great Britain by Clays Ltd, Elcograf S.p.A.

www.orionbooks.co.uk

To little Nicole, who was always enough exactly as she was

CONTENTS

Author's Note   xi

Introduction 1

PART ONE
YOUR INNER CHILD

1. Beyond Attachment Style 17
2. Your Origin Story 46

PART TWO
THE IMPACT OF YOUR ENVIRONMENT

3. The Truth About Stress 93
4. The Traces of Your Ancestors 112
5. The Culture That Shaped You 130

PART THREE
THE SCARS WE CARRY

6. Your Wounded Inner Child 153
7. The Shadow of Shame 188

PART FOUR
REPARENTING AND INTEGRATION

8. The Total Healing Tool 221
9. Becoming Whole..................................... 283
10. Building Resilience 319

Acknowledgments 341
Notes 343
Index 349

AUTHOR'S NOTE

The stories shared in this book come from many sources. Some are composites that reflect common patterns I've encountered in my clients, while others are woven from conversations, shared experiences, or comments in response to a post. Names and identifying details have been changed. What unites them all is that each story is rooted in real experiences, real voices, and real lives.

REPARENTING
THE
INNER CHILD

INTRODUCTION

In my childhood home, there was a staircase that curved at the landing. If I stood on a high enough step, I could grab the upper railing and swing from it like a monkey. I liked to place a beanbag chair at the bottom and launch myself off, landing with a dramatic thud. I loved that split second where I felt light, almost weightless. It wasn't just a game; it was how I moved through the world. My family still jokes about me as a kid, always laughing and saying, "Nicole bounced off the walls!" And it's true. I was always in motion, always doing something, always begging someone to play with me.

From as early as I can remember, I carried this intense, unstoppable energy. It wasn't something I learned; it just seemed to live within me. In childhood, before we're told to sit still, to be quiet, not to take up too much space, we express ourselves with our whole being. I expressed myself by running, leaping, spinning, and flinging my body around. Physical motion was the only language I knew. Before I was taught who I should be, I just *was*.

To keep me busy, my parents signed me up for just about every structured activity they could find—art classes, dance, every sport imaginable. My mom used to joke that if there were eight days in a week, I would've had every one of them scheduled with different activities. These became channels for all that intensity, spaces where my movement and focus were not only allowed but celebrated. I was consistently praised for how "easily things came to me," which made effort feel like evidence of inadequacy and struggle feel like failure. Over time, I learned to stick with the things I was good at, equating worth with performance rather than presence—a pattern that persisted into adulthood.

Even when my body was calm, my mind was never still. At night, I'd lie in bed worrying that my mom might fall asleep and never wake up.

The same energy that showed up during the day as playful movement or constant activity became, in the quiet and darkness, a loop of anxious thoughts—my mind scanning for what might go wrong next. You could call this my nature. But you could also look at the environment I grew up in and begin to trace the connection between that restless drive in my body and the unspoken tension that lived in my childhood home.

I was the youngest in my family by many years—my sister was fifteen when I was born, and my brother was eighteen. My sister had serious health challenges throughout her early childhood and adolescence, which required constant medical attention and multiple major surgeries. Though I was too young to understand the details, the stress around her health shaped the emotional tone of our household. It wasn't just her experience; it was a family experience. As a result, the energy in our home often felt tense, distracted, and preoccupied.

When my sister was eighteen, my family traveled to Cincinnati for one of the big surgeries. While I don't have any memories of the trip itself, I've been told I was there, staying with them at the Ronald McDonald House. While I know my family tried to shelter me from what was happening as best they could—my mom and dad taking turns caring for me and my sister—I was still affected by what was taking place around me. I imagine what it must have felt like for me as a three-year-old: being surrounded by so much uncertainty, by adults who were understandably worried, and by an unspoken sense that something very serious was happening. The surgery was a success, but the emotional imprint of that time settled into me in ways I couldn't name, only feel.

What I do remember is waiting for my mom at daycare. When I was four years old, she enrolled me in a half-day preschool program called Children's Time Out, meant to help "socialize" me. But I didn't adjust well. I spent much of my time hiding under tables, speaking to no one, and counting down the minutes until she came back. Which she always did every day, often arriving five minutes early. When dismissal time came, and I peeked out hoping to see her face, it was always there. Her consistent presence became an anchor for me. But one day, she wasn't on time. I don't know how late she actually was—maybe ten minutes, maybe thirty—but what I *do* remember is the panic. My immediate thought wasn't that she had gotten stuck in traffic or lost track of time. I was certain she had died. My teacher probably had no idea I was scared. I didn't cry. I didn't say anything to anyone. But inside, my heart was racing. I was envisioning my mother's death and worrying about what that would mean for me. That small moment says a lot about how I experienced the world as a young child. Another kid might have seen the delay as a few extra minutes to play. I went straight to loss, to fear, to finality.

A similar experience happened when I was around fourteen. One Christmas week, my family took a ski trip to the Poconos. On the day we arrived, my parents dropped me off at the mountain so I could ski for an hour or two while they went to check in. They told me to meet them outside the main lodge at 4 p.m., when the ski lifts closed for the day. When I showed up at the designated spot, they weren't there. I waited five minutes, maybe less, before the same panic took over. I started running through the ski resort, scared and searching for a pay phone—this was before cell phones existed. I didn't have a way to contact my parents at the rental, so I tried to call my best friend's mom, the only other phone number I had memorized. I couldn't enjoy the mountain, soaking in the snow, the freedom, the fun. I was spiraling into worst-case scenarios—convinced my whole family had been in a car accident, and I'd been left all alone.

On both occasions, of course, my parents were just late. Reasonably late. And when they finally showed up, they brushed off my panic: "What were you so worried about? It's no big deal. We're here now. You're fine."

But I wasn't fine. Not at four, and not at fourteen. I was alone with big, overwhelming feelings and fears that rushed in as soon as anything didn't go as expected. I never found a way to ease my anxiety, so it grew with me. By my twenties, if I couldn't reach a loved one, my first, and often only, thought was that something bad had happened. That reflex didn't come out of nowhere. It came from growing up with a constant sense of crisis. Sometimes the crisis was real—a family member's medical emergencies, or an unexpected financial burden. And even when it wasn't, it felt that way. My parents lived in an ongoing state of stress, and because of that, they couldn't tell the difference between a big problem and a small one. Being short one can of tomato paste for dinner, having misplaced a form for school, or running five minutes late could spark the same chaos as a true emergency. Living this way always left me bracing for something. A phone call or a siren triggered overwhelming feelings of fear that someone I loved was hurt. Our home was so unsettled that I carried that instability with me long after I left it. I startled easily, constantly felt on edge, and had no tools to calm myself down. In many ways, I was still carrying the fears of my younger self with me into adulthood. While I looked grown on the outside, inside I was still that little girl, terrified she wouldn't survive without her parents.

Like all children, I found ways to cope with emotions I didn't know how to handle. The energy that once led me to bounce off the walls I poured into sports, keeping my room meticulously organized, and excelling academically in school. But in still moments, especially as I got older, I started turning to other ways of managing my overwhelm. By thirteen, I was self-medicating. I became close with my sixteen-year-old neighbor and started spending time with her and her friends, drinking, getting high, doing anything I could to take the edge off. My parents, who had once been stricter with my much older brother and sister, seemed oblivious or in denial. One morning after I'd come home and been sick from drinking, my parents found the mess in the bathroom and blamed it on our family dog. In their eyes, I was getting straight A's. I was the "perfect" child." My life looked impressive from the outside, but it relied on ways of numbing emotions I didn't know how to express.

Beneath it all, my inner child was running the show for decades. I grew into an overachieving perfectionist pursuing an advanced degree. I enrolled in every certification I could find, inside and outside of school. I worked as a research assistant, took on clinical work, and kept myself constantly busy. I lived in New York City—the city that never sleeps—and I didn't, either. I worked hard, played hard, and filled every chance for quiet with distraction. I jumped from long-term relationship to long-term relationship. I was never alone, never at ease, and still never feeling truly connected or fulfilled.

My attention remained tethered to my family back home, and I was always consumed by their stress, and emotionally entangled in ways I couldn't untangle. Yet I was alone in my overwhelm. On the outside, I seemed detached, sometimes maybe a little too detached. On the inside,

I was screaming *Help me* while pushing everyone away. When something or someone real or meaningful tried to reach me, I rejected it. I didn't know how to let love in. I didn't know how to feel safe in moments of stillness. To most others I looked like I had it all together, but I was unraveling. Nobody could tell what was going on with me, because I didn't show it. The only way my stress surfaced was through complaints and blame, finding fault especially with those closest to me. I grew to resent the needs and feelings of others, all the while expecting someone else to make me feel better. I was too deep in survival mode to recognize who I was or who I could connect with.

I've since realized that this is what happens when we don't resolve what's happening inside us. We adapt. We develop ways of functioning that help us survive, blend in, or succeed. But over time, these patterns only pull us further from who we really are. By the time I was thirty, it looked like this was just who I was—high-achieving, sharp-edged, maybe a little restless. But what others saw wasn't my true Self. It was a reflection of an overwhelmed, under-supported inner child doing her best to cope.

During our childhoods, we construct an emotional home base—the automatic coping strategies and reactive behaviors that help us get through life's challenges. This way of being—shaped or *conditioned* by experience—often follows us into adulthood. For me, it meant carrying the constant sense that something was wrong, that I had to stay alert, that it was all too much. For a long time, I didn't know how to feel at home within myself; that period and the work that helped me find my way back inspired this book.

Lately, I have been thinking about the idea of home, and what it means to feel whole. No matter how many different directions we go in—physically, emotionally, intellectually, spiritually—no matter how curious we are, how far we wander, how many people and places and ideas we encounter—don't we all want to feel centered, grounded, and like there is some immutable core to who we are and where we belong? I've been realizing how many of us yearn for a greater sense of belonging—in our relationships, communities, even within ourselves. What is it that separates us? What is it that creates the disconnection we feel in the course of everyday life, between who we are and how we act, what we think we want and how we feel, what we believe and how we are seen, or who we care about and how we connect with them?

Before the external world begins to shape our instincts, we exist in a state where we feel spontaneous and free, filled with wonder and awe, connected to our natural inclinations, creativity, and imagination. But as soon as we begin to explore our environment, we start picking up cues about how to belong, and with that awareness comes a slow disconnection from our natural wholeness. As children, we actively absorb objective concepts (stoves can be too hot to touch; a smile is a likely sign of friendliness), but we also continually absorb information that we don't and even can't consciously remember, like what was said to or about us, if and how we were soothed when upset, and whether we were given the opportunity to express ourselves. By the time we're adults, we have synthesized all of this information—what we consciously learned and the deeper messages that were imprinted on our unconscious—to make sense of the world that surrounds us and to discern how we fit in it. Because this constructed perspective relies on the inner world of a time we mostly cannot recall, we end up filtering the experiences of our adult life through the lens of our often blurry past. At any number of moments throughout the day, we are pulled emotionally and behaviorally back in time as a part of us—our inner child—unexpectedly takes the stage, representing the childhood emotions and unmet needs that linger in our psyche, unaddressed and uncontained.

The inner child is the name we give to the unconscious part of our mind that holds the most foundational aspects of our being—the parts that never had space to fully unfold as well as the joyful and expansive parts. Every one of us began life as an open, innocent being: connected, curious, safe in our body, and at ease in the world. We were naturally receptive to love, support, and co-creation with the people around us. Of course, that pure state of openness doesn't last forever. Life happens. Our parents meet some of our needs and fail to meet others. We have successes and disappointments, joys and sorrows. In response, we adapt. Moments and influences that shaped us may not have looked dramatic from the outside, but they accumulated over time. And it's our inner child that holds all the adaptations that occurred when our needs weren't satisfied, when safety was uncertain, or when we were taught that certain emotions or traits were unacceptable. These early strategies—finding ways to calm ourselves, bracing against chaos, or holding on to connection at all costs—formed when our natural instincts were blocked, shamed, or ignored. As children, we are wired for survival. Adaptation is our only option.

Whenever we find a path to safety—hiding to avoid a loud argument, giving up an interest because a parent dismissed it, pretending our feelings weren't hurt because our emotions weren't respected—we store that pattern in our body. The next time a similar threat appears, our system remembers. These adaptations become the protective habits we carry into adulthood, including our learned ways of feeling okay in the face of stress. They surface when we're overwhelmed in a crowded train station or facing a yelling, angry boss. These habits aren't random; they come from somewhere. Like the way I couldn't tell the difference between someone being a few minutes late and someone being in the hospital. To my nervous system, both felt like grave danger. As an adult, I often found myself reacting from the same place as that little girl—overwhelmed, uncertain, and afraid. That's how our inner child shows up: not as a memory but as a felt experience still alive in our body. In those moments, I wasn't being dramatic or unreasonable; I was emotionally flooded. My nervous system didn't know the difference between a small stressor and a real threat. You don't have to remember the fear; you relive it.

The more we repeat these responses, the more our brain strengthens the neural pathways that support them. Each time a thought, emotion, and action link together, our nervous system builds a connection—a familiar route for how to react, protect, or escape. Over time, these pathways become the basic programming of our inner child. We return to them anytime our mind or body unconsciously associates the present with something we once felt in the past, whether exciting, frightening, or heartbreaking.

This is why, as adults, we can feel emotionally unequipped in overwhelming moments, often regressing into behaviors that seem irrational or out of character. We may shut down, lash out, people-please, overreact, or self-sabotage because an old part of us is trying to get a need met the only way it knows how. In these reactive states, whether fleeting or chronic, it's difficult to access the more joyful, open side of our inner child. That part becomes buried beneath our learned survival responses.

It's within those responses that our inner child shows up—as the early parts of ourselves that are still reacting as they once did. In those moments, we're responding from our primitive impulses—sometimes playful or joyful but also fearful, angry, or protective—driven by the emotions and reasoning of that child who never had the space and safety to develop a mature way of being. This inner child still carries the imprint of our earliest experiences, shaping how we move through the world and desperately longing to be seen, heard, and accepted.

That's why understanding our inner child matters. Once we begin to access, listen to, and integrate this part of ourselves—meeting those childlike responses with compassion and curiosity—we create space for something new. We begin to reconnect with the vital parts of our inner world that hold joy, wonder, play, and our original instincts, even alongside our earliest wounds. From this place, we can respond to life as it's happening instead of reliving the emotional residue of our past.

Over time, I've come to understand that *home* isn't just a place; it's a feeling. It's the emotional atmosphere we return to again and again, whether it nourishes us or not. The stress and disconnection that defined my childhood didn't just shape how I coped; they *became* what felt familiar. They became my blueprint for love, safety, and belonging. The protective behaviors I developed to survive those conditions? They felt like home too.

It's no wonder, then, that so many of us carry these early adaptations into adulthood. Many of our childhood homes—regardless of how they looked from the outside—lacked the emotional safety, attunement, or support we truly needed. Parenting philosophies may have shifted dramatically over the years, but one truth remains: Most of us didn't grow up with a consistent emotional presence. Whether our caregivers were controlling or permissive, distracted or overwhelmed, if there's one thing my clinical experience has shown me, it's this: Very few of us have an internal sense of home. Few of us were taught how to feel safe in our own bodies, or how to feel rooted within ourselves and our relationships. That lack—of steadiness, of connection—sends us spiraling into habits we can't break. We feel disconnected from our own inner guidance, unsure of what we want or how we feel, frozen in inaction. And in that disconnection, we suffer. Other times, we swing to the opposite extreme and are consumed by emotion, needing everyone around us to feel how angry or hurt we are. This, too, is the voice of our inner child. It's not just a part of us; it's the part through which we first learned to survive, often without the guidance, support, or safety we desperately needed.

While we can't rewrite the past, we can change the way we meet the needs of our inner child—the part of us that still holds our early emotional wounds and unmet longings. This process is called *reparenting*: the practice of giving yourself the nurturance, boundaries, and care you may not have received growing up. In this process, you'll learn to soothe yourself instead of exploding, to notice when you're uncomfortable and make a change, and to attend to the needs of your body and mind. By learning to show up for ourselves with consistency, compassion, and accountability, we begin to break dysfunctional habits and patterns that keep us stuck and to build the safety we've always needed from within. When we do this, we begin to live from a place that feels calm, clear, and connected. A home that no longer runs on fear.

This book will guide you through that return. The journey may go deeper than you expect. Together, we'll explore the environments and relationships that shaped your earliest sense of self. I'll introduce what I call the Individual Development Model—a framework that offers a new lens for understanding the impact of your childhood—not just the moments you remember but also the relationships and experiences that left a lasting imprint beneath your awareness. From there, we'll widen the view. We are all a product of our environment and are influenced by the stresses that forced us to adapt, the ancestors whose experiences live on in our genes, and the cultures that influenced our upbringing. You'll begin to see how your story is braided with the stories that came before you—how family history, unspoken trauma, and ancestral patterns shape the beliefs you carry and the way you experience the world. Next, you'll explore the wounds of your early experiences, and how you learned to cope with them by developing patterns of behavior—some that helped you, and some that are holding you back. And that's where the healing begins, not by judging these reactions but by understanding where they came from and whether they reflect who we truly are.

• • •

For years, I've been devoted to helping people reclaim their healing—because in the end, only we can do this work for ourselves. Which is why I wrote this book for anyone who's ever felt like they're just getting by—showing up, pushing through, and doing what's expected, yet never feeling at ease, always waiting for the next thing to go wrong. For anyone caught in the same painful cycles—entering relationships where they feel unseen, overworking to prove their worth, or people-pleasing to avoid conflict—only to end up resentful, invisible, and wondering why nothing ever changes. For anyone who carries unexplained stress in their bodies—headaches, jaw tension, stomach issues, fatigue, or chronic pain that no doctor can explain—sensing it's tied to something deeper than a simple diagnosis. And for anyone who turns to coping habits that ease discomfort temporarily—scrolling, eating, drinking, exercising, or staying busy to avoid feeling—only to find that the stress, shame, and loneliness return again and again.

These are all survival strategies you learned long ago to keep yourself safe when your needs weren't being met. The problem is, survival isn't the same as living. What once protected you now keeps you stuck, small, and disconnected from who you really are.

We all carry emotional imprints from childhood. And unless we learn how to work with them, we'll keep reacting to the present through the lens of the past, mistaking old pain for current danger. But it doesn't have to stay that way. Once we see that our present-day struggles are rooted in painful early experiences, we can start to respond differently. That's what this work offers: a new way forward. Reparenting is how you begin to give yourself what you didn't receive: safety, care, and compassion. It's how you release old survival patterns and rebuild an inner home—a place of safety, connection, and belonging—for the parts of you that never had one. It's what helps you move from just surviving into living fully as the grounded, connected adult you were always meant to be.

This book will offer you tools and practices to create new patterns: ones that are more intentional, more flexible, and more aligned with who you truly are. We can't change what happened in the past, but we can change how it lives within us. This change is real, and I know how overwhelming it can feel because I've lived it. I spent years in survival mode, unable to regulate, unsure how to feel safe in my body. It's hard to break old habits—to sit with big emotions, to face yourself honestly, to try something new when survival mode is all you've ever known. For me, the shift began when I started giving myself what I had once needed from others. Over time, I rewired the patterns that kept me stuck and began to thrive. This is the power of reparenting.

So now, I'd like to invite you to look back with clarity, honor the ways you adapted, and release the strategies that keep you stuck. Reparenting gives us the capacity to feel safe in our own skin, to regulate our emotions instead of being ruled by them, to build relationships rooted in honesty and trust, and to finally experience a sense of belonging that isn't dependent on others. It opens the door to choice, to joy, and to the freedom of responding to life in real time rather than repeating the past. This is how we begin to live more fully, with greater ease and connection to ourselves and to each other.

My hope is that this work helps you create lasting change in your life. The steps are clear, practical, and designed to be taken one small, manageable step at a time. I know from working within my global membership community, SelfHealers Circle, that time and energy ebb and flow, which is why the practices that are included in these chapters are meant to meet you where you are. You don't have to do everything at once. You might read this book straight through and return to the practices later or pause and reflect as you go. You might dog-ear a section and come back to it when you're ready. However you choose to move through these pages, the important thing is simply to begin. Try one small practice. See how you feel, then maybe try another. That's how change happens, by meeting your inner child with presence and giving your nervous system a new experience of safety.

Before we begin exploring your past more deeply, I'd like to start with a gentle reflection to help you reconnect with who you were as a child, before the world told you who you needed to be.

PRACTICE
INNER CHILD REFLECTION

This is where the work begins: remembering the child you once were.

1. **Find a Photograph.** Choose a picture of yourself as a child. If you don't have one, simply bring to mind a clear image of your younger self—what you looked like, how you moved, the spark in your eyes.

2. **Create a Safe Space.** Sit somewhere comfortable and quiet. Place the photo in front of you or hold it in your hands. Take three slow, deep breaths, feeling your body supported by the chair or ground beneath you.

3. **Meet Their Gaze.** Look into the eyes of your younger self. Notice their innocence, their curiosity, and also the uncertainty or hurt they may have experienced. Allow yourself to really see them—not as a stranger but as you.

4. **Acknowledge Their Story.** Whisper or write a few words of recognition:

    - I see how hard it was for you.
    - You were worthy of love then, and you still are now.
    - You didn't deserve the pain you felt.

5. **Offer Reassurance.** Place one hand on your heart and one on your belly. With each inhale and exhale, repeat silently or aloud: *I've got you now*. Let this become a mantra of safety, a reminder that your adult self is here to care for the child within.

6. **Notice Your Body.** Pay attention to sensations that arise: warmth in your chest, tightness in your throat, tears in your eyes. Don't judge them—just notice. These are signs that your inner child is being remembered and felt.

7. **Close with Connection.** Thank your younger self for showing up. With each slow, deep inhale and exhale, repeat silently or aloud: "I've got you now." If it feels right, place the photo somewhere visible—on your desk,

beside your bed, or tucked in your journal—as a daily reminder that your healing begins with this relationship.

Deepen Your Practice. Take a few moments to explore the prompts below, writing your responses in a notebook or journal:

- What do I notice in my body as I look at this photo?
- What did this child most long to hear?
- How can I offer that message now, as an adult?
- What qualities—joy, creativity, sensitivity—do I see in this child that I want to honor today?

Starting here reminds you that healing is about reconnecting with the child who never stopped deserving love. This simple act of seeing, feeling, and speaking to your inner child lays the foundation for every other practice in this book.

PART ONE

[**YOUR INNER CHILD**]

1

BEYOND ATTACHMENT STYLE

When I first started seeing clients in New York City, Aisha came to me after a string of heartbreaks, each one mirroring the last. In one session, she admitted, "My whole world revolved around my boyfriend. It's embarrassing, but I put everything on hold to help him succeed. I loved him that much."

I asked her, "Did he offer that kind of support in return?"

She shook her head. "No. He was always about himself. He didn't even celebrate when I got the promotion I really wanted. I kept giving, but there was nothing coming back to me."

I recalled a moment Aisha had shared in an earlier session. She was a child, trying to do homework in her bedroom, and her parents were fighting in the nearby living room. Afterward her father came into her room.

"I'm sorry you had to hear that," he told her.

"It's okay," she reassured him.

"Your mom—I just keep trying and trying, but it's never enough for her. Don't you see I want us to have a happy family? Everything I do, I do for you!"

Aisha had offered this to me as evidence of how devoted her father was to her, but I saw him as asking her to soothe him, to be his emotional anchor. She had learned early on that her role was to care for others, even when no one attended to her feelings.

I said softly, "Do you see how your last relationship mirrors your relationship with your dad? There, too, you were focused on his needs, keeping him calm."

She nodded. "Yeah . . . my dad and I were really close."

I paused, hearing the resistance in her answer. It can be hard to question the foundations of a relationship you hold dear. "I know it's a relationship that's important to you. But is it also true that while you gave him care, he didn't give that back? He loved you, and he told you that often, but did he ever ask what you needed?"

Aisha sat frozen, gripping her cardigan. "I've never thought about it like that . . . but it makes sense."

"It does," I said. "You learned early in life that love meant caretaking. And now, your adult self keeps reenacting that same story." For the first time, Aisha was able to see her relationship struggles as the natural outcome of her past experiences as a little girl longing for love. Instead of shaming herself for what she once believed were personal failures, she could now begin to allow herself the compassion and care she had always deserved.

What Aisha and I both recognized in that moment, and what I've observed repeatedly with clients, friends, loved ones, and even within myself, is that our inner child is always with us. It holds the lessons we absorbed early on, determining how we move through the world today. Sometimes, we're aware of these influences. We might tell our friends, "My parents hated noise, so I've always tried to be quiet," or "I felt guilty about how hard my parents worked, so now I push myself to be completely independent," or "My grandmother never celebrated my mom's birthday, so my mom went all out for any occasion."

For many of us, the connections aren't so apparent. Sometimes we're so focused on the most obvious ways we were influenced in our childhood—big issues like financial hardship or parental divorce—that we don't notice more subtle forces we haven't considered, like how our parents responded to our fears or whether they expressed curiosity about what mattered to us. And then there are some of us, like me, who only have access to a handful of childhood memories. Or we avoid reflecting on our early experiences altogether. Regardless of whether we've consciously explored where we came from, on a neurobiological level, those formative moments continue to influence how we think, feel, and relate. And the deeply ingrained habits and patterns that emerge from these experiences can feel immovable—like they are just a part of us.

Here's the truth: Awareness is a necessary beginning, but by itself, it won't create change. To truly shift long-standing patterns, you need to connect with the inner child that first learned them. That's why we're going to explore how your childhood shaped the way you relate to yourself and others, even if you don't remember all the details, so you can begin to build a relationship with your inner child. From that foundation, you can then start to release the patterns that keep you stuck, embody the fullest expression of who you really are, and break the cycle for yourself and future generations.

IT BEGINS WITH ATTACHMENT

To begin our exploration, it's helpful to understand why these early experiences matter so much. Attachment theory is one of the most influential frameworks for understanding the long-lasting impact of our earliest relationships. Developed in the early twentieth century by British psychologist John Bowlby, attachment theory suggests that the bonds we form in early childhood serve as the basis for how we connect with and relate to others throughout life.

Bowlby himself was deeply shaped by his upbringing. He was born into an upper-middle-class family, his surgeon father was rarely home, and his mother spent just an hour or so a day with her young son, leaving him in the care of a nanny. When this beloved caregiver, who was a mother figure for Bowlby, departed suddenly, he was heartbroken. Soon after, at age seven, he was sent to boarding school, a common practice among families of his social class at that time. Reflecting back later, he would say, "I wouldn't send a dog away to boarding school at that age."[1] By his own account, these early wounds fueled his lifelong quest to investigate attachment and its impacts.

Bowlby's work highlighted the unspoken language of attachment: the way a mother's gaze, tone of voice, and touch help calm her child's nervous system—a process now known as *co-regulation*. A caregiver's ability to connect with a child begins with these nonverbal cues, which are absorbed and encoded in the part of the young child's developing brain responsible for intuition, creativity, and emotional memory. When caregivers are emotionally in sync with children—a process known as *attunement*—it helps them learn to feel safe, confident, and resilient. But when attunement is inconsistent, unpredictable, or absent, the child may feel emotionally unstable. Without a sense of emotional safety, children often internalize the misattunement, forming the belief that something's wrong with them, rather than recognizing a problem within their environment. These early relational experiences form our unconscious templates for love, trust, and belonging. They shape how we respond to our own needs, how we regulate our emotions, and how we understand our place in the world. This is why attunement is so important. When children don't receive the comfort or support they need, as Bowlby observed, they often begin to ignore their own feelings and focus instead on how those around them feel. Over time, this outward focus can lead to anxiety about being left out, a sense of over-responsibility for others, or even shame around needing help themselves. These are exactly the kinds of behaviors we carry into adulthood. As Bowlby explained in his trilogy, Attachment and Loss (1969–1980), neglectful or inconsistent care can make children hypervigilant, priming them to detect even the subtlest signs of threat well into adulthood. What he understood intuitively was later confirmed by research showing that those with attachment trauma often misinterpret neutral facial expressions as threatening. In other words, our early relational experiences leave a deep imprint, forming the lens through which we view other people and the world around us.

In the 1970s, Bowlby began collaborating with American psychologist Mary Ainsworth. In their now well-known Strange Situation studies, they observed how infants responded to brief separations and reunions with their caregiver. Children between twelve and eighteen months old were placed in a playroom with their caregiver and encouraged to explore. After a short time, a stranger entered and spoke with the caregiver for a minute or two. Then the caregiver left the room, leaving the child alone with the stranger. A few minutes later, the caregiver returned and the stranger left. Researchers observed how the child explored the room with their caregiver present, how they reacted to the separation, how they responded to the unfamiliar adult, and how they greeted their caregiver upon return.

Findings from this research, along with follow-up studies, led psychologists to identify and agree upon the existence of four key attachment styles, each reflecting how early bonding experiences shape the way we relate to others and navigate emotional intimacy.

The most secure foundation develops when caregivers are warm, consistent, and responsive to our needs. As children, we feel safe to explore the world, knowing comfort and support are available upon our return. As adults, this secure attachment allows us to trust both ourselves and others. We can form lasting relationships, express our needs without fear, and regulate our emotions during times of stress or conflict. Even people with secure attachment still have an inner child. The difference is that their inner child feels seen, soothed, and supported—so its needs don't overwhelm the adult self. That's ultimately the goal of reparenting: to become more secure by learning to tune in to ourselves, stay in touch with our needs, and respond with care. In this way, reparenting helps us move closer to the kind of self-trust and emotional balance that secure attachment naturally provides.

The other three attachment styles—avoidant, anxious, and disorganized—are forms of insecure attachment. Insecure attachment signals unmet needs from childhood, like safety, steadiness, or attunement. And reparenting gives us the opportunity to meet those needs now, as adults. We do this by first noticing how our attachment patterns still play out and choosing to respond in new ways that build inner trust and stability. This is what allows us to shift from old survival strategies into a more secure way of relating to ourselves and to others.

Avoidant attachment develops when caregivers are emotionally distant, unresponsive, or dismissive. In response, we learn to depend on ourselves, suppressing our emotional needs because closeness feels unsafe or unreliable. As adults, we end up valuing independence over connection, finding vulnerability uncomfortable and struggling with commitment or asking for help. While avoidant attachment pulls us away from closeness, anxious attachment pulls us toward it. It develops when caregivers are inconsistent—sometimes nurturing, other times withdrawn or overwhelmed—and leaves us hyperaware of emotional shifts, constantly scanning for signs of connection or rejection. In adulthood, this can lead to clinginess, a constant need for reassurance, and a persistent fear of abandonment, often leaving us feeling like we give more than we receive, especially in romantic relationships. And finally, disorganized attachment emerges when caregivers are frightening, abusive, or highly unpredictable. We grow up fearing the very people we depend on, creating a deep inner conflict. We end up craving closeness but distrusting intimacy, caught in a painful cycle of pulling others close and then pushing them away. Relationships feel chaotic, and our emotions feel overwhelming and hard to manage. As with all attachment styles, these patterns trace back to the emotional availability and responsiveness of our early caregivers—the foundation that shapes how we attach and relate in the present.

Though widely accepted now, Bowlby's ideas were revolutionary for his time and often dismissed by a society that paid little attention to children's emotional development. It wasn't until after his death in the early 1990s that other pioneers built on his visionary work. One of them was American psychologist Jeffrey Young, the creator of Schema Therapy, with whom I had the honor of training during my PhD program. Working with clients facing depression, anxiety, eating disorders, and complex trauma, Young expanded attachment theory by identifying what he called *schemas*, or deep, negative thought patterns that form when a child's core attachment needs aren't met. For example, a child who experiences loss, separation, or neglect might develop an abandonment schema, always anticipating that others will leave them. These early beliefs can have lasting influence, though Young reminded us they're not permanent. When we recognize and reframe these schemas, we begin to build healthier ways of coping and connecting. While schema therapy offers valuable insight, it doesn't fully address the role our body plays in our healing. So now we'll take a holistic approach to reparenting that works with your body and your mind to help you break old patterns that have been ingrained over time.

Healing our attachment wounds requires us to return to the language in which they were formed: relational presence. The way someone looks at us, speaks to us, and helps us settle teaches our brain what it feels like to be safe and secure. If we didn't grow up with the ability to calm ourselves or feel grounded, we can learn it. Through tone, gaze, co-regulation, and emotional attunement, we slowly begin to reshape our inner world.

Real change happens when we allow ourselves to feel, name, and remain present with all our emotions, offering our inner child the understanding and care we may have always longed for but never consistently received.

ATTACHMENT IS THE ROOT OF JOY AND SUFFERING

We are all biologically driven to seek love, comfort, and connection from the attachment figures in our lives. But when those needs aren't met in childhood and we don't learn how to regulate our emotions or soothe ourselves in healthy ways, we develop other coping mechanisms to get by, often reverting to behaviors that might be immature or childish.

Early in my clinical training, I started to realize these coping patterns aren't random; they're rooted in our early relational dynamics. As I sought to better understand how our early years shaped us, I had the privilege of working with Miriam Steele and Howard Steele, founders of the Center for Attachment Research at the New School for Social Research and recipients of the Bowlby-Ainsworth Award for their contributions to attachment theory. Under their mentorship, I studied mother–infant interactions and wrote my dissertation on how a mother's emotional state directly influences her baby's ability to self-regulate.

At the same time, I was gaining hands-on experience in clinical settings, where I began to witness how these early attachment patterns show up later in life. As part of my training, I worked at Beth Israel's inpatient rehabilitation center for substance use disorders. There, I led groups where participants shared their feelings, examined their habits, and explored their relationships. Over and over, I saw the same underlying thread: Unresolved attachment wounds lay at the heart of so many patients' stories. While their struggle with alcohol or drugs may have brought them into treatment, many had turned to addictive substances as a way to soothe a nervous system hijacked by deep-rooted wounds—early attachment disruptions, unprocessed trauma, and chronic shame—all of which we'll explore more deeply in later chapters. Research now supports these clinical patterns: Individuals with insecure attachment styles are significantly more vulnerable to addiction.[2]

And my own work continued to confirm this connection. After years of running inpatient groups, I transitioned into private practice in Philadelphia. My clients came in with a range of concerns, from their relationships, to anxiety, to trauma, but at the root of most issues was an unspoken question: *Am I worthy of love?* Many carried deep-rooted shame, feeling somehow broken or not good enough. They weren't just seeking answers; though few of them would have framed it this way, I came to recognize that they were seeking safety. What I started to see firsthand was that our longing to be seen, accepted, and affirmed—our need for secure attachment—stays with us for life.

I saw this clearly in Jasmine, forty-two, who came to me with a diagnosis of schizophrenia and bipolar disorder. She often appeared a bit scattered, with crumbs on her shirt and an overflowing purse. But she always knew exactly what she wanted to explore during our session—a conversation she'd had with her mother or a thought she'd had about what we'd talked about in the previous session. It gradually became clear that her most persistent struggles stemmed from deeply insecure attachments. Jasmine grew up without consistent emotional attunement. Her father left the home when she was seven, and she described her mother as being emotionally cold and perpetually critical. Jasmine often tried to provoke emotional engagement—sometimes even calling her mother during our sessions in an attempt to be heard—but the calls always ended in conflict. She spoke of self-hate, risky sexual encounters, and substance use, all of which I came to understand as survival strategies rooted in a desperate yearning for connection. Her repeated requests for me to speak with her mother were driven by her deep longing to be seen and loved. Her rage masked a wounded inner child who had long been abandoned by her father and unseen by her mother. Jasmine's mental health struggles were not just symptoms of a diagnosis but also expressions of a disorganized and unmet need for safe, relational connection.

I saw this same theme play out in very different circumstances with Aaron, twenty-four, a gifted athlete who came from a financially privileged background. He was put together, with an air of accomplishment and power. He brought great focus to our sessions—with a notebook always in hand, he was ready to solve his problems. But his emotional foundation was far from stable. When he was still quite young, his father had been caught mismanaging funds at his job. Although he was never convicted of a crime, this was a massive blow to the family financially and emotionally. Under public scrutiny, his father lost his job, and the entire family system unraveled. His mother fell into a depression, rendering both parents emotionally unavailable. Aaron, left to deal with the mounting stress on his own, did what he had always done. He performed, pushed forward, and remained stoic. But when a shoulder injury ended his athletic career, and he was prescribed OxyContin, he described the medication as the first thing that made him feel calm, revealing to me just how much tension he had been carrying beneath the surface, even in the midst of high performance. Over time the relief that the medication gave him turned into dependence. Underneath it all, Aaron's substance use was a way to manage the emotional pain of a fractured attachment that couldn't yet hold the weight of grief, lost identity, or raw emotion. Like many, he hadn't been taught how to process emotions, only to suppress them.

Another client who reinforced my observations about attachment was Joon, a twenty-one-year-old student at an Ivy League school who came to me with intense social anxiety. He excelled academically, but was isolated, ashamed of his emotions, and deeply unsure of his worth. This was reflected in his timidity. He dressed in muted colors, spoke softly, and had noticeably low energy. He reported that he was struggling with depression. Joon had grown up in a high-achieving immigrant household where he had received little emotional validation. When he tried to open up to his mom about his issues with his friends, she dismissed his feelings, saying, "You shouldn't be worrying about that. You should be studying." Later, after finding a note from a woman that hinted at his father's affair, Joon confronted him and was met with rage, then silence. These key moments—dismissal, deflection, disconnection—shaped Joon's internal model of relationships. He learned that emotions were irrelevant, and that connection came at the cost of rejection or shame. Though he had achieved his family's dream, he felt hollow inside. His anxious and avoidant attachment patterns made intimacy feel unsafe, and he was unable to connect deeply with others.

An individual diagnosed with schizophrenia, someone struggling with substance use, and an Ivy League student may seem, on the surface, to have nothing in common. But beneath their unique life stories, I saw the same theme: Early attachment wounds don't just fade but instead follow us into adulthood, shaping how we trust, cope, connect, and relate, forming our very sense of self. This is how our inner child shows up—in the habits and patterns that we carry from childhood and reactions that are too big or too small for the moment. Whatever the source, when our inner child's needs are unaddressed, they result in cycles of undesired and often dysfunctional behavior. This is where reparenting becomes essential. It gives us the awareness and tools to break these cycles and develop new habits that better serve us and all our relationships.

The patterns I observed in my clients' stories reflected what research was beginning to confirm. In the 1990s, the Centers for Disease Control and Prevention (CDC) and Kaiser Permanente launched the groundbreaking Adverse Childhood Experiences (ACE) study. Published in 1998, the study produced a tool called the ACE questionnaire, which helps clinicians quantify the impact of early trauma and its link to chronic physical and mental illness. While John Bowlby passed away before the study's release, its findings validated a belief central in his work: Our early relationships shape not only how we feel as children but who we become as adults.

The original ACE study measured ten categories of trauma, grouped into abuse, neglect, and household dysfunction. Questions included: "Did you often feel that no one in your family loved you or thought you were important or special?" and "Did a parent or adult in the household often swear at you, insult you, or put you down?" At their core, each question pointed to relational harm, or how safe, seen, and supported a child felt in their earliest environment. The results were staggering. Two-thirds of adults had experienced at least one ACE. And the higher the score, the greater the risk for nearly every major health issue, including depression, addiction, diabetes, heart disease, and cancer.

The ACE study reconceptualized the idea of trauma in psychological circles and research, calling our attention to its prevalence, its manifestation in physical symptoms, and its long-term impact. These findings brought trauma into mainstream conversation. There was now a widespread understanding that childhood trauma wasn't rare; it was shockingly common. It wasn't just a mental health issue; it was a public health crisis. And it wasn't only about the impact on our mind, because trauma reshaped our brain, our body, and how we moved through the world.

The implications were clear across the field of psychology. We began to understand that preventing adverse experiences and supporting healthy emotional development in families could transform individual lives and the health of our entire society. Trauma is a silent epidemic that has gone ignored for too long. But when we name it, when we face it with clarity and courage, we begin to break generational cycles that we've carried across lineages. And in doing so, we open the door not just for personal healing but for collective transformation.

PRACTICE
ATTACHMENT TIMELINE

By mapping out a visual timeline of important attachment moments, you can begin to see how past experiences shaped the reactions that live in your body and show up in your relationships today. This practice is about compassionately witnessing and understanding the ways you adapted to stay.

1. **Create a Horizontal Timeline.** Start by drawing a line across a page, from left to right. On the far left, mark the beginning of your life (birth), and on the far right, your current age. You can divide the timeline into developmental phases, such as early childhood, school age, adolescence, and adulthood, or you can mark specific years, milestones, or ages based on what you remember.

2. **Plot Significant Attachment Moments.** Now begin noting moments along your timeline that involved your primary caregivers (biological or adoptive parents, grandparents, guardians, or other adults who played a caregiving role). These moments don't have to be dramatic and are often everyday experiences, like being dismissed when you were upset or only noticed when you achieved something. Include a mix of both joyful and painful experiences, such as:

- Moments of connection, warmth, attunement, or support
- Times of separation—starting school, moving, hospitalization, divorce, or death
- Experiences of conflict, rejection, emotional neglect, or inconsistent care

3. **Add Emotional Responses and Coping Strategies.** Beneath or beside each event, write a few notes about:

   - How you felt (e.g., comforted, afraid, angry, alone, safe, invisible)
   - What you did to cope (e.g., shut down, tried to be perfect, became overly self-reliant, clung to others, turned to food for comfort)
   - Whether you felt seen, soothed, or supported, or if your feelings were dismissed or misunderstood

4. **Look for Patterns.** Once you've filled out your timeline, take a step back and observe:

   - What emotional themes or patterns show up repeatedly?
   - How did you learn to relate to closeness, vulnerability, or independence?
   - What roles did you take on (the helper, the quiet one, the achiever, the caretaker) to feel safe, loved, or in control?

Deepen Your Practice. Take a few moments to explore the prompts below, writing your responses in a notebook or journal, or directly beside events on your timeline:

- What was your relationship like with each parent or caregiver? Which parent (or adult) felt safest to you, and why?
- How did you feel most often in those relationships? Which emotions were welcome, and which felt dangerous or unacceptable?
- How did experiences of loss, absence, or separation shape the way you learned to trust others or yourself?
- When you were upset as a child, how did you respond—and who (if anyone) came to comfort you?

Remember, this is a process of reconnecting with your inner child. Take your time with it, giving yourself room to feel, reflect, and be kind to what comes up. You may find yourself coming back to your timeline and adding new insights as they arise. Use this practice to help you understand what shaped you and what you can now begin to heal and release.

Looking at your timeline often reveals more than individual memories. It shows the patterns underneath—moments when your needs were met and moments when they weren't. Fundamentally, we all start out with the same core needs: physical, emotional, and spiritual. Whether those needs are fulfilled depends largely on our parents' ability to recognize who we truly are, not who they imagined or hoped we'd be. We need them to mirror back unconditional love, to take genuine interest in our emerging thoughts and values, and to create space for us to explore who we were becoming, even in moments of disagreement or discomfort. So, if like many of us, you didn't have that kind of consistent presence growing up, the first step is recognizing that your inner child feels unseen, unheard, and unacknowledged.

PRACTICE
LETTER TO YOUR INNER CHILD

Writing to your inner child helps you acknowledge what they lived through, what they needed but didn't receive, and what parts of them are still waiting to be seen and accepted. After naming their experiences, you can invite your inner child to speak the truths they never got to say. This process creates space for both compassion and release by offering care, safety, and validation, and then giving your inner child the chance to express what's been held inside.

1. **Write a Nurturing Letter.** Take a few moments to explore the prompts below, writing your responses in a notebook or journal.

    - How did I express my emotions as a child?
    - What parts of me were silenced, shamed, or hidden?
    - What brought me joy or made me feel most like myself as a child?

◁ Who might I have been if I had been nurtured, protected, and emotionally attuned to?

Now, using your reflections, write a letter to your inner child from the perspective of your adult self, who can offer love, safety, and reassurance. You might include:

◁ What they should have received but didn't, like soothing, support, or consistent presence.
◁ What they did receive, even if small, like a moment of joy, connection, or strength.
◁ A reminder that their feelings and needs were always valid, even if the adults around them couldn't meet them.

2. **Write a Truth-Telling Letter.** When you feel ready, write a second letter. This time, imagine your inner child has the safety and courage to speak directly to the person (or people) who caused harm, withheld care, or made them feel unseen. Allow yourself to be raw and uncensored without worrying about grammar or making sense. Use short phrases, images, or any form of expression that feels natural. You might write:

◁ What I needed from you and didn't receive . . .
◁ The ways you made me feel unsafe, unseen, or unworthy . . .
◁ What I want you to know about me now . . .

Optional: When the truth-telling letter is complete, you may choose to tear it up, burn it safely, or bury it, saying: *This is no longer mine to carry.*

Deepen Your Practice. Try writing this letter with your nondominant hand to connect more directly with your inner child. If you notice the urge to judge, perform, or minimize, pause and practice speaking to yourself as you would to a child you deeply care for.

Visualization (Before or After Writing): Sit quietly for five to ten minutes with one hand on your heart. Visualize your younger self beside you, at the age they most needed support. Imagine turning to them and whispering: *I believe you. I see you. I hear you.* Reread your truth-telling letter and picture your inner child speaking with clarity and strength.

Return to these letters whenever you need to reconnect with the parts of you that have always deserved to be seen. And as you do, keep in mind that what was missing in your childhood was never proof that something was wrong with you. It reflected the limits of the people raising you—their own struggles, blind spots, and unhealed wounds. Very few of us had parents who could consistently meet our emotional needs. Not because they didn't love us but because they often didn't know how or were carrying the weight of their own unresolved pain.

OUR IMPERFECT PARENTS

To truly understand our inner child, we have to look honestly at our imperfect parents and the circumstances that shaped them. In many ways, our earliest attachments are reflections of our caregivers' emotional capacity—their ability to notice, soothe, and respond to us. Because caring for a developing child is incredibly demanding, even the most loving and well-meaning parents will miss moments of attunement. But why are ACEs so common as to be "normal"? Have we normalized a certain "acceptable" level of emotional neglect as to be expected? The truth is, few of us grew up with parents who had the emotional bandwidth to be fully attuned to us, to model resilient responses to life's stress, and to help us express ourselves authentically. This is in part because so many of our parents carried their own unhealed wounds: insecure attachments, unresolved trauma, and inherited pain passed down through generations. It is also because far too many of us live in a society that undervalues caretaking and provides little support to parents. Taken together, these factors can help us understand that childhood trauma is widespread. Most parents are not intentionally neglectful, but they are often working with very limited internal and external resources.

The truth is most parents aren't failing because they don't care about their children. In my work with families, I never encountered a parent who held the intention of harming their kids or letting them down. But many of them carried the weight of their own imperfect childhoods. They passed these wounds on to their children by unconsciously repeating the parenting they experienced. Inherited patterns of pain, coping, and emotional shutdown are so routine that they become familiar, accepted as "just the way things are in our family."

This was illustrated in the story of Ted, whose father, Allen, had always wanted his son to be just like him. He pushed Ted toward sports, hoping to bond over football or weekends at the batting cage. But Ted was more drawn to spending time alone in his room playing his guitar. Allen didn't know how to take interest in what mattered to his son; his own father was a distant presence in his life, often away for months at a time in his work as a truck driver. Allen had no model for emotional connection, so he avoided the risk of rejection by trying to connect in the only ways he knew how. But Ted experienced his father's push toward activities he didn't enjoy as pressure—and his father's lack of interest in the rest of his life as disappointment and disapproval. "Dad is upset that I don't want to toss around a football or be in a frat," he told his mom one day. "That's not true, honey," she said gently. "Your father loves you. He just doesn't always show it." They were both right.

Then there was Kara. When she was growing up, her parents both had jobs with unpredictable hours. As a toddler, she went to the neighbor's while her little brothers were at daycare, but by the time she turned ten, Kara became responsible for her younger siblings once the school bus dropped them off at the end of the day. She supervised homework, intervened when they fought, prepared their dinner, and put them to bed if her parents didn't make it home in time. Kara's parents often praised her for being so responsible, and she felt proud of her maturity. But in learning to prioritize her brothers' and her parents' needs over her own, she missed out on the opportunity to simply be a child.

As you deepen your understanding of attachment, you may begin to recognize patterns like these in nearly every family you encounter. And if you're a parent, you may notice some of these behaviors in yourself. That realization can bring up shame or frustration, especially as we often catch ourselves repeating the very behaviors that once hurt us. But this isn't about shame or blame. It's about awareness, and with awareness comes the opportunity to choose differently. Reparenting begins with offering your inner child the compassion you've always deserved, so you can shift the patterns rather than pass them on. Our parents often didn't know how to meet our emotional needs because they themselves were shaped by cultural norms and survival pressures that conflicted with what children actually require to feel safe and connected.

Mary and Adam are powerful examples of how "regular life" can put overwhelming demands on parents, making attunement nearly impossible. When their daughter Ruby was born, Adam, a restaurant manager, wasn't granted paternity leave. Mary, a hospital social worker, received eight weeks of paid maternity leave and access to a childcare reimbursement account. On paper it sounded promising until she realized most daycares cost more than half her monthly salary. When she finally found an affordable option, she worried: Would her two-month-old get the attention she needed? The caregiver was kind, but clearly overwhelmed. Ruby was one of eight children in her group, and Mary couldn't shake the image of her infant, who until now had always been in her arms, now spending eight hours a day in a playpen.

Mary and Adam's story is not unique. Parents and babies are biologically wired to bond to one another, but our current systems do little to support or protect that connection. There's a fundamental mismatch between the needs of developing families and the demands of modern life. We're often taught that love alone is enough, and while having a loving parent gives us an important core strength, love by itself doesn't meet all of a child's or a caregiver's needs. Parents need their own stability, resources, and space in order to provide it to their children. They need housing they can afford, communities that can support and uplift them, and time to bond with their children without worrying about making ends meet. And yet, many are forced to work multiple jobs, stretch themselves thin, or parent in isolation. This burden falls especially hard on mothers. Today, over 40 percent of women with children under eighteen are the primary or sole earners in their household. In the face of these growing responsibilities, they're trying their best: Despite working more hours than previous generations, today's mothers also spend more time directly caring for their children.

In the United States, however, structural support is severely lacking. The average paid maternity leave is just ten weeks, and paternity leave is often only one week. Meanwhile, countries like Norway, Croatia, and the UK offer far more support—343 days, 196 days, and nearly forty weeks of fully paid parental leave, respectively. These policies aren't luxuries but are structures that support secure attachment.

When a caregiver is overwhelmed, unsupported, or constantly worried and distracted, their emotional absence shapes how that child understands love, safety, and whether their needs matter. Many of us carry those imprints into adulthood, often unaware of just how deep they run. To truly understand them, we also have to look at the people who raised us. Our parents' ability to show up was shaped by what they did—or didn't—receive themselves.

EMOTIONALLY IMMATURE PARENTS

Our parents may have faced hardships that interfered with their ability to attach to us, but the disconnection may stretch back even further. Our parents were once children too, often left with their own unmet needs. Social and cultural norms (like John Bowlby being sent away to boarding school at a very young age) may have interfered with their natural capacity for attachment. They may have experienced their own stress, neglect, and trauma.

Like all children, our parents depended on their caregivers to help them feel safe and calm. During the first year of life, infants rely on this shared regulation more than at any other time. This has always been true, but meanwhile, parenting trends come and go and often aren't scientifically backed. The once popular "cry it out" method of sleep training encouraged parents to "train" their babies by leaving them to cry alone for increasing periods of time, an approach that directly contradicts what we now know about nervous system development.

Skin-on-skin contact, co-sleeping, babywearing, and breastfeeding are all wonderful ways for babies and parents to co-regulate. They help regulate a baby's heart rate, breathing, and temperature, and these practices also support healthy emotional development and secure attachment. Oxytocin, released during moments of close contact, helps an infant's brain register safety and connection. Of course, every parent makes the best choices they can with the abilities, resources, and support available to them. And yet at various times there have been cultural trends or other obstacles interfering with these approaches, making it difficult to attune to their children's needs in the earliest years. In these ways and others, our parents may have been, figuratively and literally, pushed away at the exact time they were most in need of closeness.

When they weren't given the support or the space they needed to mature emotionally, they became emotionally immature parents who were unable to self-reflect, regulate their emotions, or repair after conflict. Emotional immaturity is often rooted in insecurity, low self-worth, and an underdeveloped sense of Self. Unable to regulate their emotions or reflect on their behavior, emotionally immature parents may act impulsively, break promises, or become defensive and reactive. They struggle to see the world through someone else's eyes, which makes it hard for them to empathize, tune in, or truly meet their children's emotional needs. Over time, their children carry a painful truth: *I don't feel seen, heard, or emotionally met.*

This dynamic was evident in Daphne's family. Daphne grew up with parents who catered to her every whim. When she was a teenager, they gave her a credit card that she was allowed to use freely; she had no curfew, even when her grades suffered because she stayed out late on school nights; and when she spoke to her parents dismissively, they let it slide. By the time she was a senior, her mother was asking *her* for permission to use the car and not the other way around. Daphne's parents' emotional immaturity showed up as conflict avoidance and a lack of boundaries. Rather than risk her displeasure or face uncomfortable conversations, they prioritized their own ease over her need for structure and guidance. What looked like freedom—a credit card with no rules, no curfew, and no accountability—was really a lack of support. This kind of role reversal is a hallmark of emotional immaturity, leaving the child to carry responsibilities the parent is unwilling or unable to hold.

"You have the coolest parents," her friends would gush. Daphne felt lucky not to have the rigid rules many of her peers complained about.

But by her early twenties, her lack of boundaries began to impact her relationships. She hadn't grown up hearing "no," so when others didn't meet her needs or expectations, it felt jarring and personal, and she reacted in a childlike manner. One night, when her boyfriend said he couldn't come over because he had to study, she snapped: "Fine, you know what? Forget I even asked." The disappointment of not getting what she wanted felt intolerable. Daphne had never learned that relationships are reciprocal, that both people have needs. She didn't yet understand that true intimacy requires give-and-take. Instead of staying connected to her feeling of disappointment, she defended against it with blame. Her boyfriend began to pull away, describing her as controlling, unaware, and unwilling to make space for anyone's needs but her own.

Daphne didn't realize she was reenacting a dynamic shaped long ago. Though her parents loved Daphne and thought they were doing their best, they lacked the emotional maturity their daughter needed to guide her and create emotional safety. Emotional immaturity can be hard to identify—people are often quite capable and even high functioning in many areas of life—but their coping strategies remain underdeveloped. So while they may be successful doctors, teachers, or otherwise high achievers, they struggle with maintaining healthy relationships, and this extends to parenting, where their inability to tolerate stress can make them reactive and emotionally unpredictable.

While each family is different, emotionally immature parents often fall into recognizable patterns. The descriptions that follow aren't meant to shame or label but to help you recognize your parents' emotional limitations and how those limitations shaped your experience of love, safety, and connection. You might see aspects of your parents in more than one pattern. If you're a parent yourself and notice some of these traits in your own behavior, remember: The work you do to reparent yourself doesn't end with you; it ripples outward. The goal here is awareness because awareness creates choice, and choice is what empowers us to break cycles.

The Reactive Parent: This parent relies on others to regulate their emotions. When overwhelmed or triggered, they erupt, often disproportionately. Their mood sets the tone of the home, and children learn to tiptoe around their volatility. Over time, family life becomes less about connecting and more about avoiding the next outburst. As adults, these children often become hyper-alert to shifts in others' moods, anxious about triggering conflict, and unsure how to express their own emotions without fear of backlash. They may struggle to trust stability, equating love with volatility and finding calm relationships unfamiliar or even uncomfortable.

The Disconnected Parent: This parent is often physically present but emotionally shut down, functioning on autopilot rather than attuned connection. They may provide stability and meet material needs yet struggle to share genuine warmth or emotional presence. Interactions can feel hollow or mechanical, leaving children feeling unseen even when cared for. As these children age, they may crave closeness but find it difficult to stay open or emotionally engaged, pulling back when intimacy deepens. They often learn to appear self-sufficient while quietly longing for real connection, equating emotional independence with safety.

The Status-Oriented Parent: This parent's self-worth is tied to image. Success, performance, and achievement become conditions for love. Children in these households often feel they must earn affection by excelling, making them vulnerable to anxiety, perfectionism, and burnout. A cultural example of this is the "Tiger Parent," a highly controlling parenting style that grooms children for success while denying them the freedom to develop a healthy sense of self. Overemphasis on achievement can lead to emotional repression and even self-harm.[3]

The Critical Parent: This parent finds fault easily, often under the guise of "tough love." Chronic criticism sends the message that the child is inherently flawed. Over time, children internalize this harsh lens and grow up with self-doubt and a powerful inner critic that mirrors their parent's voice. As adults, they may fear failure, overachieve in pursuit of approval, or avoid taking risks altogether. Even when they succeed, they often struggle to feel proud, bracing instead for judgment or disappointment.

The Peer-like Parent: This parent is more peer than authority and looks to their child for emotional reassurance and approval. They avoid conflict and boundaries, turning to the child for comfort or companionship instead of modeling stability and leadership. While praised for being "mature," their children grow up missing the freedom to simply be a child. When they get older, they often struggle to say no, set boundaries, or prioritize their own needs, fearing that doing so makes them selfish or unlovable. They may continue to take responsibility for others' feelings, confusing caretaking with connection.

The Uninvolved Parent: Sometimes absent physically, though more often absent emotionally, this parent may be consumed by their own struggles, including addiction, trauma, or mental health issues. They meet basic needs inconsistently, or overlook them entirely, leaving children to grow up fast without steady guidance, support, or reflection. As adults, they may feel chronically overlooked, hyper-independent, and convinced that comfort and care are scarce, overextending themselves to secure connection or resources before they run out.

The Over-Permissive Parent: This parent avoids setting boundaries, often out of guilt or a desire to give their child the freedom they never had. Rules feel restrictive, so they emphasize choice and expression over structure. But in trying to protect their child from disappointment, they also remove the limits that teach responsibility and emotional regulation. Children raised in this environment often struggle to tolerate frustration, expect others to accommodate their needs, or feel unsettled and unprepared when life doesn't go their way. Without consistent guidance, they may confuse freedom with love and find boundaries—both their own and others'—difficult to respect or maintain.

The Helicopter Parent: Overinvolved and anxious, this parent micromanages their child's every move in an effort to prevent pain, failure, or risk. Though often well-intentioned, this stifles resilience and undermines a child's ability to trust their instincts. The child learns that the world is too dangerous to navigate on their own, and that they need constant monitoring to stay safe. As they mature, they may feel paralyzed by the need to make a decision, fearful of failure, or dependent on others for reassurance. They often doubt their own judgment and struggle to cultivate autonomy, finding independence both desirable and frightening.

The Authoritarian Parent: This parent is rigid and controlling, and believes obedience is love. Discipline is emphasized over connection, and strict rules dominate the household. While the child may "behave," they learn to suppress their feelings, disconnecting from their inner world in order to survive a fear-based environment. This can foster resentment, secrecy, or rebellion. When these children become adults, they may struggle to assert themselves, default to passivity in relationships, or swing between compliance and resistance. They often carry a deep fear of making mistakes and may equate self-expression with danger rather than authenticity.

It can be painful to realize that your parent may still be a child in an adult body. While emotionally immature parents may have good intentions, that doesn't excuse the harm they can inflict. Awareness, however, helps us see the impact of emotionally immature parenting—not only in how we felt as children but in the roles we were forced to take on. When parents couldn't provide the guidance or stability we needed, many of us became the ones holding things together.

PARENTIFICATION

Childhood is fleeting and precious. Developmentally, these early years are meant for play, expression, and discovery—for learning to meet our own needs through curiosity and connection. They are a wild and wondrous landscape of firsts. From the beginning, we're wired to explore who we are, what we value, and how to connect with the world around us. And as children, we're remarkably perceptive. Constantly scanning our environment for cues, we watch our parents closely to determine whether they are dependable and whether we are safe. Even before we have the words, we can sense if the adults around us are emotionally steady or overwhelmed. When our parents were emotionally mature, we felt free to explore, to be different, to make mistakes. We had space to be ourselves. But if they weren't, we noticed. We felt their withdrawal, unpredictability, or dependence on us. We looked for a stable guide through stress and often had to become our own.

In time, their inability to manage themselves or create stability in our environment heightened our anxiety. We noticed things like: "Mom looks to me to calm her down," or "Dad shuts down when I express how I feel. I can't go to him, so I have to handle things on my own." Many of us were forced into roles far beyond our developmental capacity. We regularly found ourselves being the ones who offered emotional support, stability, and even care to our caregivers. But this isn't the role of a child. Children are meant to receive care, not provide it. This role reversal is known as *parentification*, a term introduced by family systems therapist Salvador Minuchin. It refers to a dynamic where a child assumes adult responsibilities, stepping in to care not only for themselves but also for the emotional or physical needs of others in the household.

More broadly, parentification occurs when a parent is unable to meet their own needs—physically, emotionally, or practically. This may stem from unresolved trauma, lack of support, mental illness, addiction, or overwhelming stressors like poverty or single parenthood. Often, these parents were parentified themselves and grew up believing this dynamic was normal. Some may even know better—but still find themselves unconsciously repeating the cycle with their own children.

Parentification can show up in two main ways:

- Instrumental parentification happens when a child is expected to perform tasks beyond their age, like cooking, cleaning, paying bills, or taking care of siblings.

- Emotional parentification occurs when a child becomes the therapist, confidant, or emotional support for a parent, listening to adult problems, absorbing their emotional pain, or managing conflict within their relationships or the home in general.

Instrumental parentification is common in immigrant households, where children are often expected to take on translation duties, financial responsibilities, or caregiving roles. Though these expectations may arise from necessity, they can still create a deeply rooted belief that love must be earned through labor, or that rest is selfish. These culturally shaped forms of early adultification are forms of parentification.

Over time, these patterns shape how a child sees themselves and relates to others. Underneath a child who seems wise, capable, even independent is often one who had to grow up too fast, learning to suppress their own needs in order to care for another's. What looks like strength in adulthood—hyper-independence—is a survival strategy born from the belief that it's not safe to ask for help.

Liza is an example of emotional parentification. Raised by a passive father and a reactive mother, her home was unpredictable. Her mother's temper could erupt over anything—once it was a yogurt container in the wrong bin. After that, Liza obsessively checked the trash to avoid setting her off. She became hypervigilant, always managing her mom's moods, never her own. This is emotional parentification in action: a child forced to regulate the emotional climate of the household when the adults could not. By the time Liza reached adulthood, the pattern was deeply ingrained. As an adult, she was efficient and reliable at work but emotionally walled off. A friend's offhand comment—"Liza's like a robot"—echoed what her ex had said: He couldn't connect with her. That's when it hit her. She had spent her whole childhood managing everyone else's emotions and never learned how to feel her own.

Parentification doesn't always look like over-functioning. Sometimes it results in emotional paralysis, including difficulty setting boundaries, a chronic fear of disappointing others, or a failure to launch—a child who never leaves the home to establish an independent life. Parentified children often feel intense sympathy for their parents, seeing them not as strong and stable but as fragile or overwhelmed. This role reversal disrupts a child's sense of safety and belonging. To feel accepted, they may become people-pleasers who are attuned to everyone's needs but their own, weighed down by guilt, and unsure how to feel at ease. Because when you spend your early years tending to others, caring for yourself can feel unfamiliar, even unsafe.

This is where healing begins, with awareness. By compassionately noticing the parts of you shaped by early relationships, you begin to understand what happened and how it lives in you now. And from awareness comes choice. The power to create new habits and the capacity to care for yourself in the ways no one once did.

Before we can rewrite our relational story, we have to understand how it was formed. The practice that follows invites you to meet the parts of yourself that adapted to love by over-functioning, hiding, chasing, or going without. As you explore, offer those parts what they needed all along: presence, compassion, and care.

PRACTICE
RELATIONSHIP REFLECTION MAP

Our earliest relationships taught us how to connect, protect, and belong. This practice helps you trace those roles with compassion so you can begin choosing new ways of relating.

1. **Map Your Relationships.** Take a blank page and write "Me" in the center. Around it, write the names (or initials) of your early caregivers and three to five of your most important relationships. Next to each name, add the role you played—such as *Peacemaker, Invisible, Helper, Performer,* or *Troublemaker.*

2. **Explore Each Connection.** Next to each person, note:
   - How you felt most often (safe, anxious, drained, dismissed)
   - What you feared most (abandonment, rejection, not being enough)
   - How you responded to conflict (withdrew, chased, people-pleased, froze, got reactive)
   - Which needs went unmet (validation, safety, consistency, freedom to express yourself)

3. **Notice the Patterns.** Step back and look at your map. Circle the roles, fears, or feelings that repeat. Ask yourself:

- Do I tend to chase closeness or avoid it?
- Do I silence myself to keep the peace?
- Do I lose track of my own needs?

4. **Reframe with Compassion.** Choose one role or pattern that feels strongest right now. Ask yourself:

   - When did I first learn this habit or pattern?
   - How has it helped me?
   - Where is it limiting me now?

Remember, these habits and patterns were once survival strategies that helped you stay connected or feel safe. Now, with awareness, they become insight, giving you the choice to build more balanced, authentic relationships.

As I hope is becoming clear, our early years are greatly influenced by the environments we grow up in, including the attachments we form with caregivers and the difficulties and hardships we face. Small and repeated moments over hours, days, and weeks gradually influence how we come to understand the world and form the blueprint for how we think, feel, and relate, not only to others but to ourselves. Life teaches us the same lessons again and again, and these repeated experiences solidify into unspoken rules about what's safe, what's possible, and who we believe we have to be in order to belong.

These patterns might come from clear family expectations, like never raising your voice at the dinner table, or subtle norms, such as downplaying your achievements to avoid appearing boastful. These influences may also come from the larger community—extended relatives, culture, religion, or school. They become guidelines we unconsciously write for our own survival. With time, these scripts can feel indistinguishable from who we are. But beneath our conditioning, a question lingers: *Is this truly me, or am I just a reflection of where I've been?*

Our first relationships literally shape the wiring of our brain. When a distressed baby is consistently soothed by a caregiver's gentle touch, the pathways between the amygdala (which flags fear) and the prefrontal cortex (which helps regulate emotion) grow stronger. With each calming touch, the child learns—at a neural level—that they can settle. The more this connection is reinforced, the more the child is able to trust their own ability to calm or soothe themselves. But soothing touch is only one example. Our nervous system constantly takes its cues from experience, learning how to respond to a raised voice, a skinned knee, a joke, or a barking dog by watching, listening to, and feeling what's happening around us.

And when love feels scarce or safety uncertain, that wiring becomes wary: Be careful, stay small, or something might go wrong. Childhoods marked by emotional unpredictability or fear create inner maps where danger feels constant, and trust becomes a risk. Even though these patterns run deep, our brains remain capable of change throughout our lifetimes. At any age, your brain can always begin to form new neural pathways, reshaping how you think, how you feel, and how you respond. One of the most powerful ways to create these changes is through what researchers call *relational* neuroplasticity, our brain's capacity to rewire itself in the context of new, nurturing relationships.

Take Shauna, for example. She grew up with a father who criticized her openly, regardless of who was around. Eventually, her friends, who felt uncomfortable with how harshly he spoke to her, avoided coming to visit. Her mother tried to sympathize with what was happening, often telling her that she wanted something different: "I wish he could see how much his words hurt you." Instead of giving Shauna a sense of the kind of love she deserved, those words only deepened her hurt. Shauna began to believe her father's behavior was her fault and that she was somehow unworthy of love.

As an adult, she found herself in romantic entanglements with emotionally distant men, unconsciously reenacting her cycle of chasing love she didn't feel she deserved. Until, one day, she met someone different. He didn't disappear or yell when things got difficult. Instead, he wrote reassuring words for her in the steam on the bathroom mirror, and he stayed. In his consistency and steadiness, she encountered something new and profound: a corrective emotional experience. When you anticipate pain or rejection but instead receive care, safety, or connection, your nervous system begins to rewire its response. This is relational neuroplasticity in action. With her new boyfriend, Shauna began to learn at a brain and body level that love could be secure, that conflict didn't mean abandonment, and that tenderness could be trusted.

This kind of healing is possible for you too. Self-understanding is the starting point of growth. When we see our past clearly, we can create space to move beyond it. Whether it comes through a romantic partner, a therapist, a mentor, a sibling, a coach, or a friend, when you revisit old wounds in the safety of new relationships, your nervous system gets a chance to reprocess your pain with new awareness, to respond differently, and to lay down new neural pathways of connection and resilience. By shifting the stories that your body has accepted as absolute, you can slowly change how you think and feel, developing new habits oriented toward the life you hope to live, and the person you have always been beneath the imprint of your early experiences. And in that process, you begin to believe that you are worthy of care and compassion.

The first step is honoring where your story began. To guide that process, I'll introduce a model built around five key spheres of development that influence who we are and who we have the power to become. Each sphere captures a core aspect of what we all need as children, and each one offers a pathway for healing as adults.

2

YOUR ORIGIN STORY

Our first attachments lay the foundation for how we see the world and how safe we feel within it. But development doesn't stop in our childhood; it continues throughout our entire lives. We're always taking in new experiences, refining our expectations, and reshaping our emotional landscape and patterns of response. We are evolving, always. At different stages, some of our needs are met, and we grow with a sense of ease; in other areas, our needs go unmet, pausing our development. These unfinished parts of us become the places where our inner child still longs for care, and reparenting gives us the opportunity to provide it so that we can grow in the ways that were once not possible.

Regardless of our circumstance as adults, our unmet needs often show up in our daily lives, in how we cope, connect, and care for ourselves. I saw this clearly when I first met Tanya. She was in her thirties and was strong, resourceful, and determined. On paper, Tanya's life looked full and stable: two jobs, a roof overhead, food on the table for her kids. But beneath that stability was a constant hum of tension. She moved through her days as if the ground could give way at any moment. Every bill, every school notice, every late bus felt like a potential disaster. There was never time to pause because there was always another shift to work, another meal to stretch, another problem to solve. Even when life slowed down, Tanya's body didn't. She read bedtime stories with one eye on the clock, folded laundry while dinner simmered, and answered work emails in the grocery line. She told herself she was just "being responsible," but her chest ached, and her sleep was restless. Rest felt unsafe, indulgent, like something she hadn't yet earned.

Slowly, a deeper story began to emerge. Tanya had grown up in a single-parent home where money was scarce and stability never certain. In that environment, slowing down meant bills might go unpaid or there might not be enough food to eat.

Over time, those early realities hardened into unspoken rules. What once kept her safe as a child became a belief she carried into adulthood. Her nervous system learned that survival depended on constant movement, that exhaustion meant safety and rest meant failure. Decades later, her body still acted as if danger were near. Tanya often wondered why she couldn't relax, not realizing that the persistent sense of urgency she felt was her body's way of trying to keep her safe after years of instability and uncertainty.

Tanya's story is just one example of how our early experiences leave lasting marks. Psychologists have long studied this connection, asking how our past shapes who we become. Over the years, many have developed models to explain why people think, feel, and act the way they do and why we're drawn to certain beliefs, behaviors, or partners.

Some, like B. F. Skinner, imagined humans as creatures reacting to their environment—much like mice in a box—responding to rewards and punishments. His theory of "operant conditioning" showed how behaviors could be shaped by consequences. But Skinner's model didn't account for our inner world, the complexity of our emotions, the pain of our unmet needs, or the cost of living without emotional attunement.

As psychology evolved, attention began to shift from behavior alone to the mind that drives it. Another developmental theorist, Jean Piaget, a Swiss psychologist, viewed children as active builders of knowledge. His work highlighted their cognitive development and intelligence, yet still overlooked their inner emotional world, attachment relationships, and overall environments.

Psychoanalyst Erik Erikson built upon these ideas with a model that captured more of our emotional depth. He emphasized the interplay between our inner world and the social environment, viewing human development as a series of stages, each marked by a core conflict or challenge like trust versus mistrust, autonomy versus shame. His work showed that a child's surroundings shape not only their emerging sense of Self—their identity and confidence—but also the personality patterns that guide how they think, feel, and connect with others. Yet even Erikson's framework, profound as it was, overlooked the role of the body—how it holds on to what the mind cannot and stores experiences we may no longer remember. Today, our body has become impossible to ignore. While traditional psychological models focused on thoughts and behaviors, modern research has consistently shown that our environments, especially chronic stress experienced in childhood, leave lasting imprints on our biology. This can look like a nervous system caught in survival mode; an immune system on high alert; or an imbalanced gut microbiome. Our development doesn't happen in the mind alone; it's etched into the fibers of our being.

For this reason, I believe it's time to embrace a model that includes biography *and* biology, emotion *and* environment, mind *and* body. A model that acknowledges healing is not only possible but also natural. Because we are built to adapt to our circumstances, to reach, and to grow.

To help map this evolution, I developed the Individual Development Model, a framework of five interconnected spheres, or core influences, that shape who we become. These spheres aren't linear stages tied to specific abilities to be mastered by a certain age, or to complete in a certain order. Instead, they're more similar to our five senses: distinct, yet constantly interacting with, informing, and responding to one another. As you learn about the five spheres, you'll be exploring where your growth might have been paused—what needs were never met and what necessary skills never had the chance to fully develop. You'll begin to understand how your nervous system adapted to the world around you in ways that were once protective but may now keep you from a deeper connection with yourself and others. Because lasting change doesn't come from insight alone; it begins in the body, where we can gently retrain the survival patterns that no longer serve us.

And just like our body, growth itself follows its own rhythm—rarely linear or predictable. It bends and adapts to the conditions around it. Think of the trees you've seen growing around fences and rusted bicycles and through split sidewalks. They do not shrink away from the obstacles in their paths. Instead, they rise, twist, and adapt to their surroundings, always making room for life, even when their path toward the sun is blocked.

They become uniquely beautiful because of, not despite, their conditions. We're like that too.

While our earliest environments shaped our growth, they did not define our limits. Some of us learned independence too early, some of us learned silence, some of us learned to meet the needs of others before recognizing our own. These are not faults. They are adaptations. Just as a species evolves to survive its environment, we change the way we think and act to make it through the challenges of our childhood. And now, as adults, we have the power to understand those adaptations and to choose what to keep, what to adjust, and what to grow beyond.

My developmental model and the reparenting journey that will follow invite you to explore where your habits and patterns began. To greet your inner child with compassion and curiosity. To gently revise the beliefs that once kept you safe but now keep you small, separate, or shut down. And to remember that even what feels permanent is, in fact, changeable.

So, let's begin. Let us walk together through the forest of your past. We take this journey not to get lost in the weeds but to clearly see and understand the path that brought you here. Let us remember that like trees, we reach for the light, even if we've had to grow around shadows. And let us reimagine what is possible from here onward.

The Individual Development Model

SPHERE ONE: SAFETY AND SECURITY

One of my earliest memories, and I don't have many, is lying awake in my childhood bed, too anxious to fall asleep, afraid that my parents are going to die. This existential fear haunted me, especially at night. I thought about death frequently, not just because my parents were significantly older than most of my peers' parents but also because health issues and anxiety were constants in our home. My mom carried deep, unresolved fear from her own childhood and didn't develop the tools she needed to manage stress later in life. She never truly felt safe in her own body. Because of this, it was hard for her to help me feel safe in mine, especially when I was overwhelmed by big emotions.

Later, in my twenties, my mom would sometimes joke, "Nicole was never bothered by anything." The rest of the family would laugh in recognition of my "stoic" nature while I felt an immediate flash of anger. The truth was, I *was* bothered. I was often scared . . . about many things. But because my mom was preoccupied with her own fears, she wasn't able to attune to or even notice mine. I'm sure I looked fine on the outside. I didn't scream or throw tantrums. I didn't sob or act out. Instead, I spaced out. I dissociated. My apparent indifference was misread as calm. Inside I was full of need. I needed connection, soothing, and someone to witness and help me hold everything I was feeling.

Without an attuned and emotionally responsive adult, I didn't have what psychologists call a *secure base*, or a consistent, regulated caregiver who helps a child feel safe in their body, in their home, and in their world. Long before my panic attacks began in early adulthood, I had already developed different compulsive habits—obsessively organizing my room, checking my clothes for stains, and rewriting work until it looked "just right"—all ways of trying to regulate my inner world by controlling my outer one. They were my desperate attempt to create order and safety wherever and however I could.

Our Survival Instincts

As babies, we are wired for safety and connection as a matter of survival. We're entirely reliant on the warmth, nourishment, and presence of an attuned caregiver who can decode our cries and soothe our distress. When something feels unfamiliar or overwhelming, we instinctively turn to our caregivers to help us make sense of what's happening within or around us. This is because evolution gave us the possibility of regulation through connection. An attuned caregiver helps us develop the ability to soothe and manage our emotions. Their consistent presence teaches our body and mind: I am safe, and I matter. Someone will come when I call. A warm hand, a calm voice, or the steady rhythm of a nearby heartbeat are all cues that signal safety to our nervous system. They trigger the release of oxytocin, slow the heart rate, and ease our body's guard. Over time, these experiences teach our body to settle, to trust that it is no longer in danger, and to reconnect with what safety feels like.

When we feel safe, our nervous system calms. When we don't, it doesn't. A powerful demonstration of this comes from the "Still Face" experiment, a well-known study conducted by Edward Tronick in 1975. In this study, a mother first engages warmly with her baby by smiling, cooing, and making eye contact. Then, on cue, she suddenly goes completely expressionless. Within seconds, the baby senses the disconnection and grows distressed—cooing, reaching, crying—to try to reengage her attention. When no response comes, the baby finally withdraws, shutting down in visible distress. While the baby remained physically safe throughout this experience, the rupture in emotional presence activated a survival response. Shutting down is our nervous system's way of surviving by conserving our energy and numbing our pain when it decides there's no way to escape or get what we need.

When this kind of shutdown happens repeatedly in childhood, especially with caregivers, it leaves lasting marks. If a caregiver is emotionally dysregulated or unavailable, as was the case for my mother, we grow up without a felt sense of safety. Our bodies adapt for survival, not connection. Instead of developing a steady baseline of comfort and ease, our capacity to feel safe becomes limited. We stop sharing our emotions when the response we desire never comes, and our nervous system stays on alert, minimizing our needs and scanning for danger.

When we're in this survival mode, our body takes over. Our heart pounds, our muscles brace, and our senses remain on alert for threat. Blood flow and energy shift away from our prefrontal cortex (our thinking brain) toward our brain stem and limbic system (our instinctual and emotional centers). Our thoughts narrow and we become hyperfocused on the most obvious threat in our environment—whether physical or emotional. Our ability to tap into logic becomes impaired; we may fumble over our words, lose our train of thought, or find our mind blanking out completely. We slip into something ancient, reflexive, and reactive. We're no longer functioning as a present adult; we're rendered as needy and survival focused as an infant.

If we lacked a consistent, soothing presence as a child, this dysregulation lives within us, driving our behavior. One mother described her colicky first child to me. "She cried constantly," she said. "I tried everything, but sometimes I just couldn't take it. I didn't really bond with her." Years later, she admitted that she felt more attached to her second child, a boy, who was quiet and easy. Her daughter, meanwhile, became careful and watchful, highly attentive to even the smallest change in others' faces, tones, or silences. She learned to stay alert for signs of disconnection, always adjusting herself to avoid rejection. Her vigilant attention and seeming empathy to the reactions of others was a long-relied-on survival strategy. Her brother, on the other hand, moved through life with ease, anchored by an expectation that his needs would be met. He offered others comfort from a place of safety and security, not as a means to create it for himself.

In therapy as a teenager, the daughter was asked: "If you had to spend a year in a room with one person, who would it be?" Her answer: "My mom." When the therapist shared this, her mother wept. "I don't deserve that," she said. But long-held truths were spoken, and forgiveness was offered.

This story mirrors the experience of so many families. Reality is, no parent actually treats each child exactly the same because their own emotional capacity shifts with time and circumstance. A parent might be exhausted with a newborn, calmer with the next child, more financially stressed a few years later, or emotionally distracted during a divorce—shifts that land differently on each child. And those subtle differences—a parent's stress, availability, or attunement—can reverberate across a lifetime.

There's a name for this return to one another: *repair*, or the neurobiological process of reconnecting after disconnection. In moments of physical or emotional reconnection through eye contact, soothing touch, or affectionate words, oxytocin rises, the activity in our amygdala decreases,[1] and both individuals' heart rates, cortisol, and even immune responses begin to synchronize.[2]

Repair doesn't always happen all at once. It builds slowly, moment by moment. The daughter's nervous system had been shaped by absence, but each new experience of presence helped rewrite that story. She and her mother now have a new level of understanding and a chance to build on this reconnection.

Wired for Survival

The first parts of our brain to develop are those that promote survival: our brain stem, spinal cord, and peripheral nervous system. This system operates beneath our awareness, constantly scanning for danger and asking, *Am I safe?* It pulls us away from pain, startles us from stillness, and prepares us to run or freeze. It reacts before we ever form a conscious thought.

And it learns through repetition. From the womb onward, our nervous system is shaped by our experiences, by the presence or absence of safety, attunement, and care. Over time, our brain forms patterns based on what's familiar. That's why the ways we soothe, shut down, or lash out can feel so automatic—because they are.

These habits and patterns don't just vanish with age. They continue to influence how we think, feel, and connect. I saw this clearly in myself. I used to suffer from OCD symptoms and panic attacks. I was an overwhelmed child who became an adult living on high alert. My mind and body clung to control—organizing, cleaning, replaying—as a way to feel safe in a world that often didn't. For years, I thought this way of being was "just my personality." But those thoughts and behaviors weren't who I *was*; they were how I adapted. For many of us, these adaptations become the architecture of our inner world, shaped not just by what happened but by what didn't. The comfort that never came and the support that was never received.

Safety is the foundation that teaches us we are allowed to *be*; to rest, to feel, to take up space. It gives us permission to exist, to be held, to soften into presence. This drive for safety is universal. It's the ground on which all development rests. That's why Sphere One of the Individual Development Model invites us to explore: *Do I feel safe? Was someone there to calm me when I needed soothing?* If not, that longing for safety may still live inside us, often unrecognized but deeply felt. And we may still be seeking safety in ways we don't recognize. When we didn't receive that safety as children, our task is to gradually rebuild it from within by tending to our present moment with compassion. Because safety is the beginning of everything. It's how we build a home within, a steady and rooted place we can return to when the world feels like too much. From that secure ground, we can finally move forward, toward separation, toward choice, and toward selfhood. To offer our inner child now what we most needed then.

PRACTICES FOR SPHERE ONE

Return to the Ground Beneath You

These practices offer simple tools to guide you back to your breath, your body, and the inner home you've always carried within you. Instead of pushing yourself forward, you'll compassionately meet yourself exactly where you are. Along the way, you'll learn to become the steady presence you always needed. You'll become for yourself the one who stays, the one who soothes, and the one who says, *You're safe now.*

PRACTICE
LESSONS ABOUT SAFETY, NEED, AND LOVE

Long before we had words, we learned through tone, touch, and presence. We absorbed messages about whether love was safe, whether our needs mattered, and whether the world would accept and hold us. This practice invites you to explore what your body remembers.

Ground Yourself. Find a quiet space. You might put on soft music, light a candle, or do anything else that helps you feel connected to your surroundings. Begin to slow and deepen your breath. When you feel ready, say softly to yourself or aloud: *I am safe now. I look back with compassion.*

Reflect. Take a few moments to explore the prompts below, writing your responses in a notebook or journal:

- When was I first comforted? Who was there, and what did it teach me about love and support?
- When do I first remember feeling afraid? Was someone there to help me? What did I learn about safety?
- When did I need support and feel let down? How did that shape my ability to trust others?
- When did I feel most connected—or disconnected—from a caregiver?
- What do I notice in my body as I recall these moments (tightness, warmth, stillness, breath holding)?
- How does my body show me today when I feel safe, and when I don't?

When you're done, place one hand on your heart and one on your belly. Take three slow, steady breaths, noticing how your body feels supported in this moment. Whisper to yourself: *I am safe. I am here. I am learning to give myself what I need.*

PRACTICE
WHAT STILLNESS MEANS TO YOU

Stillness is more than the absence of movement; it's our nervous system's signal of safety. When we can pause without bracing for danger, our body learns that it's okay to rest. But many of us resist rest because we're "too busy." Or because stillness once felt unsafe, and quiet meant tension in the house, disconnection, or invisibility. At other times, stillness can stir up uncomfortable emotions or self-critical thoughts. This practice helps you notice your body's relationship with stillness and reflect on where those beliefs began, so you can slowly rebuild safety in pausing.

1. **Notice Your Present Experience.** Find a quiet place, turn off distractions, and take a few slow breaths as you settle into stillness, noticing what comes up in your body (*calm, restlessness, heaviness, tension, alertness*) as you ask yourself:
   - What happens in my body when I pause?
   - What thoughts or emotions come up when I'm not doing anything?
   - Do I feel like I should be doing more?
2. **Explore Early Imprints.** Take a few minutes to explore:
   - When the house grew quiet in childhood, what did it usually mean?
   - Did stillness feel safe and comforting (like being tucked in at night) or unsettling (like being left in silence after an argument)?
   - What beliefs about rest started to form in those moments? For example: *Rest is lazy, unsafe, or something that must be earned.*

3. **Create a New Association.** Say to yourself, *Stillness is nourishing. I deserve to rest,* while resting a hand on your heart and/or belly and taking a slow, deep breath as you begin to notice what shifts inside your body.

Remember, every time you pause, you strengthen your connection to your inner knowing and rebuild self-trust. Over time, these silent moments can become a safe place to meet yourself again.

PRACTICE
AN INNER SENSE OF SAFETY

Safety isn't only the absence of danger. It's a felt sense in the body that says, *I am held. I belong. I can soften and be at ease.* Many of us didn't grow up with that feeling, but we can learn to offer it to ourselves now. This practice combines body cues, imagination, and simple tools to build an inner sanctuary you can return to anytime.

1. **Anchor in the Present.** Sit comfortably where you are. Take a few slow, deep breaths. Look around you and name:

    ◂ Five things you see
    ◂ Four things you feel
    ◂ Three things you hear
    ◂ Two things you smell
    ◂ One thing you taste

2. **Imagine a Safe Space.** Close your eyes and picture a place where you feel calm. It could be real (your bed, a childhood tree) or imagined (a beach, a glowing cave). Fill in the details: the colors, the sounds, the textures under your hands or feet. Invite a supportive presence into this space, real or symbolic, radiating warmth and protection. Notice how your body responds as you hold this image. Then, choose one object in this space that represents this safety to you—a candle, a stone, a soft blanket.

3. **Signal Safety to Your Body.** When you feel unsettled, try one of these cues to let your nervous system know it's safe to rest:

   ◁ Gently touch the spot just behind your ears.
   ◁ Hum, sigh, or sing softly.
   ◁ Massage your jaw, temples, or face.
   ◁ Apply light pressure between your eyebrows ("third eye" spot).

4. **Build Your Resources.** Reflect by asking, *What helps me soften or settle? Where in my body do I feel safety most easily?* In your notebook or journal, keep a list of two kinds of resources you can lean on:

   ◁ **External Resources:** People, animals, or objects that calm you (a friend, a pet, a place).
   ◁ **Internal Resources:** Memories, images, or phrases that ground you (a lullaby, ocean waves, "I'm safe now").

Through the practices of grounding, attunement, and rest, you've learned that safety begins within. Each time you listen and respond to your body's cues, you rebuild trust with yourself and remind your nervous system that calm is possible.

True safety is permission—to feel, to slow down, to simply be. With this steadiness, you create the foundation for all healing: the capacity to explore, to express, and to connect. Once safety has taken root, you're ready to discover who you are beyond protection and to honor your individuality with confidence and care.

SPHERE TWO: INDIVIDUATION

When Audrey was a little girl living in Washington, DC, she fell in love with the Metro. While other children headed toward exhibits at the museums, she lingered underground. She watched the trains come and go, traced the routes of the transit map with her fingers, memorized the names of stations like they were part of a secret language. Her parents didn't share her fascination. Her mother called it odd, and her father hurried her along. "It's dirty and unsafe down here," they said. "Why waste time in a place like this?"

Audrey started drawing her own maps at home, quietly and joyfully expressing her interests. But her mother held them up like jokes. "Guess what this is? Another subway map!" she said, laughing with Audrey's sister.

Audrey pretended not to care, but she got the message. She heard her parents talk about it with their friends. "It's just so weird," her mother said once. "I always thought I'd have a little girl who loved to dance." So, Audrey asked for dance lessons, and when she did, a huge smile spread across her mother's face. That smile said everything: *This is how to be lovable.* The train-loving girl got buried inside. Audrey didn't just shift her interests to please her parents; she also learned a deeper lesson that being herself wasn't safe.

We all have an innate desire for autonomy, or a deep, biological pull to become our own, separate person. And the more secure we feel, the more open we are to explore with confidence and curiosity. Curiosity is a natural force within us. It urges us to test limits, express our individuality, and discover our potential. Picture a baby crawling toward a toy, frequently glancing back to make sure their caregiver is still there, or a child climbing to the top of a playground structure while a parent stands nearby, offering a steady presence without interference. That balance between connection and freedom is what gives us the courage to stretch into new experiences.

While separating from our parents or caregivers can feel unsettling at times, it's a vital part of healthy development. Discovering our own interests and boundaries is referred to as *individuation*. It's through this process that we begin to learn what we enjoy, where our boundaries lie, and who we ultimately are. Eventually, this independence helps us identify the passions and purpose that give our lives meaning. When we are free to become ourselves within the context of ever-present safety and support, growth feels expansive rather than threatening.

When it's not, we may find independence frightening or fear it will cost us connection with those we love. Feeling free to explore our interests and getting in touch with our natural limits or boundaries is our focus in Sphere Two.

Learning to Set and Respect Limits

As children, we need both containment and freedom. To explore with confidence, we need clear boundaries that let us know the world is safe. From the start, we're equipped with an internal alarm system, or an instinctive signal that alerts us when something feels off or unsafe. In our toddler years, we begin testing limits: reaching for a hot stove, throwing toys when we're upset. When parents respond with consistency—"No, that's dangerous," or "We don't hit"—they're not just setting rules. They're helping us build internal discipline through the steady balance of structure and freedom.

Healthy boundaries act like scaffolding in development. They don't confine a child; they support them, offering a reliable framework within which a child can stretch, test, and retreat. These everyday moments reveal just how formative boundaries are, shaping behavior and wiring our nervous system. Imagine a toddler who pulls away from a relative's hug. An attuned parent might say, "You don't have to hug if you're not ready." That moment sends a powerful message: My body is mine; my instincts matter; and I am protected. Contrast that with the well-meaning but misguided encouragement: "Don't be rude; just give them a hug." The message shifts: Your discomfort is less important than someone else's feelings.

Moments like this show why it should matter when a child says no, even when they can't dictate the outcome. A visit to the doctor, for instance, still has to happen. But at every age, children need space to express preferences, have their opinions acknowledged, and witness adults modeling respect for one another's boundaries. When that attunement is missing, children are flooded with fear and shame, and their emerging sense of agency weakens. To preserve the relationships they depend on, they begin overriding their own instincts and silencing their needs.

As we grow, our need for autonomy becomes more pronounced. Adolescence and early adulthood call for even more space to explore and define ourselves—through keeping private journals, retreating behind closed doors, or choosing our own friends. Having this space—and having it respected—helps us build more than independence; it helps us learn boundaries and the discipline required to maintain them. Boundaries are the practice of saying, "This is what I need," and holding to it, even when it's hard or inconvenient. And discipline is what steadies us when impulses pull us off course. Like choosing not to look at an upsetting story on social media, to text an ex, or to let old, unhealthy habits pull us back in. But when children aren't given this space to practice choice or to see their boundaries respected, the consequences often linger into adulthood. People who lacked autonomy as children often have difficulty asserting their needs, saying no, or tolerating discomfort, and often struggle to trust themselves or feel secure in who they are.

Throughout my clinical work, I saw how deeply boundary dynamics shape development. Take Joshua, for example. His mother, who was brought up in a strict household, swung too far in the other direction when she became a parent, offering him minimal structure. As a child, Joshua lacked guidance on how to honor his own space or the space of others. He grabbed other kids' toys even when they protested. When his parents were having a conversation, he often pulled his mother's face in his own direction, demanding that she play with him, which she then did. His father remained disengaged, throwing up his hands and watching his wife tend to every single one of their son's interruptions. Without clear models, Joshua grew up disregarding the physical and emotional boundaries of others. In his twenties, he developed a reputation for crossing lines with women—missing signals of discomfort, showing up instead of calling first—behaviors he didn't recognize as violations because he'd never learned otherwise.

Without boundaries, children like Joshua struggle to develop a sense of where they end and others begin. To understand why, we have to look at what's happening inside the maturing brain.

The Emotional Brain

As we explore the world, our "emotional brain" is still developing. The limbic system, which includes structures like the hypothalamus and amygdala, drives our pursuit of pleasure and our instinct to avoid pain. This system fuels our curiosity, helping us discover our preferences, form emotional connections, and navigate early social interactions. As it matures, we gradually become better at managing difficult situations and distinguishing between what we can handle on our own and when we need support.

When this emotional system is supported by consistent care and appropriate boundaries, children develop the capacity to process challenging experiences, form healthy relationships, and pursue meaningful interests. But when safety and containment are absent, their system becomes overwhelmed. The result is often heightened reactivity, showing up as hypervigilance, difficulty managing stress, and trouble interpreting social cues. Chronic stress and emotional invalidation can disrupt the development and functioning of their limbic system, leading to symptoms such as mood instability, hyperactivity, memory lapses, difficulty with focus or impulse control, and emotional responses that may seem disproportionate to the situation.

When safety and emotional containment are in place, a child's nervous system can settle enough to engage with the world. From that sense of steadiness, curiosity naturally unfolds. Our drive to grow and express ourselves is innate. We're all born with a longing to explore, to stretch beyond what is known, and to discover who we are. This process of individuation begins the moment a child, consciously or unconsciously, asks, *Can I explore and express myself and still be loved?* The answers we received through tone, presence, and consistency shaped more than just our emotional security. They sculpted our brain's architecture, influenced our capacity for learning, exploration, and self-awareness, and laid the groundwork for discipline, agency, and ultimately emotional maturity. Our parents' comfort with our autonomy became the foundation for our ability to know ourselves, trust our instincts, and live in alignment with what we feel and believe.

The process of individuation is about building your own foundation so you can meet others from a place of wholeness. It is the dance between holding on and letting go, between belonging and becoming. Only when we are allowed to explore this balance within safe, respectful boundaries do we begin to discover who we truly are.

PRACTICES FOR SPHERE TWO

From Knowing to Becoming

These practices offer ways to reconnect with your autonomy, your edges, and your inner compass. Instead of overriding your needs, you'll practice listening to them. Along the way, you'll learn to honor your yes, protect your no, and trust that your truth deserves space. You'll become for yourself the one who respects, the one who protects, and the one who says: *You're allowed to be you.*

PRACTICE
MOMENTS OF PLEASURE AND DISAPPOINTMENT

Our bodies remember both joy and pain. Moments of pleasure expand us; our breath deepens, muscles soften, and curiosity sparks. Moments of disappointment contract us; our chest tightens, muscles tense, and energy drains. This practice helps you notice the difference, reconnect with your body's emotional language, and reflect on how these experiences shaped the way you relate to yourself today.

1. **Create Your Two Columns.** Take a notebook, journal, or sheet of paper and draw two columns, labeling one *Pleasure* and the other *Disappointment*. In the *Pleasure* column, list small things from childhood that made you feel alive, like playing outside, drawing, laughing with a friend, reading, singing, or climbing trees. In the *Disappointment* column, list times you felt let down, like being ignored, punished for expressing yourself, losing a game, or being told to be quiet.

2. **Choose and Recall.** Circle one memory from each column. Close your eyes and take a few slow, deep breaths:

- First recall the memory from the *Pleasure* column. Begin to notice the sensations in your body, asking yourself: *Does my body feel warmer? Is my breath deeper? Do I sense openness or energy?*
- Then shift to the *Disappointment* memory, noticing the sensations in your body and asking yourself: *Do I feel tightness or heaviness? Is my jaw tense? Do I feel like closing off?*

3. **Map Your Sensations.** Write down what you noticed in your body for each memory. You can use words, images, or even simple drawings. Examples: *Joy felt like a glowing sun in my chest. Disappointment felt like a heavy stone in my stomach.*

4. **Reflect on the Meaning.** Take a few moments to explore the prompts below, writing your responses in a notebook or journal:

   - What messages did I receive in childhood about joy, pleasure, failure, or emotional expression?
   - Do I allow myself to enjoy what feels good, or do I rush it away or feel guilty?
   - When I'm disappointed, how do I usually react—by shutting down, overthinking, blaming, or something else?

5. **Note Your Awareness.** Write one sentence that sums up what you discovered. Examples: *I feel most alive when I'm outside in nature. I learned to stay quiet to avoid disappointment. I notice I pull away from joy before I can fully feel it.*

By mapping these moments, you learn to recognize expansion (pleasure, aliveness) and contraction (disappointment, protection) in your body. Over time, this awareness helps you trust your inner signals and create more space for what truly nourishes you.

PRACTICE
RISK-TAKING AND BOUNDARIES

Boundaries teach us where we end and others begin. As children, we tested limits through exploration, curiosity, and risk-taking. The way our caregivers responded—by being encouraging, dismissive, or critical—taught us whether it's safe to take up space, say no, or try new things. This practice helps you reflect on how boundaries first formed in your life, what messages you internalized, and how you honor your yes and no today.

1. **Recall Your Early Exploration.** Close your eyes and take a few slow, deep breaths. Picture yourself as a child trying something new, like climbing a tree, breaking a rule, speaking up, or experimenting. Ask yourself:

    - Was I safe to explore?
    - How did the adults around me respond? Were they encouraging, dismissive, critical, or absent?
    - Was it okay to fail?
    - What support did I need that I didn't get?

2. **Explore Your Early Boundaries.** Now, call to mind a few moments in childhood when your boundaries weren't respected (being forced to hug, hearing adults' problems, being told to keep a secret that felt wrong). For each, ask yourself:

    - How did I feel in that moment?
    - Was anyone there to protect or validate me?
    - What did I learn about saying no or honoring my discomfort?

3. **Map Your Yes and No (Boundary Audit).** Grab your notebook or journal and turn to a blank page, dividing it into two columns: *Yes* and *No*. Think about the past week. Under Yes, write moments when you agreed to something you genuinely wanted. Under No, write moments when you said yes even though you wanted to say no. Circle one example from each column and notice the difference:

- Did I feel free, or did I feel pressured?
- What need was I honoring—or ignoring—in that moment?
- How did my body feel afterward—energized, calm, drained, or tense?
- Did I feel like I honored myself or abandoned myself?

4. **Reflect.** Take a few moments to explore the prompts below, writing your responses in a notebook or journal:

    - Do I recognize what "yes" and "no" feel like in my body?
    - Do I allow myself a pause before responding, or do I rush to please?
    - Do I notice when I agree out of pressure, fear, or guilt?
    - Where do I overextend, stay silent, or push past my limits?
    - What situations make it easier for me to say no? What situations make it harder?
    - How often do I override my need for comfort or boundaries in favor of duty, achievement, or perfection?

By exploring how your boundaries first formed and how they show up now, you begin to see the patterns more clearly. Each true "yes" and "no" is practice—small steps toward building boundaries that protect your energy, honor your truth, and make space for relationships rooted in mutual respect.

PRACTICE
BOUNDARIES YOU NEEDED

Sometimes we realize only afterward that we wish we had spoken up, said no, or asked for what we needed. This practice helps you explore the boundaries you wish you had set, without pressure to change anything yet. It's about noticing the boundaries you needed and exploring what would have helped you feel safe enough to honor them.

1. **Recall Moments You Needed a Boundary.** Think of three times in the past month when you felt overwhelmed, uncomfortable, or taken for granted, writing down each situation briefly.

2. **Imagine the Boundary You Wanted.** For each situation, write the boundary you wish you had set. Examples: *I wish I had told my friend I was too tired to talk. I wish I had said no to extra work.* Then ask yourself: *Why didn't I set the boundary?* Examples: *I was afraid of conflict. I was worried about rejection. I was unsure if I had the right.*

3. **Notice Your Feelings.** Explore what emotions come up when you imagine setting those boundaries—guilt, fear, relief, sadness, strength—asking yourself:

   ◁ What would have helped me feel safe enough to set that boundary?
   ◁ What inner resource (like courage, clarity, or calm) would I have needed in that moment?
   ◁ What reassurance or reminder could have helped me honor myself then?

4. **Plant a Small Seed.** Choose one of your examples. Write one short sentence beginning with: *Next time, I'd like to . . .* Example: *Next time, I'd like to pause before saying yes so I can check in with my energy.*

Each small, consistent act of clarity—pausing before you act, honoring what feels true—helps you stand in your truth without losing connection to others.

Individuation is the process of discovering where you begin and others end, balancing autonomy with connection. With your individuality taking root, you're ready to move into Sphere Three: cultivating empathy and connection in order to develop the ability to attune to your own emotions while staying open to the feelings of those around you.

SPHERE THREE: AGENCY AND EMPATHY

"I don't want to go back to Kyle's house," Aidan says quietly from the back seat as his dad, Steven, drives them home. Steven glances in the rearview mirror. "Why not, bud? Did something happen?"

Aidan, a thoughtful first grader, pauses. "His mommy made us a snack that looked like a face, and I didn't like it."

Steven tries to piece it together. "You didn't like how it looked?"

"No, it was a waffle. I like waffles."

"Okay..." Steven says, still unsure.

Then Aidan asks, "Is *my* mommy going to be home?"

Steven softens. "Not tonight, buddy. She has to work late."

Aidan doesn't respond. His small legs start to kick against his car seat. Steven looks back again and sees tears starting to pool in his son's eyes.

Now it clicks. It's not about the waffle; it's about who made it. Kyle's mom was home, making snacks. Aidan misses his mom, and what he really longs for is that same kind of presence. Steven feels the tightness rise in his chest, the sting of helplessness. But he stays grounded, steady for his son. "I know, sweetheart. I wish Mommy could be home more too. She wants to be. But work makes it hard. And I know that doesn't help. What matters is ... she's not here right now, and that hurts. It's okay to feel hurt."

He reaches a hand back and rests it on Aidan's knee. Aidan places his small hand on top. That touch, that acknowledgment, it calms him. When they pull into the driveway, Steven doesn't rush. He unbuckles Aidan, lifts him out of the car, and holds him close. Aidan melts into his father's arms, his breath slowing as he rests against the steady beat of his dad's heart.

It doesn't always go this way. Aidan might not calm down ... this time. Still, in these moments, when a child is allowed to feel, is where empathy begins. In that exchange, simple and unremarkable to anyone passing by, Aidan begins to understand that his feelings matter, that he is being seen, heard, and held. Steven doesn't try to fix his son's sadness or dismiss it. He makes space for it and becomes the safe harbor in his son's emotional storm. Even if he doesn't see the effect on the spot, he trusts that consistent validation of Aidan's feelings will pay off in the long run.

His father's steady presence becomes a model that Aidan will carry into his friendships, his partnerships, and perhaps one day into his own parenting. Moments like these teach a child to name their emotions, empathize with others, and show up fully in relationships. From these early experiences, emotional maturity develops.

Developing Empathy

As Aidan processed his feelings in the back seat that day, something profound happened: He learned that his emotions could be shared and met without judgment. His father didn't change the facts—his mother was still at work—but he changed the meaning. He made room for Aidan's disappointment. That space, that acknowledgment, helped Aidan feel better. But more than that, it taught him that his feelings had an impact, that his words reached another, and that he had the power to influence his connections and relationships.

This is the foundation of agency. Children don't develop agency in isolation. They develop it in the presence of caregivers who reflect their emotional worlds back to them with attunement and compassion. When that happens, they begin to realize their voice matters. Out of these moments, *agency* emerges. Agency is more than simply acting—it's the felt sense that your perspective matters, your emotions carry weight, and your presence has impact. It shows up in everyday moments: choosing a group activity, taking the lead on a project, or cleaning up so the space feels welcoming for others. But these small acts only happen when children have first been shown empathy—when their own inner world has been acknowledged and respected enough that they can extend that same care outward.

And when that empathy is missing, the results can be painful. I once watched a little boy at an orchard, overwhelmed and dragging his feet in line for a hayride. His parents, flustered, pulled him forward. When the attendant asked if he was ready, the boy hurled his ticket and screamed, "NO!" His parents, faces red with embarrassment, called him a brat and yanked him away. He dissolved into tears.

To most, it looked like defiance. To me, it looked like distress. What he needed wasn't punishment. He needed someone to kneel beside him and say, "You seem upset. Want to take a break?" Even in those difficult moments when an overwhelmed child lashes out or shuts down, what they need most is connection, not correction. You can't talk a child through or out of a meltdown because they literally can't "hear" you. Their limbic system is overactive, and their body needs to discharge energy before their prefrontal cortex can come back online and function. A child whose parent supports them through difficult moments learns, *I can struggle and still be loved. I can feel big things and still be safe.*

We don't build resilience by being told to push through discomfort. We build it when someone sits with us until we feel better and we're ready to try again. Parents who carry their own unresolved trauma often misread these moments, mistaking fear or sadness for aggression or defiance. In fact, research shows that survivors of abuse are more likely to perceive anger in neutral facial expressions.[3] This inability to perceive others' emotions gets passed down. When a parent repeatedly sees disrespect instead of distress and punishes a child for needing help, the child learns that their needs are dangerous and their emotions are wrong.

True empathy isn't just feeling badly or sorry for someone. It's staying present with their pain and tolerating discomfort alongside them. It's saying, "I'm here," not "Hurry up and stop feeling that way." And it's what teaches a child to not only understand others but to understand themselves. Real empathy grows in the emotional rhythms of a secure relationship. As adults, when we pause to really listen to someone's feelings without trying to fix them, we begin to rewire the parts of ourselves that are still learning it's safe to feel.

The Emotionally Attuned Brain

Human beings are social animals, and our brains evolved to support interpersonal relationships. We have special brain cells called *mirror neurons* that attune to the actions of others and prompt us to imitate aspects of their behavior, like movements, facial expressions, or vocal tones. This is part of why someone's laugh can make us smile, seeing someone get hurt can make us flinch, or hearing about someone's heartbreak can bring us to tears. This neural mirroring is the biological foundation of empathy, allowing us to sense, anticipate, or understand others' emotions without a word being spoken.

Our brains are wired to sync—that is, when we're closely connected to someone, our brains and bodies naturally align, reflecting their feelings, focus, and even physical rhythms. Mirror neurons allow us to absorb emotional cues from others, and when someone meets us with presence, authenticity, or care, it helps us feel seen and connected. This soothing isn't just emotional; it's biochemical, with the release of hormones such as oxytocin and dopamine, which lower stress and increase connection. When someone meets us with authenticity, it puts our body at ease, allowing us to be more authentic ourselves.

Aidan may not remember that drive home with his dad in perfect detail, but his nervous system won't forget it. Each time his father names a feeling, holds steady, and stays close, Aidan's inner world becomes a little more organized, a little more safe. And from that safety, empathy, initiative, and resilience can grow.

When we pair empathy with agency, or the awareness that our words and actions can soothe, support, or inspire, we step into truly reciprocal relationships. We begin to ask ourselves: *Do my actions matter to someone else? Do my words, my choices, my presence make a difference in the world around me?* When the answer is yes, we move beyond basic emotional intelligence into emotional intimacy, or the deep connection that leaves us feeling grounded, alive, and fully known.

PRACTICES FOR SPHERE THREE

Cultivate Agency and Emotional Resilience

These practices help you reconnect with your inner authority, experiment with choice, and practice taking meaningful action even in small ways. Without agency, life feels like something happening *to* you instead of something you're influencing. Instead of silencing your impulses or waiting for permission, you'll practice honoring them. Along the way, you'll learn to trust your decisions, follow your curiosity, and take steps that reflect who you truly are. You'll become for yourself the one who chooses, the one who acts, and the one who says, *My life is mine to create.*

PRACTICE
YOUR FAMILY LESSONS—MISTAKES AND EMOTIONS

The way mistakes and emotions were handled in your family influence how you treat yourself today. By looking back with compassion, you can see where old patterns began and start to create new ones.

1. **Reflect on Childhood Experiences.** Take a few moments to explore the prompts below, writing your responses in a notebook or journal.

   - When someone made a mistake in my family, how was it handled—through punishment, denial, or as a chance to learn?
   - How were emotions expressed at home—welcomed, dismissed, or punished?
   - When I had a strong reaction, was it acknowledged, minimized, or ignored?
   - Did I learn to comfort myself, hide my feelings, or expect criticism?
   - In my family, did "I'm sorry" signal real repair, an attempt to brush things aside, or a hollow phrase said without sincerity?

2. **Notice the Messages.** Write down one or two lessons you internalized about mistakes or emotions. Examples: *Mistakes mean I'll be punished. Feelings make me weak. Apologies don't mean change.*

3. **Connect to the Present.** Ask yourself:

   - How do these lessons shape the way I treat myself today?
   - Do I criticize or shame myself when I make a mistake?
   - Do I swallow my feelings instead of sharing them?
   - Do I know how to soothe myself when I feel overwhelmed?

Looking back at how your family responded in challenging moments can help you uncover the messages you internalized and how they influence your current habits. With that awareness, you can begin to respond differently—treating mistakes as opportunities to learn, allowing feelings to be expressed, and practicing repair that feels genuine. Each small shift helps you build a more supportive relationship with yourself.

PRACTICE
YOUR POWER CHECK-IN

Moments of powerlessness can become opportunities to practice agency. This check-in helps you pause, notice your patterns, and reframe them into grounded action.

1. **Recall a Recent Moment.** Think of a time when you felt small, stuck, or unheard.

2. **Notice Your Automatic Response.** What happened inside you in that moment? Did you shut down, avoid, overwork, or please others? What story did you tell yourself about what was possible?

3. **Reframe with Choice.** Ask yourself: *If I could go back, how would I support myself differently?* Write one or two sentences beginning with:

    ◁ If I could go back, I would support myself by _____.
    ◁ Next time, I will choose to _____.

4. **Remember Your Strength.** Think or write about a time when you felt capable and in charge of your life. What actions or supports helped you feel steady, clear, or in control?

Agency grows when you realize you are not defined by your first response—you can always choose again. Each time you pause and reframe, you strengthen your inner authority and widen your capacity for choice. Over time, these small shifts create a steadier sense of self-trust: the knowledge that even when life feels overwhelming, you have tools to meet it differently.

PRACTICE
A STEADY PRESENCE

Becoming a steady presence means offering yourself the stability and compassion you always deserved. It's about showing up for yourself in the moments you once felt most alone and being the one who stays, soothes, and supports.

1. **Recall a Hard Moment.** Think of a recent time when you felt anxious, ashamed, or emotionally overwhelmed.

2. **Visualize Your Inner Child.** Close your eyes and picture your younger self in that moment. Ask: What did they need—comfort, reassurance, space, or someone to stay?

3. **Offer What Was Missing.** Place a hand on your heart, cheek, or belly, letting your touch comfort you while saying silently or aloud: *This is hard, and it makes sense. I'm with you. You're not alone anymore.*

4. **Reinforce with Daily Self-Acknowledgment.** After practicing this in the moment, carry it into your everyday life. Every night before bed, think about how you honored yourself that day. Examples: *Offering myself kindness when I felt overwhelmed, asking for help when I needed support, allowing my feelings without judgment.* Place your hand over your heart or belly and breathe slowly and deeply as you repeat silently or aloud: *Every act of self-care matters. I see my own effort.*

Through these practices, you're learning to stay connected to your own feelings while remaining open to others. Each time you practice empathy, you strengthen agency as you choose your response with awareness and care. Together, empathy and agency create emotional safety, rebuilding trust in yourself and in your capacity for healthy connection.

With this steadiness, relationships become more honest and nourishing. You begin to trust connection as something you can sustain without losing yourself. Now you're ready for Sphere Four—authentic expression, where you learn to bring your inner world outward through voice, creativity, and presence.

SPHERE FOUR: AUTHENTICITY

Chuck was coming undone. Some called it a midlife crisis. He was dressing younger and hitting the bars and got caught in a string of affairs. To Sandra, his wife of twenty-five years, it was a shattering betrayal. They had built a life, raised three kids. And now he was blowing it all up.

"I'm finally doing what's best for me," he snapped at her when confronted about his behavior. "I spent my whole life catering to you and got nothing back."

Sandra was stunned. "Where's the man I married?" she wondered out loud.

The roots of Chuck's crisis ran deeper than his marriage. His stepfather was a successful banker who led the household through control rather than care and rarely seemed to approve of, appreciate, or even see his stepson. His mother, kind but fearful, taught Chuck to keep quiet, stay small, keep the peace. So, he did just that and ended up following his stepfather into banking. When his girlfriend, Sandra, got pregnant, his stepfather said, "You know what you have to do." And Chuck obeyed, again, marrying before he was sure of what he wanted.

Chuck learned early to swallow his hurts, bury his needs, and steer clear of conflict. On the outside, he was steady and reliable, though underneath, his resentment grew. Now, in his mid-fifties, the mask he had worn since childhood had begun to crack. His stepfather's recent death had hit hard. Chuck realized he'd spent decades chasing the approval of a man who would never give it—and now he never could. Chuck looked at his life, at decisions he'd made to please his stepdad, and saw someone else's story.

We like to believe we've made all our biggest life choices ourselves, but if we look a bit deeper, we can see that some of those choices were motivated by a need for validation from the people we loved. We may have feared disappointing them or making them angry, showing how powerful and important attachment and connection are to us. We will do just about anything to be loved and accepted, even if it means denying parts of ourselves in the process.

Chuck's unraveling wasn't a midlife crisis but rather the eruption of a life lived in silent compliance, a teenage rebellion delayed for decades. What looked like recklessness from the outside was really a man breaking down from the inside.

Authenticity

Chuck, like so many of us, was living out a version of life shaped by expectation. This is how our conditioned self develops. From a young age, we learn which parts of us are welcome and which aren't. We're praised for being agreeable, quiet, or helpful and criticized or shamed when we're loud, emotional, or different. So, we adapt and begin to mask our natural behaviors with whatever we think will be best received by those around us.

Masking doesn't mean we stop feeling; it means we stop expressing what we feel. A boy scolded for crying around his father may hold it in, even as his body aches to let it out. With a more accepting caregiver, his emotions may surface again as he continues to learn what's safe to feel, where, and with whom. But if we have to mask constantly, it becomes automatic, and we end up forgetting who we were before the performance began.

By adulthood, many of us are so disconnected from our authentic Self that one day we wake up and realize how disoriented we feel. It might happen at thirty or fifty, but the pattern is the same: We feel passionless, stuck, or like we're living someone else's life. This isn't failure; it's the beginning of a return to Self.

In therapy, I've seen this moment spark real transformation. When we weren't given the freedom and agency to explore and be ourselves, we began to repress and mask based on who we believed we needed to be. And that has a cost. Emotional repression is linked not only to anxiety, burnout, and depression but also to stress-related illness, immune dysfunction, and early death.[4] For many of us, the longing to "find ourselves" is really the desire to unearth what we buried to survive.

Authenticity begins in relationship to others. We come into the world with a unique emotional signature, but to know ourselves, someone must first be curious about us. When a parent asks, "What do you think?" or listens closely to what excites us, they help build the bridge between our inner and outer world. I once met a mother who was extremely uncomfortable with her daughter's love of bugs. "What could I do?" she told me, shaking her head. "She really wanted a Madagascar hissing cockroach. It nearly broke me, but I loved that she wanted to care for another creature." Not all families offer that kind of room for everyone to explore their unique interests and identities. Some, like Chuck's, demand conformity. Others, like Eleanor's, enforce routines so tightly that Self-expression suffocates.

Eleanor grew up in a small town where life followed an unspoken script: community college, steady job, marriage, children. No one questioned it—it was safe, familiar. For a while, she followed the path too: local college, hometown boyfriend, part-time work at her aunt's bakery. On paper, life was good. But something always felt slightly off, like a jacket that didn't quite fit. She would linger in the campus library long after closing, losing herself in books about abstract expressionism, postwar sculpture, and women surrealists no one in her town had heard of. She clipped pages from art magazines and kept them in a shoebox under her bed. Still, she told herself it was just a hobby, nothing worth reshaping a life for.

Then, on a class trip to a nearby city, she saw a replica of Picasso's *Guernica*. The sheer scale of it, the emotion, the unflinching grief. Something cracked open, and she didn't just want to look at art; she wanted to understand it, live in it, create from it. She came home glowing, eagerly sharing her experiences. Her parents smiled politely, nodding while clearing the dinner table. "That's nice, honey," her mom said, before asking if she was still planning on majoring in business. That night, Eleanor sat with the shoebox of images and finally asked herself the question that had been quietly forming for years: *What if I want something different?* Over time, she began quietly gathering recommendations, researching scholarships, and applying to out-of-state programs. She didn't ask for permission. She didn't dramatize it. She simply acted from the truth that had been growing inside her.

Authenticity can involve making bold choices or following our passions. It is equally about aligning with our values and being true to ourselves even when we're upset or uncomfortable. Take Anna. She believes in treating people with respect. But when a miscommunication at the auto shop triggered her frustration, she lashed out at the employee behind the counter. Later, she felt ashamed because her behavior didn't reflect her deeper values. We've all had moments like this. Moments when reactivity overrides intention. That momentary shame we feel afterward is a signpost, pointing us back to our true Self. If Anna had paused, named her frustration, and responded with calm honesty instead of contempt, she would've honored both her emotion and her integrity.

Regulating our emotions, especially when we feel wronged, isn't easy. But it's essential to living with authenticity. It means feeling the emotion without letting it control our actions. It means choosing who we want to be, not just reacting to what's happening in the moment.

And that choice, repeated over time, is how we reclaim our Selves. It's how we step out of the conditioned self and into the truth of our being.

Our Brain's Inner Compass

Our prefrontal cortex, which is responsible for our brain's most advanced thinking, allows us to pause, reflect, imagine, and act with intention. But it doesn't fully mature until around age twenty-five, and its development is supported by safe, attuned relationships. When a child feels seen, soothed, and supported, this part of their brain functions optimally. But in the face of trauma or chronic stress, its functioning can become disrupted, making us more reactive, impulsive, and stuck in survival mode.

When activity in our prefrontal cortex is reduced, we lose some of our ability to choose. Our executive functions, like planning, problem-solving, and self-control, falter, and we default to old habits and patterns. We return to what's familiar, even when it no longer serves us, because the familiar feels safer than the unknown.[5]

With enough safety and support, we can learn to observe those impulses without being ruled by them. We can begin to act from our true alignment, not from our conditioning.

Delaying an emotional reaction creates the space we need to respond intentionally instead of reacting habitually. From that grounded space, we can then make choices that reflect our values, including our inherent compassion, curiosity, and respect toward others. We allow others to be fully themselves, just as we claim the freedom to be fully ourselves. And in that space of mutual freedom, we begin to face one of life's most essential questions: *Who am I, really?*

PRACTICES FOR SPHERE FOUR

Cultivate Authenticity

Before we can reconnect with who we truly are, we need to look at the blueprint we inherited. Families, through spoken rules and unspoken dynamics, shape how we learn to stay connected, succeed, and stay safe. Without awareness, the self we show the world is often built on survival strategies, while our authentic Self stays hidden. These practices help you uncover the messages you absorbed and separate what was inherited from what is truly yours. You'll become for yourself the one who sees clearly, the one who chooses differently, and the one who says, *I get to decide who I am.*

PRACTICE
YOUR FAMILY BLUEPRINT

Your first sense of who you "had to be" came from your family. Families teach belonging through spoken rules ("Don't talk back") and unspoken signals (the look that meant "stay quiet"). This practice helps you notice how those early lessons still shape your choices today.

1. **Prepare your space.** Find a quiet spot with your notebook or journal. Take three slow, deep breaths, letting yourself become present.

2. **Reflect.** In a notebook or journal explore the following:

   - What happened when people in my family were honest? Examples: *We argued. We ignored it. We laughed it off.*
   - How were differences handled—through conflict, silence, or subtle tension? Examples: *We yelled and then pretended nothing happened. We stayed silent.*
   - How did my family respond to accomplishments? Examples: *They praised achievement. They ignored it. They compared me to others.*
   - When I was upset, did anyone notice or comfort me? Examples: *I was told to stop crying. I was hugged. No one noticed.*

3. **Step back and scan.** Look over your answers. Circle any responses that feel especially familiar or that still show up in your current relationships.

4. **Write one sentence:** "In my family, I learned I had to be _____ in order to belong." Examples: *the quiet one, the achiever, the peacemaker.*

By tracing these patterns, you begin to see the blueprint that shaped how you relate to others and to yourself. What once helped you survive may now limit your freedom to live authentically. Awareness is the first step in loosening these old roles so you can decide which patterns to keep, which to release, and how to show up today as your truest Self.

PRACTICE
YOUR CONDITIONED SELF

As kids, we learned to adapt. You might have hidden your anger, exaggerated your helpfulness, or stayed quiet to stay safe. Over time, these adjustments can turn into masks. This practice helps you see the difference between the self you performed and the Self you actually felt inside.

1. **Set up your page.** Draw two columns, labeling the left side *What I Hid/Changed* and the right side *What I Felt Inside*.

2. **Fill in examples.** Think about moments when you modified yourself to fit in:

    ◁ I hid my anger. → Inside I felt protective of myself.
    ◁ I cared for others. → Inside I felt scared of being a burden.
    ◁ I stayed quiet. → Inside I felt creative and full of ideas.
    ◁ I acted "strong." → Inside I felt sad and needed comfort.

3. **Underline truths.** Look at the *What I Felt Inside* column. Underline the qualities that feel most alive and authentic to you today.

4. **Write a reminder sentence:** "These parts of me were never wrong—they were waiting to be seen."

When you look at what you hid versus what you truly felt, you begin to see how much of your inner world was never lost—only covered. This awareness allows you to peel back the masks and reconnect with the parts of you that are most authentic. With practice, you'll start honoring those parts openly, letting them guide your choices, your voice, and your relationships.

PRACTICE
"WHOSE LIFE IS THIS?" MAP

As adults, many of us live by rules we didn't choose, like family expectations, cultural pressures, or survival strategies. This practice helps you separate those borrowed rules from your own authentic desires.

1. **Draw your map.** On a new page in your notebook or journal, draw a line down the middle. On the left, write *Expectations I Absorbed*. On the right, write *Desires That Are Mine*.

2. **Fill in both sides.** Use concrete examples:

   ◁ Expectation: *Get a steady job and never take risks.* → Desire: *Live creatively. Try new things. Travel.*

   ◁ Expectation: *Always put family first.* → Desire: *Have boundaries and honor rest.*

   ◁ Expectation: *Don't talk about feelings.* → Desire: *Express emotions openly.*

3. **Circle your top three desires.** Which ones feel most alive right now?

4. **Reflect.** Take a few moments to explore the prompts below, writing your responses in a notebook or journal.

- Which side (expectations or desires) feels heavier or more familiar?
- What fears come up when I imagine following my desires?
- What excites me about taking one step toward them?

Through practices of honesty, creativity, and self-expression, you've begun reclaiming the parts of yourself once hidden or edited. Each time you allow your real thoughts, feelings, and impulses to surface, you align your inner and outer worlds. These acts of authenticity build confidence, integrity, and freedom—the sense that your life finally reflects who you truly are.

With this alignment taking root, you're ready to expand outward. Sphere Five invites you to connect your authenticity to meaning and belonging in order to discover purpose and fulfillment beyond the Self.

SPHERE FIVE: TRANSCENDENCE

Finley sat at the kitchen table staring at the canvas in front of her. The art class had been her coworker's idea, a casual invitation she almost turned down. "Come on, it'll be fun," her friend had urged. Fun wasn't something Finley thought much about. She was the dependable one, the planner, the woman who never missed a deadline. At forty-two, her life was built on discipline and responsibility.

Now, with a brush in her hand, she felt foolish. "I'm not an artist," she muttered under her breath. The blank space seemed to taunt her. She thought about leaving, about packing it up and going back to the safety of her to-do list. But her hand moved almost on its own, dragging a streak of blue across the page. Then yellow, then red. She paused, startled by the small smile tugging at her lips.

"You're good at this," the instructor said as they passed behind her. Finley laughed, shaking her head. "I'm not. But maybe that's not the point."

As the colors blended, something inside her loosened. For the first time in years, she wasn't working toward an outcome. She wasn't performing or proving. She was simply present—messy, imperfect, alive.

Raised in a home where she learned that one had to be serious and careful to survive, Finley had learned that play was indulgent, and joy was a distraction. She carried that belief into adulthood, trading spontaneity for productivity, play for perfection. Now, sitting in front of a canvas, paint on her hands and laughter in her throat, she realized she had been starving for moments like this. Finley's healing wasn't about earning another achievement. It was about remembering that joy, too, is necessary. That play was not wasted time but a doorway back to herself.

Our conditioning runs deep. Sitting in front of a canvas that should have felt like an invitation to play, Finley had almost walked away. She was so disconnected from creativity that she struggled to feel at ease in a moment meant to bring her alive. And even surrounded by encouragement, she found it hard to believe she deserved it. For so long she had been shaped by someone else's definition of what mattered, not her own.

Many of us arrive at a similar place. We follow the script, check the boxes, do what's expected, and then one day, something feels off. Not necessarily wrong, but unfulfilling. Sphere Five is where we tap into our own souls to initiate a search beyond ourselves for fulfillment.

Fulfillment

There comes a time—maybe now, since you're holding this book—when we feel pulled inward. We begin to ask not just *Who am I?* but *What am I doing?* Because as we begin to search for ourselves, we also start to glimpse the thread that ties us to something larger.

Without reflection, we chase hollow goals, like status, wealth, or the next fleeting rush of happiness. As Eugene O'Neill wrote, "Obsessed by a fairy tale, we spend our lives searching for a magic door and a lost kingdom of peace." Sometimes we don't even know why we're chasing what we chase. We inherit ideas about success or worth without ever questioning their origin. I remember my father once telling me how he joined the army. "I didn't know what I wanted," he said. "My buddy was going, so I went too." What struck me wasn't the story itself but the absence of intention. There was no sense of direction, no internal compass. Just movement without meaning. It's a pattern many of us fall into, living on autopilot, following paths laid out for us by others, not by our own deeper knowing.

This journey inward is about finding meaning through alignment. It's about making choices that reflect an intention and a purpose reaching beyond just yourself.

That's the work we all must do. Purpose doesn't have to be impressive or public, and it can be found in many places, some of them quiet and private: raising a child, creating art, caring for animals, tending a garden. What matters is that we connect with a pursuit that is genuine and truly ours, which often begins as a gentle tug and can eventually guide you toward connection, contribution, and a greater sense of belonging in the world.

Connecting to our purpose is difficult, sometimes impossible, when we're stuck in survival mode. When we're overwhelmed, depleted, or burned out, we can't access the parts of ourselves that are imaginative, open, or curious. Over time, this can leave us feeling empty or disconnected, a state many describe as *spiritual hunger*. Spiritual hunger is a state of chronic dissatisfaction that arises when we lack purpose, passion, pleasure, or joy. It often begins in childhood, especially in homes where joy, creativity, or emotional expression weren't welcome. If we were taught to be quiet instead of curious, or helpful instead of playful, we may have learned to shut down the parts of ourselves that once brought us alive. Over time, we adapt to the world around us, yet we still feel empty inside.

To fill this void, we desperately seek peace to quiet our inner unrest, and happiness to ease our deep discontent. We overperform or overconsume, diving into work, achievements, or extreme activities, or seeking comfort in food, substances, relationships, or endless information. But overconsumption keeps us from appreciating what we have or fully digesting our experiences, leaving us stuck in a cycle of striving and dissatisfaction. I've felt it myself, struggling to enjoy something I intentionally created, like a slice of my favorite cake or a weekend getaway. Instead of feeling present, I find myself anxious that the moment will end too soon, and that fear makes it hard for me to fully enjoy the experience.

The reality is, true healing doesn't come from doing more. It comes from slowing down enough to feel and experience what's already here. What Finley needed wasn't more seriousness but permission to play and to trust that joy had a place in her life. Ultimately, our path to our purpose isn't about striving or pushing harder. It's about coming home to ourselves. Home to the parts of us that once dreamed, created, and cared deeply. Those parts still exist, even if buried. Fulfillment doesn't come from having more. It comes from *feeling* more: presence, alignment, aliveness, and connection.

From Autopilot to Awe

Neuroscience shows that our ability to access meaning, wonder, and spiritual connection depends on the state of our nervous system. One way this connection opens is through the experience of awe—those moments of amazement or vastness that shift our perspective, whether in nature, art, stillness, or spiritual insight. When we experience awe, activity decreases in a part of the brain called the *Default Mode Network* (DMN). The DMN is like our brain's autopilot: It keeps us anchored in our habitual thoughts and sense of identity, helping us move through daily routines. But it also traps us in familiar loops, replaying the same stories about who we are. Awe interrupts this cycle. With the DMN quieted, our inner chatter softens, repetitive self-focused thoughts fade, and we can feel more present and connected to the world around us. We stop clinging to who we're supposed to be and begin to sense our place in something larger. Biologically, awe activates the parasympathetic nervous system, increasing oxytocin, reducing stress, and enhancing empathy, patience, and presence. In these moments, we often feel and act more generous, more open, and more alive.

But when our nervous system is overwhelmed, awe and connection to something greater feel far away. Because we've lost touch with our sensations, intuition, and our place in the world, our inherent curiosity contracts and our intrinsic joy fades. Disconnected from our inner and outer worlds, we lose touch with the sense of belonging and wonder. We shift into survival mode, where external accomplishments replace deeper purpose.

Yet it is often in the collapse of this survival-driven life—through burnout, loss, or despair—that a new opening appears. When what once drove us no longer satisfies, we begin to long for wholeness and meaning. As Holocust survivor and psychologist Edith Eger, whom I've had the honor of interviewing, once said, "Your pain is not your fault, but your healing is your responsibility." Her insight, as well as Viktor Frankl's, reminds us that even after profound suffering, it is still possible to create meaning, not because we have to but because we're capable of it. In fact, a study of Holocaust survivors found that 65 percent received high scores for their resilience.[6] These impressive results show that suffering and trauma don't only harm us; they can also awaken our capacity to transcend our individual Selves.

And when we tap into something larger than ourselves—something spiritual, shared, or sacred—we rediscover true belonging. We move beyond survival-driven instincts and start asking a different question: *How do I fit into the greater whole?*

PRACTICES FOR SPHERE FIVE

Reconnecting with Wholeness

These practices help you slow down, listen inward, and notice what genuinely lights you up. Instead of waiting for a grand revelation, you'll learn to return to yourself in small daily ways through curiosity, choice, and presence. Along the way, you'll learn to distinguish between what was inherited and what is truly yours, and to trust the quiet voice within. You'll become for yourself the one who listens, the one who honors what matters, and the one who says, *My purpose is here, already living inside me.*

PRACTICE
CONNECTION AND BELONGING

Belonging is more than fitting in with people. It's the felt sense that you are part of something larger—a family line, a community, the earth itself. This practice helps you explore the layers of belonging you've known, longed for, or avoided, and reconnect with the web you're already a part of.

1. **Rooted Reflection.** Sit quietly with both feet on the ground. Place your hand on your heart and belly. Breathe slowly and deeply while asking yourself:

    ◁ Where in my life do I feel most seen and accepted?
    ◁ Who or what helps me feel safe to be my full self?
    ◁ Are there places where I still hold back from belonging?

2. **Expanding the Circle.** On a page, draw three circles: *Me, Community, World.* Fill each with what comes to mind:

    ◁ People, groups, or spaces where you feel connected (Community).
    ◁ Larger forces you feel part of—nature, culture, humanity, spirit (World).
    ◁ Notice: Where do the circles feel full, and where do they feel sparse?

3. **Reflect.** Take a few moments to explore the prompts below, writing your responses in a notebook or journal.

    ◁ What emotions surfaced as I explored belonging?
    ◁ What does belonging mean to me right now?

4. **Belonging in Action.** Choose one small step to deepen connection this week. Examples: *Call or visit someone you miss. Spend time in nature and let yourself feel a part of it. Share something true with someone you trust. Volunteer or offer kindness to a stranger.*

Belonging isn't something you earn; it's something you return to. Each time you notice where you're already connected, you strengthen your roots and remind yourself that you have a place here.

PRACTICE
A SENSE OF AWE

Awe is the felt sense of touching something vast, mysterious, and greater than yourself. It can shrink your worries, expand your perspective, and remind you that you belong to something infinite. This practice helps you explore awe directly through breath, imagination, and sensation.

1. **Settle and Soften.** Find a quiet place where you won't be interrupted. Sit comfortably and take five slow, deep breaths, letting your body relax with each exhale. Close your eyes and feel the ground holding you.

2. **Widen Your Awareness.** Imagine your awareness expanding outward like ripples on water. First, notice the room around you. Then, picture your neighborhood, city, country, the earth beneath your feet. Keep expanding to the sky, stars, and galaxies, allowing your sense of self to stretch with it.

3. **Enter the Vastness.** Ask yourself silently: *What happens when I imagine being part of something infinite?* Notice the sensations in your body, like chills, lightness, tingling, tears, even fear. Let yourself stay with whatever arises, breathing into it.

4. **Open to the Mystery.** Now bring to mind something you can't fully explain—the night sky, the miracle of birth, the beat of your heart. Say silently or aloud: *I don't need to understand everything to be moved by it.* Connect with the sensations of awe as both humility (*I am small*) and connection (*I am part of something vast*).

5. **Anchor Your Experience.** Place your hand on your heart or belly. Say silently or aloud: *Awe is safe here. Awe belongs here.*

Deepen Your Practice. Take a few moments to explore the prompts below, writing your responses in a notebook or journal:

- What did awe feel like in my body?
- What shifted in my sense of Self?
- What reminder of vastness or beauty do I want to keep alive inside me?

Each time you practice awe, you remind yourself that life is larger than your fears and bigger than your to-do list. Awe softens self-focus and reconnects you to wonder, to presence, and to the sense that you are part of something greater.

PRACTICE
TRANSCENDENCE

True meaning goes beyond individual achievement. It arises when life connects us to something larger through shared values, relationships, and purposes that ripple outward. This practice invites you to explore how meaning shows up in your life as both personal nourishment and collective connection.

1. **Tune In.** Sit quietly, place a hand on your heart, and take three slow, deep breaths. Ask yourself:

    - When have I felt most connected to something bigger than myself?
    - What experiences fill me with a sense of wonder, reverence, or belonging?
    - Where do I feel the ache of disconnection from that sense of meaning?

2. **Map "Me" and "We."** Draw a line down a page. On the left, title it *Where I Focus on Myself*. On the right, title it *Where I Feel Part of Something Greater*. Examples:

    - Me: *Working hard to succeed.*
    - We: *Mentoring someone and seeing them thrive.*
    - Me: *Seeking personal peace.*
    - We: *Joining a community effort for justice.*

    Circle the "We" moments that feel most alive or needed right now.

3. **Choose One Step Toward the Larger Whole.** Pick one way this week to move toward collective connection. Examples: *Offer your time or presence to someone in need. Join or reconnect with a group, circle, or practice. Do something creative or expressive that feels like it could benefit others.*

4. **Reflect on Your Experience.** At the end of the week, take a few moments to explore the prompts below, writing your responses in a notebook or journal:

- What shifted in me when I acted from "we" instead of only "me"?
- Did I feel more connected, purposeful, or grounded?
- How does this deepen my sense of belonging in the larger story of life?

Through these practices, you're learning that purpose isn't something to chase; it's something you live each day. Each moment of presence becomes meaning in action; each gesture of care expands belonging. By noticing beauty in the ordinary, you move beyond survival into a deeper sense of connection with yourself, others, and life itself.

From here, your reparenting journey continues beyond the Self, integrating safety, autonomy, empathy, authenticity, and purpose into a way of being that supports lifelong growth and connection.

But to live with that sense of purpose, our body must feel safe. Meaning can't take root in a nervous system that's still bracing for danger. The safety and steadiness we feel today are built on early experiences—on the presence, or absence, of support and care. Those first attachments shape how free, secure, and connected we feel in the world. And yet, even the strongest foundations are tested by stress. Whether it shows up as everyday discomfort or in moments of deep adversity, stress influences how safe we feel in the world and how easily we can stay connected to ourselves and others. When stress is overwhelming or chronic, it reshapes our nervous system, narrows our capacity for joy, and reinforces survival strategies.

In the next chapter, we'll explore the role of stress in our lives and how it influences both mind and body. You'll learn why we become stuck in certain patterns, how stress responses are passed down through families, and—most important—what you can do to shift them. By understanding stress, we begin to reclaim choice, resilience, and the possibility of living not just in survival but in connection, creativity, and wholeness.

PART TWO

THE IMPACT OF YOUR ENVIRONMENT

3

THE TRUTH ABOUT STRESS

We often think of stress as the feeling of being overwhelmed or under pressure—being "stressed out." But stress is more than just an emotion or phrase we use when we reach our mental breaking point. Stress isn't all in our heads. It's a physiological experience in our bodies that we often register as emotional strain.

Our response to stress is ancient, wired into our biology. Humans have always adapted to shifting climates, scarce resources, and other environmental pressures. Our bodies evolved to manage stress because our survival depends on it, which can be observed across populations. Sherpas, an ethnic group native to the Himalayas, have adapted to live at high altitudes. Indigenous groups from Arctic regions have developed a greater tolerance for extreme cold. These examples remind us that stress isn't always harmful. Beneficial stress, known as *eustress*, triggers adaptations that actually improve our chances of survival.

This works on an individual scale as well. For example, exercise stresses our muscles, heart, and lungs, making them respond by growing stronger. Positive stress can also accompany life changes, whether it's starting a new job, speaking in public, going on a date, or moving to a new city. Confronting and meeting these manageable challenges builds resilience and confidence. Small bursts of cortisol, our body's main stress hormone, support healthy brain development, and each return from stress to calm strengthens our confidence and coping skills.

As children, we adapt to stress, whether from unmet needs, misattunement, sudden events, or life circumstances, by developing coping strategies.

Without consistent support, we may learn to meet stress with anxiety, anger, or withdrawal—hallmark behaviors of an insecure attachment. These responses protect in the moment but don't build long-term resilience. With attuned care, we learn to self-soothe, seek help, and recover quickly.

As adults, our stress response reflects how safe and supported we felt as children and how our caregivers managed stress. A 1972 study found the strongest predictor of a child's resilience was feeling lovable to their mother in the first two years. These secure, attuned relationships reduce pain, lower blood pressure, and buffer stress, even in extreme cases like combat trauma, while isolation consistently predicts poor health.[1] Being seen as worthy of love creates an internal sense of safety; lacking it leaves us more vulnerable.[2] Secure bonds give us the trust and stability to face challenges, regulate emotions, and seek support, allowing us to develop resilience. The goal isn't just to endure hardship but to grow through it, becoming more whole, not more hardened. Trauma shapes us, but so does connection.

Who you are didn't happen by accident. You are the product of your environment and, more specifically, how you adapted to stress within it. Your nervous system learned what it needed to do to survive, and those adaptations became part of your personality. Shutting down, constant busyness, and people-pleasing are survival strategies. And if we don't develop healthy ways of dealing with stress, those same strategies keep running our lives. They show up as anxiety that won't settle, exhaustion that doesn't lift, relationships that feel draining, or a sense of being trapped in the same cycles.

Thankfully, because stress lives in both our body and the mind, healing can start in either place. When emotional work feels overwhelming, beginning with your body can be more accessible. Practices like movement, sensory grounding, breathwork, and eating nourishing foods regulate physiological stress responses and signal safety to your nervous system. As your body stabilizes, it creates the capacity to process deeper emotional experiences. That is the essence of reparenting: working with both body and mind to build a new inner environment where your nervous system can relearn safety and your inner child finally feels supported.

A STRESSFUL WORLD

Our earliest attachments prepare us to face the world, but today's world is increasingly defined by a glorification of achievement, producing a daily stress load that challenges even the most resilient. Urgency culture is everywhere: overnight deliveries, instant replies, meals in minutes. Employees are praised for working crazy hours, over weekends, and on vacations. The constant pressure to be "on" seeps into our own expectations of ourselves. Our bodies never rest as our minds carry the weight of unmet expectations, and we scramble to meet demands everywhere and all at once.

Stress isn't only about deadlines; it's also about disconnection. Modern life hides certain stressors so completely we forget they're stressors at all. For most of human history, our nervous system evolved with the elements: waking with the sun, moving over soil and sand, and resting at nightfall. In just a few generations, we've moved almost entirely indoors, cut off from the sunlight above us and the earth beneath our feet.

Without daily natural light, our circadian rhythm becomes dysregulated. In addition to providing warmth and light, the sun provides instructions for our body. Morning and evening red light signals repair and rest, and, even on cloudy days, sunlight penetrates glass and clouds, regulating cortisol, serotonin, and sleep. Daytime blue light fuels focus while artificial blue light at night overstimulates our brain, suppresses melatonin, and keeps our body in low-grade activation. We feel tired but wired—restless, anxious, and unable to fully unwind.

We are equally disconnected from the earth. Walking barefoot, lying on grass, touching a tree are physiological resets. Grounding, or earthing, allows a subtle electrical exchange with our planet, calming us, improving sleep, and even reducing inflammation. Yet most of us go months without direct contact. This disconnection may not feel dramatic, but over time it disrupts the functioning of our nervous system.

Our social world shapes our nervous system just as deeply as our environment. Loneliness is now recognized as a public health crisis. The US surgeon general reports that the lack of social connection carries a mortality risk comparable to smoking fifteen cigarettes a day and is linked to higher rates of heart disease, stroke, dementia, anxiety, and depression.

Chronic loneliness keeps the body in a state of threat, eroding both physical health and emotional resilience. We are wired to co-regulate, and without safe connection—to people, to nature, to ourselves—our nervous system struggles to find its way back to a state of grounded connection.

OUR STRESS CYCLE

Believe it or not, your experience of stress began before you were even born. While you developed in the womb, your mother's stress became your stress. Cortisol—our body's primary stress hormone—can cross the placenta, directly influencing a baby's brain and nervous system. High cortisol in pregnancy, whether from anxiety, unsafe conditions, lack of support, or other stressors, can alter brain development, especially in the prefrontal cortex, the area responsible for decision-making, planning, and emotional regulation. These early changes can make it harder later in life to manage emotions, stay organized, and handle challenges.

After birth, your ability to handle stress continued to be influenced by the presence, or absence, of attuned, regulated caregivers. Parents who feel unsupported, carry unresolved trauma, or fear repeating their own childhood patterns may struggle to provide calm, consistent co-regulation. Even something as ordinary as a baby's cry can activate a powerful biological alarm in an already overloaded nervous system, activating a parent's own unmet needs.

Over time, repeated stress without adequate support can wire a child's nervous system to stay prepared for threat, even when the danger has passed. These protective patterns can become lifelong. Once we link certain experiences with danger, we remain sensitive to them for life. When a challenge appears, like a snake in our path or a thunderclap over our head, our brain instantly asks: *What is required of me?* and *Do I have the resources to cope?* If we feel capable, our nervous system releases chemicals like acetylcholine (to help us focus), GABA (to steady us), and dopamine (to motivate us). If we feel overwhelmed, or if the situation reminds us of a past trauma, cortisol and adrenaline surge instead, activating our fight-or-flight response: Our pupils widen, muscles tense, heart rate quickens, and adrenaline dulls pain to prepare us for action.

When the threat passes, our parasympathetic system, activated by the vagus nerve, guides us back to balance: Our heart rate slows, digestion resumes, and our body recovers. This recovery can also happen through the process of repair—when we move from a state of disconnection to connection. Repair might look like a friend offering comfort after an argument, a parent softening with an apology, or a hug that helps our body settle. In our nervous system, this process shifts us out of a stressed state and back into a calm, regulated, and connected state.

This cycle of activation and recovery is how we build resilience, learning from stress rather than being worn down by it. But it depends on one thing: feeling supported and safe enough to return to calm.

OUR BODY'S STRESS SYSTEM

Stress affects our whole body, not just our mood. Ideally, our nervous system cycles between activation and recovery. But without support, it can keep us in survival mode, shutting down our emotional openness and limiting our ability to grow, connect, and heal. Let's take a closer look at what happens in our bodies when we're under stress.

HPA Axis Dysregulation

Emotionally and physically, we need to manage stress in ways that let our body to return to balance. The hypothalamic-pituitary-adrenal (HPA) axis, a network linking our brain and body to regulate stress, plays a central role in this process. When we detect a threat, our hypothalamus, pituitary gland, and adrenal glands work together to release hormones like cortisol, allowing our body to respond and, ideally, recover.

When stress becomes chronic and recovery time is scarce, our HPA axis can become dysregulated, keeping our brain's alarm system on high alert. Even minor challenges can feel overwhelming, and we may overreact or shut down entirely. Prolonged cortisol release disrupts our hippocampus, making it harder to store or recall memories, and weakens our prefrontal cortex, reducing focus, organization, and creativity. This results in executive dysfunction. Over time, constant activation creates *allostatic load*—the cumulative "wear and tear" that drains our resources, disrupts our hormones, and increases our risk for nearly every major health problem,[3] from inflammation and immune dysfunction to mood disorders and chronic disease.[4]

Gut-Brain Axis Dysregulation

While our HPA axis highlights how our brain and hormones regulate stress, it's only part of the story. Most of us aren't taught just how closely our brain and gut are connected. When I was completing my clinical psychology program, the connection between our brain and gut wasn't mentioned at all. While many cultures have long understood the importance of this relationship, modern medicine has often treated our brain as our body's command center, issuing orders from the top down. But emerging research shows that communication flows both ways, and our gut has a lot to say.

The gut-brain axis (GBA) is the communication network between our gut and our brain. It plays a vital role in digestion, in regulating our stress response, and in supporting our overall mental health.[5] When bacteria are thrown off balance by poor nutrition or when our gut lining becomes damaged by inflammation, our physical, emotional, and mental well-being all suffer. Early-life factors such as antibiotic use, lack of breastfeeding, C-section delivery, infections, chronic stress, and environmental toxins can disrupt our gut microbiome and affect our long-term well-being. One reason our microbiome is so influential is its role in producing neurotransmitters, chemicals that shape mood, focus, motivation, and emotional balance. About 90 percent of serotonin, the feel-good chemical, is made in our gut, not our brain, and gut bacteria also produce dopamine, which drives motivation and focus, and GABA, which calms our nervous system. When gut bacteria are thrown off balance by stress, poor diet, or other factors, these brain chemicals can fluctuate, making it harder to feel steady and regulated.

What happens in our gut is influenced by what we eat. Nutrient-dense foods help our body function well and help us handle stress more effectively, while processed foods, excess sugar, and chemical additives contribute to our body's stress load. Many parents have seen sugar-filled treats cause hyperactivity or mood swings in their children; adults experience similar effects, even if they're less obvious.

Stress doesn't just affect our brain; it disrupts our gut, and an imbalanced gut can make stress worse, creating a feedback loop. Under stress, eating habits often change: Some people lose their appetite, while others eat more to self-soothe. Stress can slow digestion, cause nausea, or lead to IBS-like symptoms.[6] Over time, food can shift from being simple fuel to serving as comfort, distraction, or a way to feel in control when deeper needs go unmet, sometimes leading to patterns like overeating or emotional eating.[7]

A growing body of research shows just how important gut health is especially early in life. A healthy gut supports emotional balance and overall well-being. Later in this chapter, we'll explore practical tools to support both your gut and your nervous system.

Addicted to Stress

Many of us have lived with stress for so long that we don't even notice it anymore. If you grew up in a high-stress environment, you might not register stress unless it's extreme. Research shows that people from chronically stressful backgrounds often rate their stress as "moderate" only when it's already intense because their baseline has been set so high.[8]

Which is why our ability to reset after stress matters so much. Ideally, after a threat passes, our body discharges the energy it mobilized. Animals do this naturally: After a close call, they shake, tremble, or run before returning to calm. Humans have the same capacity, but many of us suppress it. If our stress cycle doesn't complete—because we were never taught how to come back to safety or because the stress never let up—our body can get stuck in a chronic state of alert. On the outside, we may seem calm, but inside, we're flooded with trapped energy.

Over time, that trapped energy leaves its mark. Just like walking barefoot creates calluses to protect our feet, constant emotional stress builds its own kind of armor in our nervous system. That armor helps us survive, but it can also make us rigid, reactive, or disconnected. Over time, we get so used to being "on" that we stop noticing the tension in our jaw, the hunch of our shoulders, or the shallow breath we carry through the day.

For some, this becomes a kind of addiction. We wake up thinking about everything we need to do, rush through the day, and, in rare moments of stillness, reach for something, like our phone, a snack, or another task, just to keep moving. This drive to "do" or to release energy can also show up in smaller, more hidden ways. Many people find themselves biting their nails, picking at their skin, or fidgeting when stress and tension build.

Overdrive may be the only way we've ever felt worthy or in control. Our culture rewards this pace, praising productivity, ambition, and responsibility, even when they're fueled by survival mode. This addiction to stress can lead to actual addictions, either as a way to get ourselves out of the exhausting state of alertness or to fuel our compulsion to stay in it.

To break free from this survival-driven pace, we need to understand our "window of tolerance." Coined by Dan Siegel, this term describes the range where we function best, think clearly, and stay connected. A wide window allows us to stay grounded during stress and return to calm when it passes, and a narrow window means we slip quickly into extremes:

- **Hyperarousal** (fight-or-flight): overreacting to minor stress, feeling on edge, or staying compulsively busy.
- **Hypo-arousal** (freeze): shutting down, feeling numb, or unable to act even when we want to.

Lena's story shows what hyperarousal can look like. Lena's mother often disappeared for days, so Lena became the "watcher" early on. Now, as a parent herself, she struggles to turn that vigilance off. She hovers, checks every detail, rereads school forms three times, and panics over small fevers. Her kids are safe, but her body doesn't know it. Her nervous system keeps her locked in overdrive—heart pounding, muscles tense, sleep interrupted—always bracing for the next emergency that never comes.

Jolie's story shows the other extreme. After a turbulent childhood, she worked her way through school and into a marketing career. But over time, she found herself procrastinating, missing deadlines, and feeling unmotivated. She blamed herself for being lazy, but her body was in shutdown mode. In hypo-arousal, even small tasks can feel impossible as your nervous system slows you down to conserve your energy as if danger were still present.

Whether we're in overdrive, shutdown, or caught between the two, our nervous system can rewire. With consistent, compassionate practice, we can widen our window of tolerance, return to safety more easily, and meet life with grounded presence.

PRACTICE
YOUR STRESS BLUEPRINT

This practice helps you explore the environments that shaped your nervous system and stress responses. You'll reflect on past experiences, notice your body's cues, and begin to understand how those early imprints still impact you today.

1. **Consider Your Earliest Environment.** If known, reflect on your mother's physical and emotional state during pregnancy and your first year of life. Was the environment safe and supported, or stressful and unpredictable? If you don't know, write down what you intuitively sense because your body often carries this story.

    Now picture your early home environment (infancy through early school years). Take a few moments to explore the prompts below, writing your responses in a notebook or journal:

    ◁ Was it loud and chaotic or quiet and nurturing?
    ◁ Were the adults around you regulated and calm or easily overwhelmed?
    ◁ Did you feel supported or learn to manage feelings on your own?
    ◁ How was conflict handled?

2. **Reflect on Early Stressors.** Our earliest environments shape how our nervous system learns to respond to the world. Read through the inventory below and check any statements that fit your experience. As you do, notice your body: Does your chest tighten and your jaw clench? Do

you become short of breath or go numb? Do your limbs feel heavy? These sensations are your body showing you how it remembers.

Common Early Stress Inventory: Check all that apply.

- ☐ I witnessed frequent conflict, yelling, or hostility at home.
- ☐ I was physically, emotionally, or sexually abused.
- ☐ I feared a parent's reaction or walked on eggshells around them.
- ☐ I was bullied, shamed, or mocked, at home or by peers.
- ☐ I felt like a burden more often than I felt loved.
- ☐ I was expected to comfort or take care of my parent emotionally.
- ☐ I had to be "good," "perfect," or quiet to stay safe or earn love.
- ☐ I didn't feel safe expressing anger, sadness, or fear.
- ☐ My home felt chaotic, unpredictable, or emotionally unsafe.
- ☐ I lacked a consistent, emotionally available adult I could turn to for safety and support.
- ☐ My feelings and needs were often dismissed, misunderstood, or ridiculed.
- ☐ I lived with financial insecurity or housing instability.
- ☐ I witnessed substance abuse, addiction, or reckless behavior in adults.
- ☐ I had to translate, manage, or buffer cultural differences for my parents.
- ☐ I regularly heard one parent criticize, vent about, or turn me against the other.
- ☐ I moved frequently or experienced constant changes in caregivers/schools.
- ☐ A loved one had a serious illness, disability, or mental health issue.
- ☐ I experienced racism, discrimination, or cultural erasure.
- ☐ I felt like I didn't belong in my home, school, or social environment.

3. **Body Awareness Check-In.** Return again to your body. Take three slow, deep grounding breaths and ask yourself:

    ◁ What is the overall state of my body right now—agitated, heavy, numb, calm?

- Where do I feel tightness or tension? Where do I feel openness or ease?
- Do any memories bring physical sensations or reactions?

You've just taken the first step in naming your stress origin story. Remember this is not about blame; it's about awareness. And awareness is the first signal to our body that change is possible. It gives your nervous system a new message: We're safe enough now to feel and to heal.

THE IMPACT OF CHRONIC STRESS ON OUR BODY

People like Lena might think, *I'm a high-strung type A person. This is just who I am.* But the truth is, none of us are born wired that way. Living in a constant state of stress eventually takes a toll on our body, impacting how we breathe, how we digest food, and how we move. When our nervous system doesn't complete the stress cycle, we often cope by overworking, staying busy, overplanning, doomscrolling, or numbing out with food or substances. These strategies might bring short-term relief, but they don't give our body the rest and recovery it needs, so stress slowly chips away at our health, leaving us anxious, exhausted, or in pain, often without being aware that stress is at the root of our problems.

That's because our nervous system remembers what our mind often overlooks. So, let's now look at how stress gets stored in our body, and what this means for us.

The Issue's in Your Tissues: Fascia and Stress

Chronic stress doesn't just affect our thoughts and emotions, it physically reshapes our body through changes in the fascia, connective tissue that surrounds and links our muscles, tendons, ligaments, and bones. Imagine the white threads inside an orange: fascia holds everything together, giving our body its form and function. In a healthy state, fascia moves easily, expanding, contracting, twisting, and gliding to support fluid movement, relaxed posture, and a general sense of ease.

Under chronic stress, fascia tightens and locks into protective patterns. When we feel unsafe or overwhelmed, it can store that tension, which is why we often notice "knots" or tightness in the neck, jaw, hips, or lower back. Even regular stretching may not relieve this stiffness, because the tension isn't just physical; it's emotional. Over time, chronic stress and emotional tension can cause fascia to become hardened, knotted, or stuck.[9] This makes everything it surrounds (like blood, ligaments, and tendons) get stuck too, resulting in pain, stiffness, limited mobility, and decreased circulation. Tight abdominal fascia can affect digestion, core mobility, and nervous system regulation.

Signs of fascial tightness may include pain or restriction in the hips, midsection, and lower back, twisted posture or pelvic alignment, shallow breathing, TMJ, and even chronic headaches. For years, I experienced tension headaches, jaw tightness, and limited movement in my torso, until I discovered how much of it was rooted in my psoas muscle. The psoas, a long muscle that runs from your lower back through your hips, is often referred to as the "fight, flight, or freeze" muscle. When we experience fear or trauma, our body directs energy here to prepare for survival.[10] If that energy isn't discharged, it stays locked in our fascia, which is why deep hip stretches sometimes trigger unexpected emotion.

When this tension persists, it disrupts our ability to complete the stress cycle.[11] Our body may stay in a state of activation even when our mind insists we're "fine." When fascia is persistently stiff or inflamed, it can disrupt our autonomic nervous system, the network that regulates digestion, heart rate, and temperature regulation,[12] contributing to both physical discomfort and emotional distress. Research even shows that people with major depressive disorder often have higher levels of fascial stiffness, underscoring the strong connection between fascial health and mood.[13] In other words, how we feel in our body deeply affects how steady or unsettled we feel in our mind, and vice versa.

PRACTICE
STRESS RESET

Stress doesn't just live in our mind; it gets stuck in our body, especially in the fascia and in deep muscles like the psoas. When these areas stay tense, the body feels stuck "on," leading to anxiety, pain, or emotional overwhelm. This practice offers two layers of support: a quick reset for moments of acute stress, and a longer sequence to help the nervous system deeply unwind.

Part One: Quick Reset–Finding Your Off Switch. Use this when stress feels overwhelming and you need to calm your body fast.

1. Notice the first sign of stress in your body (tight shoulders, racing thoughts, shallow breath).
2. Place one hand on your chest.
3. Inhale slowly through your nose for a count of four, hold for two, exhale through your mouth for a count of six.
4. Repeat this cycle three times.
5. Say silently or aloud to yourself: *I am safe in this moment.*

Part Two: The Somatic Reset Sequence. Use when you have more time (ten to twenty minutes); move through this layered practice to reset, release, and restore.

1. **Core and Psoas Activation.** Lie on your back, knees bent. Slowly lift one knee a few inches, then lower. Alternate sides, six to eight times.
2. **Supported Psoas Release.** Place a block or pillow under your sacrum—the flat bone just above your tailbone. Let your pelvis grow heavy, legs extended. Hold two to five minutes.
3. **Reclined Butterfly Stretch.** Put the soles of your feet together, knees open. Support your thighs if needed. Breathe into your hips.
4. **Fascial Massage.** Use a foam roller or ball to slowly roll your hips, thighs, or back. Breathe into the tension.

5. **Shake It Out.** Bounce lightly on your feet, letting the shake rise into your arms, jaw, and face. Hold for one to three minutes.
6. **Vagus Nerve Support.** Massage your ears or slowly move your head side to side while breathing deeply.
7. **Progressive Release.** Tense and release muscle groups from feet to face, pausing to feel the difference.

Practicing this sequence regularly helps support your body, regulate your emotions, and create a deeper sense of safety. Each time you soften, shake, or stretch with awareness, you remind your body that it no longer has to live only in survival mode.

Cortisol: Our Body's Stress Hormone

Cortisol is one of our body's main stress messengers. In short bursts, it's protective, mobilizing our energy, sharpening our focus, and helping us handle challenges.[14] But when stress becomes chronic, cortisol lingers in our bloodstream, and our system never resets. This is when stress starts to feel less like a passing state and more like a personality trait. You may notice yourself "wired but tired," feeling alert and restless but also depleted. Sleep is disrupted, cravings for quick energy—like sugar, caffeine, or refined carbs—increase, and our emotions feel harder to manage. Over time, the wear and tear of elevated cortisol can show up as stiff muscles, recurring headaches, skin changes, gut issues, or emotional instability.

Stress and Nutrition

While stress impacts every system in the body, one of the most noticeable effects is on our appetite. Under stress, our brain craves sugar and simple carbs because they provide fast fuel. In the short term, this makes sense. But when stress is constant, the cycle of highs and crashes leaves us more depleted.

For many of us, food often becomes a way we cope. We eat to soothe, to distract, or to feel a moment of comfort when deeper needs go unmet. This isn't simply a "bad habit." It's your body's attempt to feel safe.

One of the most powerful ways we can support ourselves is through nourishment. Every meal or snack is an opportunity to send our body a signal of care. Even small shifts make a difference:

- **Protein** helps steady energy and supports resilience.
- **Omega-3s** (salmon, walnuts) reduce inflammation and calm mood.
- **Magnesium-rich foods** (nuts, beans, leafy greens) relax our nervous system.
- **Hydration** supports energy and detoxification.

Even adding one supportive food at a time can shift the message your nervous system receives: *You are cared for; you are safe enough to rest.*

Stress and Energy

Deep inside each cell, mitochondria convert food into usable energy. Under chronic stress, they are pushed into overdrive. When recovery is scarce, they produce more free radicals than the body can clear, leading to oxidative stress—a buildup of cellular damage that accelerates aging and inflammation. Over time, this wear and tear shows up as lingering fatigue, brain fog, mood swings, lowered immunity, or even a body that feels older than it should.[15]

Because stress takes such a toll at the cellular level, building resilience starts with supporting our body's energy systems. A strong metabolic foundation supports steady energy, balanced appetite, and overall resilience. Here's how to strengthen yours:

- **Fuel wisely:** Eat nutrient-dense, antioxidant-rich foods to keep blood sugar steady, protect cells, and reduce oxidative stress.
- **Move consistently:** Exercise supports circulation, improves insulin sensitivity, boosts mitochondrial function, and triggers cellular cleanup.

◁ **Recover regularly:** Practices like breathwork, meditation, and sauna therapy promote cellular repair, enhance nervous system balance, and activate heat shock proteins that protect mitochondria.

◁ **Sleep deeply:** Deep, consistent sleep is when mitochondria and antioxidant systems carry out their most important restoration work.

Stress and Immunity

Your immune system's job is to defend against illness and infection, but it's also deeply connected to your emotional and psychological well-being. This complex network includes your lymphatic system, which filters out harmful invaders, and cytokines, proteins that regulate inflammation in response to stress and disease.

When stress becomes chronic, this system can become imbalanced. Elevated stress hormones like cortisol and CRH lower the threshold for immune reactivity, triggering persistent inflammation. At the same time, they can weaken frontline defenses, making us more vulnerable to infections and slowing recovery. Over time, this imbalance raises the risk for autoimmune conditions,[16] which occur when our immune system mistakes healthy tissue for a threat and begins attacking it. The effects aren't limited to our body; chronic inflammation is also linked to depression, anxiety, and cognitive decline,[17] highlighting how immune dysregulation affects mental health. One way this happens is through mast cell activation. Mast cells are protective, but under constant stress, they can become hypersensitive, releasing floods of histamine and inflammatory chemicals. This cascade can trigger bloating, fatigue, headaches, skin flare-ups, food sensitivities, and anxiety, which make ordinary everyday triggers feel like a full-scale assault on our system.

At the same time, stress slows our body's detox and defense network: the lymphatic system. Your lymphatic system works quietly in the background, clearing out pathogens and cellular waste. Lymph nodes—clustered in your neck, armpits, and groin—contain immune cells called *lymphocytes* that detect and destroy threats. Elevated cortisol can constrict blood vessels and alter circulation, which may stall detoxification and slow lymphatic flow. When this happens, you may notice bloating, constipation, water retention, or unexplained weight gain. These are all signs your body is showing the strain of slowed detoxification and rising inflammation.

Left unchecked, chronic stress can dysregulate immune signaling, leading to excess cytokine release. The overproduction of cytokines—chemical messengers of inflammation—acts like an alarm system stuck on repeat. Instead of resolving once the danger has passed, they keep firing, amplifying inflammation even when there's no real threat. This "false alarm" state can create symptoms that mimic depression: persistent exhaustion, brain fog, disrupted sleep, appetite shifts, and heightened pain sensitivity.

Relationships and Immunity

Our immune system is impacted not only by our physical health but also by the quality of our social connections. Social isolation and chronic loneliness can alter immune function at the genetic level. In a landmark study, people who described themselves as being lonely showed changes in the expression of 209 genes, many of which are tied to inflammation.[18]

This means healing doesn't just come from diet and rest—it also comes from belonging and from reconnecting to ourselves, to others, and to practices that regulate our nervous system and restore our sense of safety. Even meditation has been shown to influence the body at a cellular level: Experienced meditators had reduced activity in pro-inflammatory genes and faster stress recovery.[19] This reminds us that true healing involves both physical care and how we reconnect and regulate.

Stress, however, doesn't just live in our body; it shapes how we see the world. When we're overwhelmed, our focus narrows, and our thoughts can swing to extremes—black-and-white judgments, all-or-nothing beliefs, or worst-case scenarios: *You never listen. Everything's going to fall apart.* These mental shortcuts are signs of survival mode, not of truth. In these moments, we lose sight of nuance, safety, and possibility. One way to restore balance is by training ourselves to "zoom out," widening our lens so we can respond with more clarity and choice.

PRACTICE
A NEW LENS ON STRESS

Stress narrows our focus. Everything feels urgent, overwhelming, or impossible. It also pushes us into all-or-nothing thinking: *I'll never get this done*, or *I always screw things up*. This practice helps you zoom out, widening your lens, softening those extremes, and reminding your body and mind that you're safe enough to pause and choose.

1. **Ground with Bilateral Movement.** Tap your hands gently on your thighs, left-right-left-right, while slowly scanning the room. Do this for one to two minutes until your body begins to settle.

2. **Reframe the Signals.** Instead of labeling stress as danger, try *This racing heart is my body preparing me. This tension is my body asking for support.*

3. **Catch All-or-Nothing Thoughts.** Notice if your mind says things like *always* or *never*. Pause and replace them with more balanced statements:

   ◁ Instead of *I always mess this up*, try *I'm having a hard time right now, and I've handled challenges before.*
   ◁ Instead of *You never listen*, try *I'm not feeling heard right now.*

4. **Shift into Observer Voice.** Talk to yourself in the third person to create space: *Jose feels overwhelmed right now and is slowing down and choosing one step to focus on. Mei is tense before the meeting and is also prepared.*

5. **Scan and Notice.** Pause for thirty seconds. Are your shoulders lower? Is your breath deeper? If not, return to Step 1 and repeat.

6. **Anchor the Shift.** Place a hand on your heart and breathe in for a count of four, out for six. Silently say: *I am safe enough to choose how I think about what's happening.*

The effects of stress ripple through every part of life—mental, emotional, and physical. They remind us that our body is an interconnected system, that our histories live in our present, and that our emotions are etched into our physiology. Our brains and bodies are in constant communication, working to keep us safe and help us endure. And while the toll of chronic stress can be profound, healing is always possible. We can't control everything that happens, nor can we rewrite the past, but we can begin now by harnessing our body's capacity to restore, repair, and grow.

In this chapter, you've traced the origins of your stress, learned how it imprints on your body, and begun practicing new ways to release tension, nourish resilience, and meet challenge with choice instead of reactivity. Healing doesn't mean eliminating stress; it means learning how to move through it with more awareness, more tools, and more empowered choice.

We began by looking at how the stress of your mother and early caregivers shaped your system. But the story doesn't start there. The roots of your stress response extend far deeper, carried through generations of survival. You are the inheritor not only of their struggles but also of their resilience. To understand stress fully, we must turn toward our ancestry—the unseen threads linking you to those who came before.

4

THE TRACES OF YOUR ANCESTORS

To fully understand the origins of our habitual patterns, we need to explore the lived experiences of generations before us. You didn't just inherit your parents' eye color or hair texture, you may also have inherited their stress responses, including their physiological reactions to danger and their learned survival habits. These inherited patterns can influence how your nervous system develops and how your body learns to regulate threat, connection, and emotion.

Science shows how direct this inheritance can be. Women are born with all the eggs they'll ever have, which means the egg that would one day become you, and any siblings you might have, was already developing while your mother was still in your grandmother's womb. In other words, your biological beginning was shaped not just by your mother's body but by your grandmother's environment and experiences. Epigenetics explores that impact, studying how environmental factors influence gene expression without changing the DNA sequence itself. These influences can affect how certain genes are turned on or off, and some of these changes can even be passed down to future generations through epigenetic inheritance.

History holds countless examples of epigenetic inheritance. Near the end of the Second World War, the Dutch in German-occupied regions of the Netherlands endured a devastating famine known as Hunger Winter. Food was scarce, forcing citizens to rely on soup kitchens and bread rations. As resources diminished further, people resorted to eating potato peels, grass, and leaves. Bread was even made using sawdust as a substitute for wheat. This famine led to severe malnutrition, claiming an estimated twenty thousand lives through starvation and disease.

Researchers studying women who were pregnant during this famine found that their children's DNA carried the effects of these environmental factors—including alterations in their metabolism, a higher likelihood of obesity, and an increased risk of developing diabetes—even though the food shortage ended before they were born. They also displayed a heightened stress response and an increased likelihood of developing mental illnesses from depression to schizophrenia.[1] Even more remarkably, researchers found that these effects extended to the *next* generation. Their DNA showed similar genetic changes, revealing just how deeply stress and survival leave their mark on our biology.

This groundbreaking study illustrates how collective trauma can alter biology for generations. But this inheritance doesn't only happen during rare historical crises; it unfolds in our everyday lives.

WHERE NATURE AND NURTURE MEET

In utero, a fetus's developing nervous system is influenced by the mother's life experiences, including her stress, anxiety, and of course trauma. If an expecting mother is in an abusive relationship, or battling depression, for example, elevated cortisol levels can cross the placenta, impacting the formation of neural pathways involved in emotional regulation and executive function. Many of us who feel unsafe in our own bodies or whose minds feel stuck on high alert may actually be carrying a legacy of maternal stress in our nervous systems. We might experience unexplained symptoms, heightened reactivity, or emotional heaviness with seemingly no direct cause. Even if our parents worked hard to break dysfunctional behavioral cycles, the biological imprint of their stress, suffering, or survival strategies still lives within us.

This is because, long before we take our first breath, our body begins learning about the world it will enter. And that learning continues across generations, shaping how we adapt to the environments that raise us. Our stress responses develop in relation to our surroundings, and are influenced by the conditions around us from the geopolitical (famine, war) to the personal (insecure attachment, maternal stress). Sometimes our inheritance is easy to see, as it was for Malik. Malik grew up in a house where silence was necessary for survival. His grandfather had fled war, his father battled undiagnosed PTSD, and the pain carried through their lineage was too unspeakable. Silence became the only way to contain it. In a family marked by intense fear and loss, quiet meant safety because speaking or asking questions risked awakening memories no one knew how to face. So Malik learned early on to keep the peace by keeping his mouth shut. It wasn't until his daughter was born—loud, expressive, emotionally open—that something shifted. Her aliveness was beautiful, but it overwhelmed him. In therapy, he began to untangle a lineage of suppression he had inherited.

Other times, the imprint isn't obvious at all. Zahava always felt inexplicably afraid of being hungry. She stocked snacks in every bag, panicked if a meal was delayed, and berated herself for these behaviors. When she finally asked her mother about it, Zahava discovered that her grandmother had nearly starved during the Second World War. The family had rarely spoken of it, but the effects lingered, not just in memory but in her body.

Inherited stressors may be known to us or traceable. But often, they remain buried or unnamed and are passed down through behavior, biology, and belief. Whether or not we know the story, epigenetic changes still manifest. And even if we don't remember or know what happened, our bodies do. This is especially true for those whose lineage has been disrupted by adoption, secrecy, or displacement, as it was for Merrin. Her family fled their homeland of North Korea during a period of political and economic upheaval. She was born soon after in a new country—safe but far from the land, language, and community that had once rooted her family. Growing up, Merrin often felt a quiet longing she couldn't name, a sense of being untethered. When she began exploring somatic work in adulthood, unexpected waves of sadness would arise during certain body-based meditations, especially when placing a hand over her heart or belly, as if her body were remembering what it once called home. She realized she was grieving more than personal loss—her body was remembering the rupture her family had lived through. Through guided visualizations and intuitive journaling, Merrin began to honor that disconnection, reclaiming her right to belonging in both body and lineage.

Stories like Merrin's show us what science is now confirming: Our bodies carry more than just our own experiences. What our parents and grandparents lived through—famine, migration, war, grief, or silence—doesn't vanish with time. It can leave biological traces that influence how we process stress, regulate emotion, and experience safety. Current science now shows that these effects aren't only psychological; they can be passed down in the body across generations. This discovery marks a profound shift. For much of modern history, we believed our genes were destiny, fixed blueprints that determined everything from our health to our habits to our fate.

The "Age of Genetics," beginning in the early twentieth century, centered on DNA sequencing and the hope of finding single-gene explanations for disease. In 1990, the Human Genome Project set out to map all the human genes, fueling the widespread belief that if we could locate the right gene, we could understand and predict health outcomes.

But today's research tells a more complex story: In reality, very few conditions are triggered by a single gene. While disorders like cystic fibrosis and Huntington's disease are clear exceptions, most common illnesses like diabetes, heart disease, and cancer result from a combination of factors, including the interaction between multiple genes and, notably, the environment. In fact, only 5 percent of cancer and cardiovascular diagnoses can be attributed to heredity.[2] Even in conditions with well-known genetic risk factors, like the BRCA mutation (an inherited condition that significantly increases your chances of developing breast and ovarian cancer), inherited cases only account for less than 5 percent of breast cancer diagnoses.

Our focus on gene mapping has significantly shaped how we approach emotional and mental health treatment. Yet despite decades of research and millions of dollars in funding, no single gene has been definitively linked to conditions like depression, anxiety, schizophrenia, bipolar disorder, and many other psychiatric diagnoses.[3] While mental illnesses often appear to "run in families," there is almost always a deeper story of inheritance beyond genetics alone, one that includes environment, attachment, stress, and relational patterns.

Despite these findings, much of the field of psychiatry continues to focus narrowly on symptoms and diagnoses, often overlooking critical factors like nutrition, lifestyle, trauma history, and nervous system regulation. When you visit most psychiatrists, you'll likely be asked about your symptoms, assigned a diagnosis from the *DSM* (*Diagnostic and Statistical Manual of Mental Disorders*), and prescribed medication to manage those symptoms. Psychotherapy is often treated as optional, outsourced, or secondary, and in some cases, discouraged altogether. Even when therapy is recommended, recent research has shown that processing trauma in the context of traditional talk-based psychotherapy is not always effective. For lasting change, especially in cases of early or chronic trauma, somatic interventions, or those that involve the body, are often essential. Sadly, lifestyle factors that support healing, like sleep, movement, social connection, and nutrition, are still rarely addressed in conventional mental health treatment.

This narrow approach reinforces the belief that mental illness is something you were born with and must simply manage. And that belief leaves people feeling helpless. But what if the story can be revised?

The long-standing debate between nature and nurture has taken a surprising turn, with science now showing that nurture can actually influence nature. In the 1990s, David Barker, a British physician and epidemiologist, challenged the dominant belief in genetic predetermination with a groundbreaking theory. He proposed that some chronic diseases, such as cancer and heart disease, are not solely the result of genetics or an unhealthy lifestyle. Instead, he suggested that the mother's nutrition during pregnancy could have a lifelong impact on her baby's health. This idea radically shifted how we understand human development. It laid the foundation for a new era of research, leading to the epigenetic revolution.

Epigenetics explains not only how past generations have shaped us but also highlights our power to alter genetic expression in ourselves and future generations. This discovery reshaped science. We once believed ourselves to be pre-wired for illness or dysfunction, but we now know that mental health is shaped by a dynamic interplay of genetic predisposition, environment, and lived experience.

Epigenetics research gained momentum in the early 2000s, when scientists discovered that environmental factors—everything from neglectful caretaking and child abuse to a high-fat diet and air pollution—can result in the addition or removal of chemical tags on DNA, turning genes on and off. In fact, as Barker proposed, this process begins even earlier than pregnancy. The final stages of egg and sperm development in prospective parents influence the activity of specific genes, shaping characteristics of a child who is *yet to be conceived*.[4]

This growing body of modern research is reinforced by twin studies showing that even genetically "identical" individuals can develop different health and psychological profiles.[5] Identical twins share the same DNA, but they don't have perfectly identical epigenetic profiles. What's most remarkable is that these differences become more pronounced with age. The longer twins live apart, the more their medical and psychological profiles diverge. This further illustrates that differences in environment can significantly alter gene expression over time.[6]

Building on this understanding, cell biologist Bruce H. Lipton explored the dynamic interplay of nature and nurture in his book *The Biology of Belief*. He writes, "If you only focus on the blueprints, as scientists have been doing for decades, the influence of the environment is impossible to fathom."[7] Epigenetics now shows us that gene expression is constantly shaped by our surroundings. Our life experiences trigger biochemical signals that influence how our genes respond, a process guided in part by methylation, adjusting a gene's responsiveness to what's happening inside the body. Methylation patterns can be passed down from one generation to the next, further illustrating that we inherit not only our DNA but also a biological imprint of our ancestors, their environment, and their lived experiences.

Epigenetic changes influence how our genes are expressed, and our DNA holds the codes for everything from the formation of individual cells to the overall functioning of our body. Our cells hold biochemical memories of what has happened to our ancestors, and to us, long after the original experience has passed.

It can be easy to view our epigenetic inheritances as a burden to overcome, but it's important to remember that these adaptations can also be beneficial. And we're not powerless to this legacy; we can influence how our genes are expressed, for ourselves and for future generations.

PRACTICE
MAP OF YOUR ROOTS

Family patterns don't start with us, and they don't end with us unless we bring them into the light. This practice helps you trace the emotional threads passed down through your family so you can notice what you've carried, what has shaped you, and what you may be ready to release.

1. **Map Your Family Themes.** On a blank page in your notebook or journal, draw a simple family tree—include parents, grandparents, siblings, or anyone who feels significant. Next to each name, write one or two words that capture what you most associate with them—*quiet, worried, strong, angry, loving*. Step back and look at the whole page. Do certain words repeat? Do you notice themes, like silence, resilience, or distance? Circle the one that feels strongest in your own life.

2. **Reflect on What You Carry.** Write a few sentences about how this theme shows up for you today. For example: *Silence shaped me because in my family no one spoke openly. Now I still struggle to say how I feel with people I love.*

3. **Expand the Story.** Ask yourself what was happening in your family before you. Don't worry if you don't have all the answers. Write down what you do know. Even guesses, gaps, or silences carry meaning. Take a few moments to explore the prompts below:

   ◁ Where did my ancestors come from geographically (countries, cities, villages)?
   ◁ Did they migrate by choice, or because of hardship (war, famine, poverty, displacement, enslavement)?
   ◁ What major stress or trauma did my grandparents or parents experience as children?
   ◁ What was happening in my family when my mother was pregnant with me—was her experience calm or stressful?

Deepen Your Practice. This step helps you connect your map to real stories or intuitive knowing.

- **Interview if possible:** Pick a few questions from the list above and ask a parent, grandparent, or elder relative. Listen with curiosity, not judgment. Write down key phrases or stories, adding what you learn directly onto your family tree. For example: *Immigrated in 1945. Survived war. Lost a sibling. Struggled with depression.*
- **If interviews aren't possible:** Turn inward. Notice what stories, films, or histories stir something deep in you—tears, anger, or resonance. Write down what feels true in your body, even if you don't have "proof." Your felt sense matters too.

As you step back and look at your map, notice the threads that connect you to those who came before. Some patterns may feel heavy or limiting, while others may reveal strength, resilience, or love that carried your lineage forward. Remember: Your family story doesn't end with what you've inherited. By bringing awareness to these patterns, you open the door to writing a new chapter—one where you consciously choose what to carry forward and what to lay down.

WHAT SHAPES OUR EPIGENOME

While your DNA is the fixed blueprint you inherit, your epigenome is the system that decides how that blueprint is read and expressed. It doesn't change your genetic code itself, but it adds "markers" that turn certain genes on or off. Your epigenome continuously responds to your internal and external environment, sending signals that influence everything from inflammation and immunity to emotional regulation and metabolism. One common way this shows up is when physical activity, like lifting weights, activates genes that promote muscle growth and repair. If you live a more sedentary lifestyle, your epigenome may activate genes related to fat storage instead. You can think of your epigenome as the manager of your genetic blueprint, responding to your experiences, adapting over time, and helping shape how your body and mind function.

But what influences it most? Our epigenome is especially sensitive to prenatal conditions. While maternal health has traditionally been the focus of this research, science now shows that fathers also pass down epigenetic instructions that help script the next generation. A father's environment, nutrition, stress, and early life experiences all influence the health of his sperm, which in turn can impact a child's long-term development. Toxin exposure, from air pollution, heavy metals, smoking, or endocrine disruptors, can alter sperm DNA, increasing the risk of metabolic and neurological conditions in offspring. Research has found that children of fathers with high stress or obesity levels are more likely to develop insulin resistance, high blood pressure, and greater vulnerability to depression, showing how these consequences are passed down through generations.

Many fathers pass down not only their biology but their emotional patterns. Take Daniel, for example. His father, a Vietnam veteran, was physically present, but not emotionally available. Though his lack of attunement looked like indifference, it was in fact an adaptation, a survival strategy used to distance himself from overwhelming emotions he had never learned to express. Daniel's father came to every school play, but never once said, "I'm proud of you." As a boy, Daniel interpreted his silence as disapproval. Now, as a father himself, he finds that he struggles to express affection, even though he loves his children very much. In therapy, he came to realize that his father's restraint wasn't rejection; it was a form of protection passed down through behavior and biology. For many men, emotional expression was never modeled, only managed. What gets passed down, then, is a nervous system trained for suppression. Slowly, Daniel is learning to give what he never received—to himself and his children—and to speak aloud what was never spoken to him. He is reparenting himself, and parenting others, in unison.

The emotional inheritance Daniel experienced is supported by science. Men with high Adverse Childhood Experience (ACE) scores show altered DNA methylation patterns in their sperm, alterations that can affect stress regulation, immune function, and disease risk in their children. All of this underscores a truth that's long been overlooked: Fathers help shape their children not only after birth but long before. And just as paternal experiences leave their mark, maternal and ancestral traumas can do the same—rippling through families in ways that extend far beyond one lifetime.

THE LONG SHADOW OF TRAUMA

Your immune system, brain plasticity, stress reactivity, and emotional regulation are shaped not just by your genes but by how those genes are expressed. Trauma, especially when unresolved, can influence this expression and travel across generations. This is what's often called *transgenerational trauma*—when wounds that weren't fully processed live on in descendants, shaping their biology, behaviors, and beliefs. Even if the trauma didn't happen to us directly, it can influence how we cope, connect, and regulate. And without conscious reflection, we may unknowingly pass these patterns on to our own children.

One of the clearest ways this inheritance shows up is through our attachment patterns. The way we form relationships—how safe we feel with closeness, how we handle distance—may be shaped not only by our caregivers but by the emotional residue of generations before us. Their grief, fear, and survival strategies can become our own, passed down through both biology and behavior.

I felt this personally. As a child, I sensed something missing. My memories were hazy, my body uneasy, and my parents rarely spoke of their pasts. I knew only fragments of our heritage and family history, while silence filled in the rest. In adulthood, I began piecing together what was unspoken: my parents' experiences of emotional neglect, the sibling my mother lost before birth, the cultural and economic strain both families endured as immigrants in a new country during tough economic times. None of these stories were openly named, yet they were alive in our home—in the way my parents reacted, in what they avoided, in the tension I carried in my body. Their unspoken trauma did not disappear; it became part of me.

Our ancestors' struggles live on not just in our stress responses but also in our daily rituals. When trauma is collective, such as that caused by colonization, war, genocide, or exile, it leaves imprints not only on individuals but also on entire bloodlines. Their unprocessed grief may result in our anxiety. Their silence as our self-doubt. Their suffering influencing how our families grieve, celebrate, or survive scarcity. Some over-prepare or hoard, while others avoid planning altogether or let things fall apart. Some laugh at funerals; others forbid mention of the dead. These behaviors are memory made visible, survival strategies etched into routine. Left unexamined, they harden into unspoken rules: how to stay safe, how to earn love, how to disappear.

But rituals can also be reclaimed. With awareness, we can choose which patterns to carry forward and which to release. In this way, healing becomes about untangling biology from biography, honoring the stories our bodies hold while consciously shaping new ones for ourselves and future generations.

Yet not all of what we inherit is visible. Some wounds leave no words or memories, only sensations and beliefs that carry across generations.

PHANTOM TRAUMA

Luis grew up in a conservative household where the rules of what it meant to be a man were clear and inflexible. When he came out at eighteen, his family cut him off. From this rejection came a deep wound and a constant question: *Am I only lovable if I hide who I am?* On the outside, he looked confident and successful. Inside, shame convinced him that belonging was always conditional. Luis learned that love was contingent on compliance, that authenticity carried a cost. His nervous system absorbed this rejection as danger. But the fear wasn't only his. It came from generations of silence and unspoken rules about who could be fully seen, and who had to stay hidden. What Luis carried was not just his wound but a reflection of conditional belonging passed down through his culture and family.

This is the essence of what's often called *phantom trauma*: the inherited emotional and physiological imprint of past trauma, carried in our body's stress responses even when our mind holds no memory of it. It's called *phantom* because it hides in plain sight, showing up as pain we can't explain, reactions that feel disproportionate, or stories that seem like they don't belong to us at all.

In my clinical practice, I witnessed this kind of trauma frequently. Sometimes it appeared as chronic health issues that resisted every intervention. Other times, it emerged as persistent anxiety that felt unshakable. Phantom trauma doesn't just affect us emotionally; it finds a home in our body.

Marcus is a great example. He spent most of his adult life chasing relief from relentless digestive pain. He tried everything: gastroenterologists, elimination diets, supplements. Nothing worked. The flares always returned as tight knots, nausea, cramping, especially after conflict or stress. Doctors diagnosed it as IBS or said it was psychosomatic. Marcus began to believe this was just his body's default. But something deeper stirred. In therapy, during a somatic session on early attachment, Marcus was invited to place a hand on his belly and simply notice. Almost instantly, a wave of grief surfaced. A crying infant appeared in his mind, followed by sorrow that had no clear origin. He'd always known he was adopted. His parents were loving and supportive. And yet, his connection to them had always felt fragile, like he had to earn it. As therapy unfolded, so did the story his body had been carrying all along: For his first three months of life, Marcus had been in foster care, without a consistent caregiver. His mind held no memory, but his gut, his fascia, and his vagus nerve remembered that lack of safety and attachment. His body had been wired to expect disconnection. When the source of his suffering was finally named, Marcus wept deep, shaking sobs. For the first time, he was listening to his body rather than trying to fix it. His healing began with grief for the mother he never knew. For the touch that never came. For the part of him that had waited in silence, hoping someone would return for him.

Marcus's story is not uncommon. Studies show that fear and stress responses can be passed down generationally, even without direct exposure. One study found that when a mother's fear activates the infant's stress response and amygdala, the child may learn to associate fear with certain cues, even if they've never experienced danger firsthand. For instance, if a mother tenses or startles at the sound of a loud noise, her baby's body may also begin to register that same sound as a threat without understanding why.

The past lives in our bodies, shapes our stories, and waits, sometimes silently, for the chance to be seen, felt, and finally released. But we are not doomed to carry more with each generation. This is where the science offers hope; the answer lies in nurture.

EPIGENETICS AND RESILIENCE

As you've seen, attachment and caregiving have a profound impact on our epigenome. Research shows that consistent, responsive caregiving in infancy influences a child's epigenetic markers for emotional regulation, effectively "programming" their body to manage stress more efficiently. This means that if your parents made a conscious effort to be more nurturing than their own parents were, they may have helped shift your biology toward greater resilience, offering proof that positive caregiving can also be carried throughout an entire lineage.

One of the ways this happens is through the oxytocin system, the hormonal system responsible for connection and safety. Consistent, loving care—soothing touch, warm eye contact, affectionate words—enhances oxytocin activity through epigenetic changes, strengthening our body's capacity for trust and regulation. Inconsistent or inadequate care, on the other hand, can reduce oxytocin sensitivity, making a child more reactive to stress or emotionally guarded. These shifts may also heighten sensitivity to sensory inputs, such as noise, texture, or light, contributing to challenges with attention, social connection, and even language development.[8]

Our early environment powerfully shapes who we become, but epigenetic change remains possible across our lifespan. Our relationships, in particular, offer an opportunity to shift our biology. Becoming a parent, for example, can open a profound window of neuroplasticity, rewiring brain regions involved in attachment, emotional regulation, and stress response, and research shows these shifts occur in fathers as well as mothers. We can also reshape these brain circuits through intentional relationships, nurturing communities, and conscious reparenting. Each generation has the capacity to create new experiences, form new memories, and influence how genes are expressed. We can all widen our window of tolerance, regulate our emotions more effectively, and rewire our habits.

We can even influence our DNA through our daily lifestyle choices. Exercise has been shown to have a protective effect on our DNA. For example, a 2012 study published in *Epigenetics*[9] revealed that just six weeks of consistent physical activity led to gene modifications that support energy metabolism[10] and fat regulation, as well as epigenetic changes that help protect against disease. Exercise doesn't just change our bodies in the moment; it creates epigenetic shifts that support healthier metabolism and lower disease risk. Remarkably, some of these adaptive benefits can be carried forward to future generations.

Psychotherapy can offer another path to alerting our epigenome and has been shown to influence gene expression in people with PTSD, anxiety, and phobias. Treatments like cognitive behavioral therapy (CBT), eye movement desensitization and reprocessing (EMDR), and mindfulness-based stress reduction (MBSR) change thought patterns and can also improve our body's ability to regulate emotional and physiological responses to stress,[11] impacting DNA methylation and helping the body unlearn what it once encoded as danger.

Perhaps the most powerful evidence of epigenetic change comes from the long-term follow-up studies of the Dutch Hunger Winter. You'll remember that babies who were exposed to famine in utero showed increased risk for obesity, heart disease, and diabetes in adulthood. But subsequent generations, raised in environments with stable nourishment, showed signs of reversal in some of these epigenetic patterns.[12] Again, we find evidence that our present choices have the power to repair the biological imprint of the past.

Across generations, humans have endured war, famine, displacement, and deep personal loss. We've survived, adapted, and protected what mattered most. Sometimes, the coping strategies that once kept our ancestors safe become patterns that hold us back. But healing is also inheritable. Just as pain can be passed down, so can strength.

This can be seen in Javier's lineage. His grandfather crossed the border with nothing but a suitcase and a secondhand prayer. He took any job he could find, fixing fences, washing dishes, and rebuilding broken engines. He didn't teach Javier through lectures but rather through consistency. "Show up, even when it's hard," he'd say, handing him a wrench to help out with household repairs at the age of ten. Now, when Javier faces setbacks, it's not just his own strength he draws on; it's the legacy of grit wired into his nervous system through nature and nurture. The story of survival didn't end with his grandfather; it lives on within Javier, a reminder that resilience itself can be inherited, steady and alive in our body.

Our genetic inheritance may shape our beginning, but it doesn't define our future. Each day, through the ways we nourish, move, connect, and care for ourselves, we influence which patterns continue and which end with us. Because change doesn't happen in a single moment—it's a daily choice to live with greater awareness, compassion, and intention.

PRACTICE
ANCESTRAL RELEASE THROUGH VISUALIZATION

What lives in you often began long before you. This practice uses imagery and inner dialogue to connect with your lineage. Through visualization, you'll explore what may have been passed down, release what doesn't belong to you, and consciously reclaim the strengths that serve you.

1. **Settle and Ground.** Sit or lie in a comfortable position. Place one hand on your heart, one on your belly. Take five slow, deep breaths, saying silently or aloud: *I am here. I am safe.*

2. **Imagine the Tree of Your Lineage.** Imagine standing at the base of a wide, ancient tree. Its roots stretch deep into the earth, holding the lives of those who came before you. Notice the qualities you sense there—strength, endurance, silence, sorrow. Whisper: *Thank you for what you endured.*

3. **Invite a Presence.** Picture one ancestor stepping forward. They may appear as a face, a feeling, or simply an energy. In your mind, say: *I see you.*

4. **Speak the Unspoken.** Ask silently or aloud, pausing to listen without forcing or judging:

    ◁ What gift did you pass to me?
    ◁ What burden am I carrying for you?
    ◁ What helped you survive that I no longer need?
    ◁ What would you want me to know now?

5. **Release the Burden.** Imagine your ancestor handing you something heavy—a stone, a bundle, a box. Picture yourself placing it at the base of the tree. Whisper: *This is not mine to carry.* See the earth take it in, transforming it into something new.

6. **Receive the Strength.** Ask: *What wisdom or strength do you want me to carry forward?* See this strength as light or warmth entering your body. Silently or aloud, say: *I carry this with love.*

Deepen Your Practice. Take a few moments to explore the prompts below, writing your responses in a notebook or journal:

   ◁ What did I release?
   ◁ What strength do I choose to carry forward?
   ◁ How does my body feel when I imagine this shift?

Take a final breath and notice what has shifted, even if only slightly. Acknowledge yourself for taking the time to connect with and honor the stories carried in your body, soften what no longer belongs to you, and choose what you want to carry forward.

PRACTICE
ANCESTRAL RELEASE THROUGH SOMATIC PRACTICE

This practice explores how your family history lives in your body today through tension, breath, or restlessness. It teaches you to soften what isn't yours and reclaim steadiness through movement, breath, and self-soothing.

1. **Body Check-In.** Sit comfortably with one hand on your chest and the other on your belly. Slow and deepen your breaths as you call to mind what you know about your family history. Ask yourself:

   ◁ Where do I feel tight, heavy, or restless?
   ◁ Where do I feel open, calm, or steady?

2. **Self-Soothing Signals.** If you notice tension, agitation, or heaviness, choose one way to comfort your body and continue the soothing action for one to two minutes:

   ◁ Gently rock from side to side.
   ◁ Hum softly or sigh audibly.
   ◁ Tap your chest in a steady rhythm.
   ◁ Hold a warm object (mug, blanket) and breathe into its comfort.

3. **Reframing the Imprints.** Call to mind one family message or belief that still feels alive in you (e.g., *I must stay small to be safe*). Place your hand on the part of your body where you feel that belief most strongly. Take three slow, deep breaths into that spot. Silently or aloud, say: *This helped me once, and it's not mine to keep.* Then place your hand on your heart and add: *What I choose to carry forward is* _____ (e.g., *courage, tenderness, creativity*).

4. **Anchor the Shift.** Take three more slow, deep breaths. Notice how your body feels now—lighter, softer, steadier, or calmer. End by silently or aloud saying: *I honor where I come from. I release what is not mine. I carry forward what gives me life.*

Each time you notice tension, offer yourself comfort, and choose what to carry forward, you remind your body that it's safe to soften, safe to release, and safe to live in alignment with what truly sustains you.

Reparenting isn't about erasing the past but about learning to hold it with compassion while ending cycles that were never yours to keep. And you don't have to have all the answers to begin. What matters is that you're listening, with your body, your heart, and your soul. The past shaped you. But you are the one who gets to decide what comes next. When you meet inherited burdens with understanding, you free yourself from the roles you never chose. Letting go is an act of remembrance. It's honoring what came before while choosing a path that is lighter, truer, and fully your own. In doing so, your nervous system learns to associate rest and ease with safety.

While epigenetic imprints may live in our cells, we also inherit something less visible but just as powerful: core beliefs, cultural stories, and collective expectations. In the next chapter, we'll explore how those unseen legacies shape our identity, and how we begin the sacred work of reclaiming it.

5

THE CULTURE THAT SHAPED YOU

We are socially driven creatures; we thrive in groups: families, communities, and cultures that share a common way of life. In these groups, we naturally absorb ideas through shared routines, roles, and rituals. These beliefs—about ethics, culture, religion, relationships, and ourselves—create meaning and identity, providing a sense of belonging. Our beliefs help us make sense of the world around us and understand our place within it. They give us a sense of safety by offering a framework for how to act and connect, and an understanding of right and wrong that helps us live harmoniously with others.

We've relied on such shared understandings since our earliest ancestors roamed the land, searching for safe places to live, avoid predators, gather food, raise families, and build communities. Along the way, they formed beliefs to guide their decisions. If a particular area seemed dangerous, they avoided it, boosting their chances of survival. If it offered abundant resources, they stayed. Over time, simple survival beliefs like these—"This land is good" or "This land is bad"—evolved into more complex systems of meaning, from mere cautions into tools of cooperation that allowed us to build systems of mutual care, trust, and collective survival. "Some of us will guard the village while others gather food." "When a baby is born, we'll share caregiving so the mother can rest." What began as instinctive choices for survival gradually became shared understandings, or customs, agreements, and moral codes. These shared beliefs became the scaffolding of society, and today, all over the world, they guide behavior, shape values, and teach generations how to live in harmony with one another.

BELIEF SYSTEMS

The shared understandings we accumulate from society are what we call *belief systems*. They are the written and unwritten rules that define what is acceptable, taboo, or considered morally right or wrong. They are often tied to safety, health, identity, and belonging. They may be influenced by the powers that be, but they are also deeply grounded in lived experience, shaped not only by logic but by generations of adaptation, survival, and meaning-making.

In Finland, for example, visiting saunas is central to the national lifestyle. For generations, saunas have served as communal spaces where people gather to release, reflect, and reconnect. Nudity in these spaces is viewed as normal and nonsexual, a reflection of cultural values that translate into how comfortable people feel in their bodies. In Germany, social norms dictate that smiles are saved for friends rather than strangers, an unspoken expression of emotional boundaries. In Japan, the near absence of public trash cans reflects a post-1995 shift following the sarin gas attack in the Tokyo subway in response to fear that the cans could be used to hide chemical weapons or explosives. But the success of this shift was supported by a long-standing cultural belief in personal responsibility and collective cleanliness—citizens are expected to carry their trash home and sort it mindfully.

In some cultures, belief is born from intergenerational memory and the wounds of survival. The Sentinelese people, an isolated Indigenous tribe who live on an island in the Indian Ocean, are known for aggressively resisting outside contact. At first glance, this might appear as hostility, but history offers more context. In 1880, a British naval officer kidnapped six of their people. Two adults died, and when the children grew ill, they were returned to the island, likely bringing with them illness that devastated the community. Their present-day stance may be a carried belief, passed down through inherited fear and the shared memory of past devastation.

Belief systems like these are living stories shaped by time, trauma, geography, and necessity. And often, they're carried forward because someone, somewhere, once needed them to survive. We all carry some level of awareness about our beliefs, whether it's our religious values, political leanings, personal ethics, or even what's considered polite at the dinner table. These are the beliefs we hold consciously—the ones that shape how we see ourselves, where we fit, and how we relate to the people around us. But beneath the surface of these more obvious beliefs lies a vast network of subconscious beliefs that shape how we think, feel, and behave. Many of these were formed long before we even understood what beliefs were.

Our subconscious mind begins absorbing and storing information from our earliest experiences. It learns through what we're told, what we observe, and how we interpret the world as children. If you grew up with a parent who was constantly overworked or stressed but never asked for help, you may have internalized the belief that you have to handle everything on your own and that needing support is a weakness. If your mother, shaped by her own relational experiences, repeatedly warned you not to trust men, you might have been conditioned to believe that intimacy with men is unsafe. And if someone consistently encouraged you by saying, "I know it's hard, but you can do it," you likely developed a belief in your own strength and resilience.

The cultural, generational, and societal environments we grow up in greatly impact our subconscious beliefs. Remember Luis, the gay man who grew up in a conservative community with the firm belief that belonging was conditional on adopting traditional masculine behaviors—a belief that had been passed down through his culture and family. Culture influences how emotions are expressed, how safety is communicated, and how attachments are formed. Generational patterns, like inherited trauma or attachment styles, often pass from one generation to the next through parenting styles that are rooted in cultural norms, teaching infants what connection does or doesn't feel like.

At the same time, larger forces, such as poverty, systemic oppression, or political instability, can deeply affect a caregiver's emotional availability. When caregivers are overwhelmed by the stress of their daily survival, their capacity to attune may shrink, leaving children to navigate safety and self-regulation on their own. These early patterns imprint themselves on our nervous system and become the scaffolding for what we come to believe about ourselves and the world. As neuroscientist Stephen Porges reminds us, "Safety is not the absence of threat. It is the presence of connection." Even in calm environments, a child without emotional attunement may still feel profoundly unsafe. We are always responding to what happens around us and what happens within us. And safety lives in felt sense, in co-regulation, and in the quality of the relational presence of those around us.

Culture shapes our experience of safety. It tells us what emotions are acceptable, how we should express ourselves, and what belonging looks like. This becomes even more complex for those raised between cultures, where the rules for safety and connection may conflict. For first-generation and bicultural individuals, identity often becomes a balancing act. At home, you may have been expected to honor your cultural roots, while at school or work, you were pressured to assimilate and adopt the norms of another culture. You might have spoken one language with your family and another in public or been encouraged to hide certain traditions or values to avoid standing out and protect yourself from discrimination. These opposing forces can create an inner dissonance marked by guilt, confusion, shame, and the ache of never fully belonging anywhere. The belief systems of each culture may clash over everything from emotional expression to success, independence, or family roles.

A similar kind of dissonance exists for those living with disability or chronic illness. In societies that glorify productivity, independence, and physical perfection, your body can become a source of judgment, both from others and from yourself. In many societies, rest can be perceived as laziness and asking for support can be mistaken for weakness. And when you can't meet these narrow standards of success, shame can take root, leaving you feeling both too much and not enough at once.

The same can be true for those raised in rigid religious environments, where identity is shaped under the shadow of judgment and conditional love. Take Sofia, who grew up in a tightly controlled faith-based community where obedience was worship and doubt was rebellion. She prayed to be good, pure, and worthy, while secretly terrified she never would be. As she grew, her body became a source of shame and her desires something to silence. When she finally left the church in her twenties, she shed the doctrine, but not the guilt. It followed her into relationships, into her self-talk, into the way she apologized for simply existing. To heal, she had to do more than reject this guilt and shame. She had to confront her subconscious, conditioned beliefs and reimagine her place in the world, finding her way back to meaning through compassion, curiosity, and personal conviction.

Deconstructing inherited or conditioned beliefs is a process of separating truth from trauma and of letting go of beliefs that no longer serve you. Sofia's story reflects a broader truth: Many of the beliefs we carry weren't chosen consciously; they're survival strategies, encoded in our body. When belonging feels unsafe or conditional, we adapt by overperforming, silencing our needs, and disconnecting from ourselves just to maintain connection with others. Healing begins with a powerful question: What if my worth isn't defined by how much I produce or by how well I conform?

Cultural narratives shape our adult identities and sculpt the emotional and physiological patterns of our future generations. They shape how we define safety, belonging, trust, and value. The work we're doing here is about bringing these beliefs into the light. Because once we can see them clearly, we can begin to ask: Are these stories still helping me grow and connect, or are they keeping me stuck and disconnected?

Many of the beliefs we carry today were formed in response to our first attachments and the environment that held (or failed) us. From birth to around age seven, our subconscious mind is highly receptive, making us deeply impressionable. During those early years, our brains operated predominantly in theta, a brain-wave state similar to hypnosis, which made us especially open to suggestion. At that age, our caregivers are our entire world. We don't consciously question their moods, their beliefs, or their behavior. We internalize what they say and do as truth, taking on many of their values, fears, and expectations as our own.

Through this process, we inherited far more than habits or mannerisms; we absorbed emotional templates for how to feel, what to fear, who to trust, how to behave, and what to believe about ourselves and the world around us. These early impressions laid the foundation of our own belief systems. Even now, long after childhood, those beliefs continue to shape how we think, feel, and respond, often without our conscious awareness, and often long after they've outlived their purpose. As we grow older, we begin to see the bigger picture. We realize the strategies that once helped us survive—people-pleasing, perfectionism, emotional hypervigilance—now may be holding us back from living fully. We remain overly responsible for the emotions of others, still operating from the belief that we are the cause of disruption and must be the ones to make it right.

PRACTICE
FAMILY AND CULTURAL CONDITIONING

Before we know our own voice, the beliefs and norms of our family and culture speak for us. They shape what's acceptable, what's shameful, what counts as success, and who belongs. This practice helps you bring those invisible forces into the light so you can see which still guide you and which no longer serve you.

1. **Settle In.** Find a quiet space where you won't be interrupted. Take three slow, deep breaths, letting your body settle. Place your feet on the ground and notice the support beneath you.

2. **Reflect.** Take a few moments to explore the prompts below, writing your responses in a notebook or journal.

    - What beliefs did my family or community pass down about love, power, gender, or identity?
    - Which emotions were welcomed, and which were silenced or punished?
    - Was I allowed to question rules and traditions, or was conformity expected?
    - How were differences treated—in me, in my family, or in my community?
    - How free was I to be myself in my family or culture, and how much did I feel I needed to change to fit in?

3. **Identify a Belief.** Circle one belief or message that feels most present in your body or mind right now. Write it clearly on a new page.

4. **Check Its Impact.** Ask yourself: *Does this belief nourish me—or does it keep me small?* Write down a few notes about how it affects your choices, relationships, or sense of self today.

Your inherited beliefs will continue to shape your life until you bring them into awareness. Once you can see them clearly, you have the power to question, reshape, or release them.

Understanding how beliefs form in early childhood helps us recognize their emotional weight. To truly understand their influence, we also need to see how they operate in our brain. While our beliefs are rooted in our past, our brain uses them as a lens to predict what comes next.

BELIEFS AND OUR BRAIN

Understanding how beliefs form in early childhood helps us recognize their emotional weight. To truly understand their influence, we also need to see how they operate in our brain. While our beliefs are rooted in our past, our brain uses them as a lens to predict what comes next.

Every day, we are flooded with information and stimuli. And our beliefs act as survival-based shortcuts that help us reduce overwhelming amounts of information into manageable, actionable, and quick conclusions. Our brain is an extraordinarily efficient prediction machine, leaning heavily on pattern recognition. It quickly categorizes experiences, forms associations, and stores them as internal rules we follow, often unconsciously, to navigate a complex world. As neuroscientist Lisa Feldman Barrett explains: "Your brain does not react to the world. Using past experience, your brain predicts and constructs your experience of the world. It combines sensory input with memories and beliefs to create emotions." In other words, your brain is interpreting events in real time, and those interpretations guide how you feel.

As we grow, our subconscious mind becomes even more efficient at making quick decisions without our conscious input. Constantly analyzing every situation in the moment would drain us. Instead, we rely on mental autopilot, or snap judgments guided by what we already believe to be true. We saw this earlier when we talked about the Default Mode Network, the part of the brain involved in these automatic inner narratives. Here's a simple example: You're walking through an unfamiliar neighborhood and see a large dog running toward you, off leash. You don't pause to reflect. Your body reacts, tensing, stepping back, maybe bracing for impact. Somewhere in your neural archive is the belief: "Unleashed dogs are dangerous." That belief activates in an instant, shaping your reaction before logic has a chance to weigh in. The same thing happens in subtler, less urgent situations. Imagine you're swiping through a dating app, and, whether you realize it or not, you hold the belief that people who work in the field of finance are greedy or superficial. Without a second thought, you skip over someone who works in banking. Your subconscious is running the show, conserving energy by bypassing reevaluation, thinking it already knows what happens next.

Our brains are remarkably efficient at categorizing and making decisions with very little information, but that efficiency can limit us. Consider how the Sentinelese people, based on past experiences, react to outsiders. Though one might debate whether their isolationism is beneficial or harmful, it is certainly a very limiting choice. This kind of shortcut thinking also helps explain phenomena like the cross-race effect,[1] a well-documented tendency for people to more easily recognize faces of their own race compared to those of other races. One widely shared video[2] illustrates this powerfully: a toddler in Africa sees a white man for the first time and bursts into tears. The adults around him laugh, and it's apparent his fear doesn't come from direct experience but from unfamiliarity. He feels safest among people whose faces resemble those he's always known. Without conscious thought, his brain registers a simple equation: Familiar means safe. And this isn't unique to him. Every day, you make an estimated thirty-five thousand decisions, many of them automatic, shaped by beliefs formed long ago, often in childhood. But that toddler's story doesn't end with the clip that's circulating online. Given the lighthearted response of the adults around him, it's likely his perception will change. Our brains are highly attuned to social cues, and we absorb the emotional reactions of those around us without even realizing it. While the child may not consciously think, "My mother doesn't seem scared, so I shouldn't be," over time, as he has different experiences, his perceptions will shift and so will his beliefs.

This same mechanism of social learning and emotional imprinting continues well beyond childhood. As adults, we don't outgrow these internalized patterns; we simply reenact them in more complex ways. The same unconscious processing that once helped us feel safe now influences how we handle stress, navigate relationships, and move through our daily routines. We fall back on familiar behavioral patterns because they're tied to deeply held beliefs, rituals, and cultural norms that once made us feel like we belonged. These patterns often show up in the habits and routines of our daily life.

Routines are the consistent actions that offer stability and predictability. Rituals, by contrast, are more symbolic: repeated practices that anchor us to personal meaning, cultural identity, and collective memory. Whether lighting a candle on a Friday evening, gathering for Sunday dinners, cooking a special family recipe, or fasting in observance of religious holidays, these rituals help maintain community over time and connect us to the story of who we believe ourselves to be. The structure we crave, the practices we repeat, and the symbols we hold dear all reflect internalized beliefs about safety, identity, and belonging, whether they're communal rituals like Sunday dinners or deeply personal habits like cracking a joke when tension rises, reaching for food when comfort is needed, or taking the same path on your evening walk. Each of these patterns teaches our nervous system what safety feels like and reinforces the beliefs we carry forward.

The routines, rituals, and personal habits we carry aren't shaped by personal experience alone. One of the most overlooked yet powerful influences on them is class-based belief systems. If you grew up hearing things like "We can't afford that," "You have to work twice as hard," or "Money doesn't grow on trees," you may have inherited a scarcity mindset, one that lingers even after your circumstances improve. On the other hand, those raised in material comfort might internalize different narratives: that they can do anything (because they've always had resources); that self-worth is tied to success; or that failure equals shame. For many, class mobility creates an inner conflict where "success" can feel both like an imperative and a betrayal of their community.

As you become more aware of your habits, patterns, and related beliefs, the real question becomes: Do they still serve you? And if not, what might you choose instead? Recognizing a pattern is only the beginning. The deeper work comes in questioning the assumptions you've carried. As Bruce Lipton notes, "Our lives are essentially a printout of our subconscious programs, behaviors, and beliefs that we acquired from others, like our parents, family, and community, before the age of six." Much of what we do today is rooted in what once helped us survive or belong. But questioning what we've accepted as "normal" is how we reclaim the power to choose which beliefs and behaviors we now want to live by.

PRACTICE
RITUALS AND RECLAIMING

Rituals are the practices we carry from our families and cultures. Some bring comfort and meaning, while others can feel restrictive. By noticing which ones you've inherited and choosing new ones, you create rituals that reflect who you are now.

1. **List Your Rituals.** Write down the practices you already follow—daily (morning coffee, bedtime routine), weekly (Sunday meals, calls with family), or seasonal (holidays, fasting, traditions). Then, if any come to mind, add rituals you once practiced but let go of.

2. **Reflect on Each One.** Ask:
    - Is this ritual inherited or chosen?
    - Does it reflect who I am today—or who I used to be?
    - Does it support me, or does it hold me back?
    - Did I leave it behind out of self-protection?
    - Is there a ritual I want to reclaim, reshape, or release?

3. **Choose and Reimagine.** Circle one ritual you'd like to change or create anew. Decide how you can make it feel more aligned with your current values and needs.

4. **Create a New Ritual.** Anchor it in something simple and consistent. Examples: *Light a candle before journaling. Speak a blessing to your inner child each morning. Set aside weekly time for play, nature, or silence. Transform a daily task (like making tea, cooking, or taking a walk) into a mindful practice.*

Your beliefs and rituals are living, breathing stories, and you are their author now. As you move through this practice, remember: You're allowed to evolve. You're allowed to grieve what was handed to you and still honor those who handed it down. Belief is both inheritance and choice.

WHAT IS "NORMAL?"

In 1692, nineteen people were hanged in Salem, Massachusetts. They hadn't committed any crimes. They were hanged for who they were perceived to be. The Salem witch trials were a desperate attempt to enforce social conformity. Those who spoke out, stood apart, or lived differently were labeled—by authority figures as well as peers—as dangerous. Because that's the thing about "normal": It's a cultural construct. It's a script, one we're expected to follow, even when it means hiding who we really are. What is "normal" comes from the beliefs we've grown up with, beliefs that tell us how to behave, what to value, and who we must become to belong.

To understand how these internal rules take root, we first need to understand that beliefs are interpretations, or ideas we've accepted as truth, often without even realizing it. While we may share the same external world, we don't all experience it the same way. Our beliefs, shaped by upbringing, culture, and access to information, act as invisible filters that influence how we interpret everything from politics and religion to social cues and daily rituals. What feels "right" to one person may feel foreign, or even threatening, to another. And when information is missing or situations feel ambiguous, we fall back on these internal narratives to create a sense of order. As natural storytellers, our brains weave experience into cohesive narratives that help us navigate the world and define our place within it.

Over time and within communities, these stories grow into collective understandings—of what is polite, moral, legal, or kind—that help reduce fear, maintain social cohesion, and reinforce a shared sense of what is normal. These societal norms influence our laws and customs. And they influence how we see ourselves and how we live too. A pull toward "normal" is wired into us. Our brains are wired for social connection because, for most of human history, being isolated from community was dangerous. One of the ways the brain keeps us close to others is through shame, a built-in signal warning us when we might be moving too far from the safety of belonging. In early human history, where separation meant physical danger, this was an advantage. In our modern world, however, shame can be very damaging.

For generations, shame was relied upon as a form of discipline. "Shame on you" wasn't just a phrase; it was a moral imperative aimed at children to keep them in line. Today we recognize the damage these words can cause, but the truth is that shame doesn't always need words. Children sense disapproval in tone, withdrawal, or a look. Deviating from "normal" can trigger shame without a single correction being spoken aloud. (In chapter 7, we'll dig deep into the origins of shame, its effects, and how to let it go.)

While what's "normal" isn't the same everywhere, regardless of where we grow up, we absorb rules of belonging that influence how we understand community, safety, and ourselves, and in turn how we express care, process pain, interpret illness, and seek healing.

EARLY CULTURAL IMPACT

Nowhere is a culture's impact more visible or more enduring than in its parenting practices. From the way we soothe infants to the expectations we place on adolescents, cultural values influence how children learn to care for their bodies and express their emotions. In some families, independence is encouraged early: Children may be expected to sleep alone, self-soothe, and grow up quickly. When these behaviors are paired with emotional attunement, they can foster confidence and resilience. But when emotional needs are dismissed or shamed, children may learn to suppress their feelings or disconnect from their inner world to maintain connection. In other families, close physical contact is the norm—through practices like co-sleeping, carrying infants, and constant proximity—offering steady co-regulation and a deep sense of safety. Each approach carries its own wisdom, and its own risks, shaping behavior, the developing nervous system, and the child's core beliefs about safety, belonging, and love.

Across cultures, this search for safety and grounding takes many forms.

The ways we make sense of pain, identity, and belonging are deeply influenced by the beliefs we inherit, including how we understand illness and pursue healing. In Western medicine, health is often reduced to biology: Symptoms are labeled, diagnoses assigned, and treatment focuses on physical intervention. By contrast, many Indigenous and Eastern traditions view healing as relational, spiritual, and community centered. The reality is that neither tradition holds all the answers. And healing doesn't depend on choosing one over the other. It lives in integration and interdependence. In learning how to care for yourself without abandoning your connections. Individual healing and collective healing are connected. When we tend to our own nervous systems, boundaries, and values, we can show up more fully for others. And when we are a part of communities that honor our truth, we receive a sense of inclusion and acceptance that no one should have to earn.

Still, not everyone grows up with something to return to. For some, the ache is from being cast out, and for some, it's from never quite knowing where they belonged to begin with. Sometimes we are wounded by what was done to us, but sometimes we are wounded by what was never given to us. We respond to pressure or to silence. To rules or to their absence. In either case, we adapt. We perform, conform, survive. We shape ourselves around the contours of what's allowed or what's missing.

And nowhere is that more powerful than in our earliest relationships.

CORE BELIEFS, ATTACHMENT, AND IDENTITY

Growing up, Selena was often praised for being "the pretty one." At every family gathering, relatives commented on her size, her hair, her clothes. Compliments landed like expectations, teaching her early that her value was tied to how she looked. She remembers standing in front of the mirror as a teenager, tugging at her clothes before school, repeating to herself, *If I look good enough, maybe I'll be loved enough.*

By high school, the mirror had become a battleground. She skipped meals, overexercised, and hid her exhaustion behind a bright smile. In college, the same pattern followed her—scrolling through social media feeds of sculpted bodies, comparing herself endlessly, silently counting calories in her head. Outwardly, she appeared disciplined and confident, but inside she felt fragile, as if her belonging could vanish with the next flaw. Selena had internalized the core belief that love was conditional, and her body was the test she had to pass. Because she had only experienced love as conditional approval, she tried to "earn" it by perfecting herself.

Selena's story reflects how early emotional experiences can crystallize into core beliefs, or deep, often unconscious convictions about what we must do to be loved, seen, or safe. These beliefs don't arise from logic. They arise from repeated emotional cues that train our nervous system and shape the stories we tell about ourselves.

Core beliefs influence how we see ourselves, relate to others, and move through the world. Whereas surface beliefs are flexible preferences that shift with new experiences, core beliefs are formed early in life and tend to operate beneath our awareness. A surface belief might answer the question of whether you prefer the beach or the mountains. But a core belief asks deeper questions: *Am I lovable? Can I trust others? Is it safe to be myself?* These foundational beliefs take root in our earliest relationships, particularly with caregivers. This is especially true when our early bonds were marked by inconsistency, fear, or emotional distance. The framework of attachment theory teaches us that secure attachment fosters beliefs like "I am worthy of love" and "Others are reliable." Insecure attachment, by contrast, often leads to inner narratives like "I am unlovable" or "The world is unsafe," and to heightened vigilance toward signs of rejection, abandonment, or criticism.[3]

Nowhere is this imprinting more profound than in the messages we receive from our caregivers. A caregiver's words, tone, and emotional presence are internalized, becoming the scaffolding for a child's self-worth, emotional regulation, and relational blueprint. When those messages are warm and consistent, children come to believe: *I am safe. I matter. I can rely on others.* But when a caregiver's responses are critical, dismissive, or unpredictable, a different story begins to form. A child who hears "You always mess things up" or is made to feel like mistakes are personal failures may grow into an adult who fears risk, avoids vulnerability, and chases perfection, believing their worth depends on getting everything right. Even in the absence of overt criticism, emotional neglect or inconsistency can seed beliefs like "My needs are too much" or "It's not safe to feel."

These messages become wired into our brains. Repeated emotional experiences form neural pathways that shape how we think, what we expect, and how we protect ourselves. A parent's voice often becomes the template for a child's inner dialogue, with their tone, words, and even their silence shaping how we speak to ourselves. These early messages influence how we handle conflict, cope with pain, build relationships, and define our self-worth. If you were frequently compared to others—"Why can't you be more like your sister?"—and your excitement was dismissed or your achievements were minimized, you may have internalized the belief that you're never quite enough. Over time, this can lead to a pattern of downplaying your successes, hesitating to celebrate yourself, and constantly striving for external validation just to feel worthy.

I'm sure you can imagine how this plays out in the lives of adults who carry these early wounds into their relationships. Consider Ted. Frustrated with his love life, he often complains, "Women just want my money" or "I'm a good guy, but no one appreciates a good guy anymore." He feels used and dismissed, reinforcing a belief that he's always the victim of hidden agendas. When he meets Emma, he wants to believe she's different. He confides in her about his ex, saying, "She blindsided me and moved out, no warning. Then she's suddenly with some older rich guy. Total gold digger." Emma sympathizes, until she learns, by chance, that she knows Ted's ex and has already heard a very different version of their breakup. His ex had longed for a deeper connection, tried talking about the future, and felt consistently dismissed. When she finally brought up her needs, Ted lashed out, accusing her of being materialistic. Feeling unseen and unheard, she eventually left and found someone emotionally present and willing to build a life with her.

Ted's version of events didn't match his ex's, but it didn't come from nowhere. He had grown up watching his father shame his mother for being "money hungry," a belief that eventually solidified in Ted's mind. To question it would be to disrupt a deeply rooted survival story, one that protected his ego but distorted his reality.

OUR OWN REALITY

Once a belief takes hold, we unconsciously look for evidence to confirm it and dismiss anything that challenges the story we've built around it. Our reticular activating system (RAS) is a powerful neural filter that sifts through millions of sensory details, allowing only what aligns with our expectations and beliefs to reach our conscious awareness. Say you're thinking about adopting a golden retriever. Suddenly, it feels like every park, sidewalk, and social media feed is filled with golden retrievers. They were always there, but now your RAS has flagged them as relevant. The same thing happens with beliefs about ourselves. If you believe you're awkward in social situations, your RAS will highlight every stumble in conversation while ignoring the moments you made someone laugh or felt fully at ease. Or if you hold a core belief, whether "I'm not good enough" or "The world is unsafe," your RAS will amplify the experiences that support it and downplay or ignore those that contradict it.

This process doesn't just shape how we see ourselves; it colors how we see everyone else. Imagine two friends walking through a new city. One carries the belief that strangers can't be trusted. Despite a day filled with kind encounters—a barista remembering their name, a passerby offering directions, a child waving from a window—it's the one person who bumps into them without saying sorry that defines the experience. "People here are so rude," the friend mutters, brushing off everything else. That's how our brain works. It filters our world through our beliefs, highlighting what confirms our story and quietly discarding what doesn't.

Research shows just how powerful this bias can be. In one study, participants were shown an image of a car accident involving an expensive car and a more modest one. Even when no context was provided, when asked to describe what happened, people were significantly more likely to blame the driver of the expensive car, projecting arrogance, recklessness, or entitlement based purely on appearance. The belief that "wealthy people are careless or selfish" distorted neutral information into a narrative that confirmed that bias. Over time, this becomes a self-reinforcing loop. The more a belief is confirmed, the less room there is for contradiction. That's why core beliefs, especially those tied to identity, love, and safety, can be so difficult to change. They don't just live in our mind shaping our thoughts; they're wired into our nervous system itself, constantly scanning the world and asking, *Is my story still true?*

And yet, these stories, no matter how deeply held, can be rewritten. The shift begins with awareness or recognizing that what feels or is familiar doesn't always mean it's true. Once you see a pattern, you have the power to choose differently. But choice alone is only the beginning. Beliefs live not only in the mind but also in the body, influencing our physiology and priming our nervous system to scan for what it already expects. Over time, this loop—belief shaping perception, perception reinforcing belief—becomes embodied, making outdated narratives feel real even when they no longer serve us.

PRACTICE
THE STORIES THAT SHAPED YOU

In addition to passing down traditions, families pass down stories, both spoken and silent. These stories often become the invisible scripts for how we see love, safety, and self-worth. This practice helps you become aware of those scripts so you can begin to choose which ones still serve you.

1. **Identify the Stories.** Write down three family sayings, mottos, or unspoken rules from your upbringing. Examples: *We don't talk about our problems. Family is everything. Crying is weakness.*

2. **Reflect on Their Impact.** For each story, write:
    ◁ What did this teach me about myself?
    ◁ What did it teach me about others?
    ◁ What did it teach me about life?
    ◁ How did it influence the way I approached the world (work, relationships, risk, creativity, etc.)?

3. **Choose One Story.** Circle the one that feels most powerful or limiting today. Write it at the top of a page.

4. **Rewrite Your Story.** Beneath it, write a new version that honors who you are becoming. Example:

    ◁ Old story: *I have to do everything alone.*
    ◁ New story: *It's safe to ask for help. I don't have to carry it all myself.*

5. **Anchor Your New Story.** Place a hand on your heart, breathe deeply, and say silently or aloud: *This is the story I choose now.*

While you can't change where the story began, you have the power to decide how it continues. By rewriting these narratives, you begin to chart a path that feels lighter, truer, and fully your own.

IMPACT OF BELIEFS ON OUR BODY

The stories we carry don't stay in our heads; they imprint on our bodies, leading to emotional, psychological, and mental shifts that ripple through our nervous system, affect our immune function, and even influence our genetic expression.

One of the earliest pieces of evidence for this mind-body connection came from the discovery of the placebo effect. First recognized in the 1950s, this phenomenon occurs when people experience real improvements in health after receiving an inactive treatment, illustrating how their belief alone can trigger physiological changes. In one study, participants were told they were drinking alcohol in a social setting but were actually given nonalcoholic beverages. Still, many exhibited slurred speech, impaired coordination, flushed skin, and lowered inhibitions, all hallmarks of intoxication. Their belief that they were drinking alcohol activated the same neural and physiological pathways as if they actually had. This is our mind in action, altering our body without any pharmacological input.

In addition to social experiments, medical researchers have conducted many studies showing the powerful link between our mind and body. One striking example is a 2002 study[4] where patients were divided into three groups: two received real surgeries, and one underwent a fake procedure.

Remarkably, all three groups reported reduced pain and improved mobility, proving that belief in the healing process alone can create results that are indistinguishable from the effects of surgery.

Another study on mindset and healthy aging found similar results. Researchers followed 660 adults over age fifty and found that those who saw aging as a time of growth, wisdom, and possibility lived an average of 7.5 years longer than those who saw aging negatively. In other words, the way they thought about aging influenced their choices, their immune function, and their long-term health.

The implications of this research are powerful. In his work on optimism and performance, Shawn Achor, author of *The Happiness Advantage*, showed that positive mental states like gratitude, optimism, and connection lead to better immune function, lower stress, and improved productivity.[5] One example comes from a study on placebo treatment in patients with major depressive disorder. Even without receiving active medication, participants showed increased activity in their prefrontal cortex, the region of our brain associated with emotional regulation and decision-making.[6] Belief alone sparked changes in their brain, lifting their mood and supporting their emotional balance. These findings demonstrate that we have the ability to influence our biology. Beliefs like *I am powerless* or *My emotions are dangerous* send stress signals through our bodies, leading to tension, inflammation, and disconnection. Thankfully, the opposite is also true. When we believe we are worthy, are capable of healing, and have agency, our nervous system calms, our stress hormones drop, our brain chemistry shifts, and our body's natural healing abilities are supported.

Beliefs can't take the place of necessary medical care, but they can powerfully support and complement the healing process. Just as somatic work can support emotional healing, shifting our beliefs and internal narratives can benefit the rest of our biology. Transformation begins with awareness. Once we witness the scripts we've inherited, we gain the power to revise them.

In the next chapter, we'll turn toward the deeper roots of these stories: the emotional wounds formed in early life. These wounds live in our memory and our unconscious—they show up in our body as overwhelming feelings, sudden reactions we can't explain, or emotions that don't match our current experiences. We'll explore how to recognize these wounds as signals from our inner child, and how to begin soothing our nervous system when our emotions feel overpowering. Through this work, we create space for healing that allows us to move through life with more steadiness, clarity, and freedom.

PART THREE

THE SCARS WE CARRY

6

YOUR WOUNDED INNER CHILD

Jordan volunteers at a local community center, where, once a month, people are invited to share personal stories during a group gathering. The vibe is casual and low pressure with the intention of giving the volunteers a chance to connect.

At a recent meeting, Jordan told a lighthearted story about a family road trip. It made people laugh, especially the part about getting so lost they ended up in the wrong state. When he finished, a few people clapped as someone said, "That was great; thanks for sharing." Another added, "You've got a really natural way of telling a story."

As people were mingling afterward, one woman casually said to Jordan, "That was cute. I was wondering where it was going for a minute, but then it landed." Then she smiled and turned to grab a drink. Jordan nodded, but the woman's words ran through his mind. *She wondered where it was going?* Had he rambled or seemed scattered? On the way home, his mind didn't replay the applause or praise he'd received, just that one comment. He found himself thinking: *Was the story too long? Did I lose people? Did they laugh just to be polite?* A single, outlying observation from a stranger caused him to doubt his whole perception of the moment.

There's a reason a negative comment can replay in our minds long after we've received a dozen kind ones, and it has everything to do with how our brains operate. It's called *negativity bias*, and it's one of the most deeply ingrained aspects of our biology. Our brain is far more adept at noticing, storing, and recalling painful or threatening experiences than positive or neutral ones. This sensitivity once served us well; when danger could be hiding behind any tree or bush, remembering which paths led to predators and which berries made us sick could mean the difference between life and death. Our ancestors survived because they paid attention to what hurt them, what scared them, and what could kill them.

Our brain developed a kind of internal alarm system dedicated to promoting our survival, devoting up to two-thirds of its neurons to constantly scanning the environment for potential threats. This subconscious scanning process is called *neuroception*, a term coined by Stephen Porges. It refers to the way our nervous system detects safety or danger without involving conscious thought. We don't have to *think* about whether someone's tone feels "off" or a room suddenly feels tense—our body just *knows*, often before our mind can catch up. If something seems dangerous, neuroception triggers our survival responses and locks in the memory of the experience, just in case we encounter it again.

The challenge is that while our environments have evolved, our brains haven't quite caught up. We're no longer faced with the same existential threats on an hourly basis, but our minds remain vigilant, scanning for what could go wrong, what feels unsafe, or what threatens our sense of Self. This is why, even during a mostly positive day, a dismissive glance or moment of awkwardness can hijack our entire state of mind. Like Jordan, you might have thirty pleasant interactions, but if one person cuts you off in traffic or doesn't laugh at your joke, that's the moment your brain replays on a loop.

This negativity bias becomes even more powerful when paired with a history of emotional wounding. When we were young and vulnerable, our brains were more likely to encode painful experiences. Even if your childhood included plentiful warmth, laughter, and love, your nervous system was still wired to remember the moments that felt overwhelming or otherwise dysregulating. All the stress we experienced, the traumas passed down through generations, and the beliefs we absorbed and internalized didn't just shape how we think. They shaped how we function. Our nervous system kept the score. Every wound we carry influences how our body responds in our present moment. We've developed patterns, often unconscious, to keep ourselves feeling safe, like staying on high alert for danger or quickly withdrawing when we sense conflict. Our brain reinforces these habits by focusing more on potential threats than on signs of safety. We become hyperaware, constantly scanning for danger, so that even a small comment or gesture can trigger a big reaction, as if the old threat is happening all over again.

Real growth, then, isn't about erasing our past or eliminating all our uncomfortable feelings. It's about something more nuanced; it's about experiencing safety again and again, even while moving through discomfort. Neuroscientists call these moments *safe emergencies*; they allow you to step beyond your comfort zone without tipping you into overwhelm. When your nervous system is gently challenged and met with co-regulation or self-soothing, your brain begins to change. These small moments of stress met with safety send a new message to your body, a message that says: *This time, you're not alone. This time, it's safe to stay.* With each new experience we have the opportunity to teach ourselves different patterns, to rebuild old associations, and to grow our body's capacity to trust what safety feels like.

EMOTIONAL WOUNDS

When we experience a physical injury, it usually leaves a visible mark, like a scrape or a broken bone, something we can point to and treat directly by bandaging the wound or wrapping it in a protective cast. After the pain fades, we might have a scar that reminds us of what we went through. Emotional wounds, on the other hand, are not visible, but they are just as real, stored in our nervous system and wired into the neural pathways of our brain. Just like physical injuries, they need care and attention. But, too often, they go unacknowledged and untended.

We all carry emotional wounds from childhood that continue to impact us in adulthood. These childhood wounds can be triggered in present situations that may not seem particularly challenging on the surface but which touch on our past struggles. A *trigger* is any internal or external cue that signals danger to our nervous system, even if that danger isn't real or current. Triggers can be external, like a sound, a smell, a tone of voice, or a place. Or they can be internal, like a racing heart, a wave of hunger, a sudden feeling of loneliness, or an intrusive thought. As Bessel van der Kolk and other trauma researchers have shown, our body stores emotional memories—that is, a present-day experience can activate an old wound before our brain even has time to register what's happening. This is what leads to emotional flashbacks, or sudden, intense emotional reactions that resemble how we felt during earlier traumatic experiences. These are physiological reactions that cause our brain's limbic system (which governs emotion and memory) to become overactive, while our prefrontal cortex (which helps regulate and interpret experience) goes offline. That's why it's so difficult to think clearly, explain yourself, or make grounded decisions when you're triggered: Your body is reliving the past, and your brain is no longer in problem-solving mode.

When we are triggered, it is because our emotional body doesn't distinguish between past and present in the way the thinking mind does. I once watched a reality show where a couple was shopping for a new home. The husband was fixated on avoiding low windows and insisted that the house have a safe room. His position seemed a bit extreme until his wife explained that when he was young, his sister had been home alone during a break-in. Ever since, he had become "Mr. Home Protector," constantly thinking and planning ahead to protect his own family. While she appreciated his vigilance, she also noted that he sometimes went overboard. This was the residue of an emotional wound that had never fully healed. His hypervigilance in adulthood is a protective response shaped by unresolved feelings of fear, helplessness, even guilt from a traumatic childhood experience.

You might notice similar patterns in your own life, with hypersensitivities that don't always make sense on the surface. You might find yourself devastated by mild criticism or deeply hurt when someone leaves without saying goodbye. That criticism can bring up memories of being blamed, misunderstood, or never quite enough. And that goodbye may not just be about the present moment—it can stir old feelings of being left behind, forgotten, or unworthy of consideration. Or you might be the one who, the moment guests arrive, shifts into overdrive, talking nonstop, telling stories, making sure everyone is entertained because the thought of sitting in quiet with others feels unbearable. It might look like confidence, though underneath is a fear that simply being yourself isn't enough. Often, these tendencies point back to unprocessed emotional wounds, or times in our past when we felt unseen, unloved, unimportant, or unsafe.

Unless we process the emotions connected to those experiences, our wounds continue to influence our nervous system's perception of safety and threat. And when something reminds us of the original event, our brain reacts as if it's happening again. That man seeing low windows isn't just thinking about architecture; his body is reliving the fear he felt when he experienced that robbery in childhood.

Neurobiologically, this is how trauma becomes embedded in our body and mind. When we experience distressing or overwhelming events, our brain releases stress hormones like cortisol and adrenaline. These chemicals help our brain encode the memory as dangerous so that we can both remember and avoid similar threats in the future. Our hippocampus (which processes memory) and our amygdala (which governs emotional responses) start to work in overdrive. Eventually, both of these areas become more sensitive to anything that even *resembles* our original pain, making us more likely to become activated by similar experiences again.

This system evolved to protect us from experiencing unsafe situations, yet, at the same time, we're often compelled to revisit and re-create the very situations that hurt us. Freud referred to this as *repetition compulsion*, the unconscious drive to relive old pain in hopes that this time, it might turn out differently. It's not that we want to suffer; it's that a part of us longs for resolution, healing, and integration. Over the course of our lifetime, we may unconsciously repeat this cycle, in essence deepening the wound each time.

Recognizing these patterns is a powerful first step. Our emotional reactions are rooted in our personal history. Until we acknowledge and tend to those old emotional experiences, and until we feel what we couldn't allow ourselves to feel back then, they'll keep driving our reactions, making it harder to respond from the present instead of the past.

NERVOUS SYSTEM SURVIVAL RESPONSES

Most of us have heard of the fight-or-flight response, but that's just one piece of our body's full survival tool kit. Neuroscience now recognizes additional stress responses—freeze, fawn, and faint (also called *flop*)—as equally significant. These reactions are automatic, deeply ingrained responses shaped by our unique life experiences.

To understand why some of us tend to fight while others might freeze or fawn, it helps to look at what's running the show: our autonomic nervous system. This system controls our automatic bodily functions like heart rate, breathing, and digestion, and it constantly scans for cues of safety or threat. When we enter a survival state, our brain's priority becomes simple: *Survive this*. Higher cognitive functions, like reflection, empathy, creativity, or clear communication, take a back seat. Our thoughts may race, our senses sharpen, and everything in us shifts toward dealing with what feels like an immediate threat.

Polyvagal Theory, developed by Dr. Porges in the mid-1990s, is a framework that explains how our nervous system toggles between these states of safety, stress, and shutdown. The theory is named after the vagus nerve, which connects our brain to the rest of our body, communicating important information. It carries signals about safety, threat, and danger, helping to determine the physiological states that influence how we regulate our emotions. Our vagus nerve helps our body signal to our brain whether we can relax and feel connected or if we need to tense up and be on guard. These responses are our nervous system's way of protecting us in the moment, but they also reflect the coping strategies we developed earlier in life. These survival states are meant to protect us, but when they become our default, they can keep us stuck in cycles of hypervigilance, collapse, or disconnection long after the real threat is gone. To change these patterns, we start by noticing and exploring the feeling of safety our body can return to once the danger has passed.

STRESS STATES

Safe and Social: Our Baseline State

When we feel calm, connected, and secure, we are operating in what's known as the *ventral vagal state*, or the *safe and social* state. This is the foundation of a regulated nervous system, where we feel grounded in ourselves and able to engage openly with others. In this state, our parasympathetic nervous system is active, sending signals throughout our body that it's safe to relax, digest, and recover. Our heart rate is steady, our breathing is deep and unforced, and our muscles are at ease.

This safe and social state supports our emotional flexibility. We can experience the full range of emotions—joy, sadness, anger, excitement—without feeling overwhelmed by them. This is where connection thrives. Our voice warms, our body language opens, and we become a source of safety for others. In this state, vulnerability feels possible, trust can grow, and relationships deepen. Not only do we feel emotionally balanced, but our physical systems function optimally, making it easier to cope with stress when it inevitably arises. In this state, glimmers, or small moments of safety, comfort, or connection, are easier to notice, and these brief, soothing experiences can help guide us back to calm presence when stress pulls us away. Learning to track and expand these experiences helps build nervous system resilience.

Fight Response

When our nervous system perceives a shift in safety—real or imagined—it immediately mobilizes us for action. The fight response is one of our body's most primal reactions to perceived danger. It's our nervous system's way of preparing us to confront a threat head-on. When in fight mode, we may feel intense anger, irritation, or a surge of adrenaline pushing us to protect ourselves or those we care about. This response is essential in situations that demand defense, but when activated unnecessarily, it can make us reactive, combative, or controlling in ways that strain our relationships.

Physiologically, our body prepares for battle: Muscles tighten, jaws clench, heart rate spikes. Adrenaline and cortisol flood our bloodstream, narrowing our attention. We become hyper-alert even to subtle threats, like a change in tone or a delayed response. Our voice may grow louder, sharper, more urgent. Sometimes the fight response erupts as yelling, criticizing, or lashing out. Other times, it lurks beneath passive-aggressive remarks, micromanaging, or an unrelenting need to be right. Our body isn't trying to start a conflict; it's trying to stay safe. What others experience as intensity may feel, internally, like clarity, strength, or justified self-defense. Many people who live in a chronic fight state don't see themselves as angry or aggressive; they see themselves as competent, confident, and unwilling to be disrespected.

Andre was one of these people. Andre believed he was direct, clear, and unafraid to speak his mind. But others experienced him differently. His coworkers said he was hard to approach; his teenage son had started going quiet when Andre entered the room; and his partner said that conversations with him often felt like arguments, even when she wasn't trying to disagree. The truth was, Andre's nervous system defaulted to fight mode at the first hint of disrespect, his body tightening at even a pause, a sigh, or a look that felt dismissive. He didn't mean to hurt anyone. He just needed to feel heard, to stay in control, and to keep himself from falling apart. As a child, Andre had learned that strength and loudness were necessary to be heard or taken seriously. His father only listened when someone yelled. Emotions were met with ridicule or silence, and vulnerability was a liability. So, he adapted. He got louder, tougher, and quicker to react. In his world, if you didn't push back, you disappeared. Now, as an adult, his body still responds as if every disagreement is a threat, making even tender moments feel dangerous. Andre doesn't want to intimidate anyone, but underneath his force is a child who learned that striking first was the only way to stay safe.

Flight Response

The flight response is triggered when our nervous system perceives danger and signals us to escape. This could involve physically leaving a threatening environment or mentally and emotionally distancing ourselves from an uncomfortable situation. When in flight mode, we often feel a surge of panic, anxiety, or urgency or an intense drive to avoid confrontation at all costs. Our heart races, breath quickens, and muscles tighten as our body prepares us to flee. In this state, we instinctively seek ways to avoid discomfort. That might mean disengaging physically or mentally, avoiding eye contact, ignoring difficult conversations, or distracting ourselves with work or constant activity.

For some, the flight response shows up as chronic overdrive: always moving, overcommitting, or staying endlessly "productive" to keep anxiety at bay. For others, it's more internal, zoning out into fantasy, constantly canceling plans, or withdrawing emotionally from relationships. This reaction often masks deeper feelings of fear or helplessness. And though it may look like ambition or independence, it can leave us feeling scattered, overwhelmed, and disconnected from ourselves and others. Not everyone flees by running. Some do it by joking, charming, and managing the emotional temperature of every room they enter.

Javier is one of those people. He's a high school teacher who always keeps the conversation going, ready with a punch line or clever observation. At thirty-five, he is known for his wit and is beloved by his students, the life of any staff meeting, and the guy who can make even tense moments feel lighter. But underneath his humor is a nervous system that learned to flee through charm. As a child, Javier's sensitivity was a liability. He remembers being laughed at when he cried in front of his classmates and how his uncle called him soft as his father looked away. Both at home and at school, emotions were met with teasing, mockery, or dismissal. So, Javier got ahead of it. If he could turn his feelings into a joke, no one else could use them against him. If he could keep things light, no one would see the weight he was carrying.

By the time he was a teenager, Javier had mastered emotional escape. He avoided anything that made him feel exposed, like new experiences, vulnerability, even compliments. He learned to control the narrative: always entertaining, never too serious, and never too real. Humor became his way of disappearing in plain sight. As an adult, Javier still flees intimacy, not by running away but by staying onstage, joking through his discomfort, changing the subject when things get personal, and deflecting care with a laugh. Deep down, he worries that if he stops performing, what's underneath won't be enough. Javier's flight response keeps him moving, constantly one step ahead of being seen.

Fawn Response

The fawn response is an adaptive strategy that develops when our nervous system learns that the safest way to survive is by pleasing or appeasing others. This response is especially common in environments where conflict, disapproval, or assertiveness feels dangerous or leads to emotional withdrawal. In such settings, our body learns to suppress personal needs, ignore boundaries, and focus entirely on appeasing others in order to avoid harm. We may say yes when we mean no, take on too much responsibility, or consistently prioritize others' needs at the expense of our own. We often become hyper-attuned to the emotions of those around us, trying to anticipate what they want or need before they even say it. This can create a sense of over-responsibility, as though another's well-being depends entirely on us. Our ability to set boundaries becomes compromised, and our fear of conflict or abandonment can be so strong that asserting ourselves feels unsafe or even selfish. As this pattern repeats, it often leads to burnout, resentment, and a blurred sense of identity, where our own wants and needs become secondary, or are forgotten or ignored altogether.

For most people, this instinct to soothe others starts in childhood, in moments when telling the truth feels unsafe or when protecting the comfort of others becomes the only way to protect yourself. Fawning is a protective response often used by survivors of assault as an attempt to reduce danger by appeasing the perpetrator who has power over them. This was true for Talia. She was nine when she told her mother that her uncle had touched her, and that it felt wrong. Listening to what Talia had to say, her mother's face froze, then tightened. "Don't say things like that," she whispered, glancing toward the kitchen, where the family was gathered. "He's family." At bedtime that night, her mother didn't tuck her in. The next day, everyone acted like nothing had happened. So, Talia learned to do the same and became skilled at silence. She didn't trust adults—not therapists, not teachers, not even herself. She doubted both her memory and her instincts, becoming hyperaware of every shift in mood, tone, or emotion of another. Even in safe spaces, part of her stayed curled inward and hidden, bracing to be disbelieved.

As an adult, Talia is a bodyworker who helps others reconnect with their bodies, but she still tightens when someone says, "You can relax; it's just me." She smiles when things get hard, pivots when conversations get personal, and downplays her pain to keep the peace. Her nervous system has been wired to believe that truth invites danger, and connection requires protecting others from discomfort. Talia's story reminds us that fawning or appeasing isn't always about being nice; it's about staying safe.

Freeze and Functional Freeze

When neither fight nor flight nor fawn feels like an option, our nervous system may default to a freeze state. In this state, we can feel immobilized, numb, or emotionally detached from what's happening around us. Freeze is our body's protective mechanism when it perceives that we cannot confront or escape threats. Our heart rate slows, our breathing becomes shallow or we hold our breath, and our physical response is dulled as blood is pulled away from our hands and feet, often making them feel cold, numb, or tingly. Mentally, we disconnect and feel as if we're watching ourselves from the outside—dissociated, disconnected, and unable to fully take part in what's happening around us. Some victims of abuse describe this as the experience of floating above their own body and watching events unfold as if they were happening to someone else. For many, freeze feels like being locked in place, paralyzed and unable to act, sometimes resulting in excessive sleep. This state can be deeply disorienting and frightening, as our body shuts down in an effort to distance or disconnect from an overwhelming moment, preserve energy, and avoid further harm.

Freeze, however, doesn't always mean stillness. Sometimes it shows up as *functional freeze*. Our body is stuck in a state of hyperarousal and freeze. It's like pressing the gas and the brakes of a car at the same time. Outwardly, we appear to be managing life—going to work, meeting obligations, doing what's expected. Internally, though, we feel numb, flat, or hollow, cut off from meaning and disconnected from the people and things that matter most. All the while, we're scanning for danger, tracking every shift in someone else's tone, mood, or expression. The world loses its color, and each day becomes something we push through on autopilot instead of something we truly live.

Take Ali, for example. A successful attorney in her mid-forties, she's fast-talking, energetic, and widely admired at her firm. She runs five miles every morning, keeps a spotless home, and works more than eighty hours a week. Her coworkers joke that she makes them all look bad. "I do my best under pressure," she says, and it's true. Stress is all she's ever known. Ali's childhood was filled with instability. Her mother was an alcoholic, and her father enabled it. She still remembers her mom arriving drunk to her high school graduation. Her father was dismissive, saying, "She's just tired," and no one talked about it again. Ali coped by excelling in school, pouring herself into her studies and achievements. This worked, because on paper, her life is a success story. But internally, she feels empty. Though she's financially secure, she's deeply unfulfilled. She wants a family, but there's no space in her life for connection. She prides herself on avoiding alcohol, but she's addicted to busyness. Stillness feels intolerable. So, like many stuck in functional freeze, Ali turned to food, caffeine, social media, and an overfilled calendar—anything to keep the adrenaline flowing and distract from the inner chaos.

Faint (Flop) Response

The faint or flop response is our nervous system's most extreme form of shutdown, its final survival strategy when all other options are gone. In this state, our body may go limp, leaving us feeling weak, dizzy, or disoriented, and physically unable to move or respond. Our breathing becomes shallow, and our mind feels foggy or far away. Much like an animal "playing dead" to survive, our faint response can appear as sudden exhaustion, emotional or physical collapse, or an intense numbness. Though distressing, it's our body's way of trying to preserve our life in the face of overwhelming threat. One extreme version of this response is known as *vasovagal syncope*, or a sudden drop in heart rate and blood pressure triggered by emotional stress or physical stimuli like pain, fear, or the sight of blood, causing us to faint.

Recognizing early warning signs, like blurred vision, dizziness, or weakness, can help individuals respond proactively, for example, by lying down and elevating their legs to restore blood flow to their brain. Although the episode usually passes quickly, the collapse is a primal signal that, while frightening in the moment, is the body's way of saying: *This is too much right now.*

PRACTICE
PRESENCE DURING ACTIVATION

Our stress responses often show up as subtle (or not-so-subtle) sensations or impulses in our body. By learning to notice and name these states without judgment, we begin to build the capacity to stay present and regulate ourselves through them.

1. **When you notice that you feel triggered, overwhelmed, or emotionally reactive, try to compassionately name the experience.** Use the following language to separate your identity from the feeling:

    - I notice a part of me that wants to hit or lash out is active right now.
    - I notice a part of me that wants to run or disappear is active right now.
    - I notice a part of me that is going through the motions on autopilot, feeling disconnected or flat, is active right now.
    - I notice a part of me that feels numb, stuck, or unable to act is active right now.
    - I notice a part of me that wants to please or make others comfortable is active right now.

2. **Place one or both hands on your chest or belly, and breathing slowly and deeply, say to yourself:** *This is a part of me. I hear you. I'm listening.*

3. **Choose one grounding action:**

    - Press your feet into the floor.
    - Gently hum.

- ◁ Shake out your hands.
- ◁ Push against a wall with your palms.

4. **Notice and Reflect**: What changed in your body? What does this part of you need right now?

Before moving on, take a moment to honor what just surfaced. These small shifts, naming, pausing, grounding, are the foundation of healing. Each time you respond to yourself with awareness instead of judgment, you're creating safety where there was once threat.

MISUNDERSTANDING SURVIVAL STATES

Because our survival responses are instinctive and automatic, they're often misunderstood, both by those experiencing them and by those around them. The way someone reacts, or fails to react, during a moment of crisis may be questioned by others who don't realize they're witnessing a nervous system in defense mode, not a conscious choice. Take, for example, the man who receives devastating news that his wife has died in an accident. He appears stoic, speaks in a flat, monotone voice, and continues to make coffee or fold laundry as if nothing happened, his face blank and expressionless. Without an understanding of our nervous system, others might say, "He doesn't seem upset" or "He's not even crying." But in reality, the shock of the loss has triggered his nervous system to shut down in order to protect him from overwhelming pain. The same misunderstanding happens with women who've experienced sexual assault or interpersonal violence. People often ask, "Why didn't you scream or fight back?" What this overlooks is that our body can become immobilized, speech can stop, and our ability to act disappears, all as our nervous system shuts down to survive.

The truth is, we don't always know how we'll respond in crisis. But trauma or chronic stress can push our nervous system into any of the survival states—fight, flight, freeze, fawn, or flop—without warning and without explanation. This is why understanding polyvagal states is vital. When we mistake survival responses for personality traits, we make unfair judgments. We can end up labeling people as cold, dramatic, lazy, hysterical, weak, or aggressive when what we're really seeing is a body protecting itself. This lack of understanding can escalate conflict and deepen disconnection. In high-stress professions, like law enforcement, first responders, healthcare, or the justice system, this awareness can be the difference between harm and help. A trauma-informed, polyvagal-aware lens changes how we interpret behavior, intervene in crisis, and hold space for pain. When we understand the nervous system, we stop asking, "What's wrong with you?" and start asking, "What happened to you, and how can we help you feel safe again?"

STUCK IN SURVIVAL MODE

As I hope is now clear, trauma lives in our nervous system. When we experience early or repeated trauma, our bodies begin to anticipate danger around every corner. This makes it difficult to feel safe: in our bodies, in our relationships, or in the world. We may long to feel calm or grounded, but our bodies simply won't allow it. This dysregulation changes how we perceive and respond to stress.

In a well-regulated nervous system, we can pause, assess, and determine what's minor and what's serious. But when we carry unresolved emotional wounds, even small frustrations can feel like emergencies. I remember once being on vacation with my father. Midway through the day, he learned that the person who was supposed to mow the lawn back home hadn't shown up. What could have been a minor annoyance became a full-blown crisis. He was glued to the phone, treating the situation as if it were an emergency. It wasn't really about the lawn. His nervous system was already on high alert, and it grabbed on to the first disruption it could find. That tension needed a story, and the missed lawn care became it.

When we're in an activated state, everything feels urgent. Waiting for someone who's running late can feel intolerable; misplacing your keys becomes catastrophic; being cut off in traffic feels like a personal attack.

When your nervous system is in survival mode, your brain can't distinguish between true danger and everyday stress. This is why when someone tells us to "just calm down," it can feel absurd. Their assessment of the moment may be more accurate, but most of us would rather not be told to calm down, especially when the reminder conflicts with everything our body is telling us. Often our body's response isn't even about what's happening now; the present moment is a reminder of a past event.

Here's an example: A friend of mine, Amy, recently reached out to an old friend, Vince, hoping to reconnect over a phone call. When they finally spoke, the first thing Vince asked was, "Are you okay?" Amy was confused; she had simply wanted to catch up. But for Vince, a surprise phone call from a loved one felt ominous. As a child, he had lost his father to cancer, and more recently, his girlfriend had gone through her own health scare. For him, a phone call out of the blue could only mean bad news. The same cue—"let's catch up"—carried completely different meanings for each of them, shaped by their individual histories. While Amy felt warm anticipation, Vince's nervous system was already bracing for grief. His body was reacting to an old imprint of loss and fear.

Our past doesn't stay in the past; it lives in our bodies. Our nervous system remembers our history. Early-life wounds can resurface years later as emotional triggers that feel just as real in the present. Here are some examples:

- If you experienced abandonment in childhood, you might panic or shut down when someone seems emotionally distant or doesn't text back.
- If you were criticized, shamed, or bullied, even gentle feedback might feel like an attack, leaving you tense or defensive.
- If you went hungry as a child, feeling hunger now might activate anxiety or fear.
- If you experienced verbal, emotional, or physical abuse, things like a raised voice, someone crying, or a sudden movement can feel threatening.

◁ If you experienced sexual abuse, arousal or intimacy can feel unsafe, triggering fear, confusion, or distress.

When these emotional responses are so intense that they overwhelm our nervous system, we experience a state known as *emotional flooding*. This term was popularized by relationship researcher John Gottman, who observed how, in moments of conflict, people could become so emotionally saturated that they shut down or became reactive. In his work with couples, Gottman found that during flooding, one partner often couldn't hear, absorb, or respond to the other, not because they didn't care but because their nervous system had entered a defensive survival state that prevented them from being able to take in what was happening.

During flooding, our brain's amygdala over-activates, while our prefrontal cortex goes offline. This is why, in moments of overwhelm, we may struggle to speak, lash out, shut down, or react in ways that feel out of character. Emotional flooding can occur in any situation that feels threatening or destabilizing, especially when something in the present, like a tone of voice, a look, or a smell, echoes a painful memory and triggers a full-body response.

While we can't control every trigger, we can grow our window of tolerance, or the range where our body and mind can handle strong feelings without getting overwhelmed. Expanding this window takes time, patience, self-compassion, and consistent practice. With support, what once overwhelmed us becomes manageable. Triggers, though painful, can be powerful teachers, pointing to what still needs our care and healing. Meeting them with curiosity instead of judgment creates space for change. We reclaim our agency, respond instead of reacting, and strengthen our ability to face life with courage, resilience, and grace. But to truly heal, we must first understand where these patterns come from.

PRACTICE
STRESS RELEASE THROUGH MOVEMENT

As stress builds, our muscles tighten, our breath shortens, and our energy gets stuck. This practice invites you to release tension physically so your body and emotions can reset. You'll try simple movements that help your nervous system discharge stress. Pick one or move through them all.

Shaking

- Stand or sit with your feet firmly on the ground.
- Begin by lightly bouncing your knees.
- Let that movement rise through your body into your hips, arms, shoulders, and head.
- Shake gently for one to two minutes. If it helps, you can imagine shaking off stress or stuck emotion.
- Notice and Reflect: When you're ready, come to stillness and take a few breaths, asking yourself: *What do I feel now? What shifted?*

Pushing

- Stand facing a wall and place your palms flat against it.
- Slowly lean your weight into your hands, pressing as if to hold the wall up.
- Feel your muscles engage, focusing on the feeling of strength and boundary.
- Hold for three to five breaths, then release.
- Notice and Reflect: When you're ready, come to stillness and take a few breaths, asking yourself: *What did this feel like emotionally? What did my body need to say?*

Yelling

- Find a private, safe space: your car, a forest, the shower, or use a pillow.
- Let out a sound that expresses what's stuck—anger, grief, frustration.

- You can yell, growl, sob, scream, or groan whatever needs release.
- Let the sound move through you and out of you.
- Notice and Reflect: When you're ready, come to stillness and take a few breaths, asking yourself: *What emotion needed to be heard?*

Breathing

- Lie on your back with a pillow under your knees if needed.
- Place one hand on your chest and one on your belly.
- Breathe in slowly through your nose, and exhale fully through your mouth.
- Focus on an area of your body that feels tense.
- With each exhale, imagine the tension softening or melting away.
- Stay with this breath for two to five minutes.
- Notice and Reflect: When you're ready, come to stillness and take a few breaths, asking yourself: *What changed inside me?*

Our bodies often speak before our minds can make sense of what's happening. When we allow that energy to move through shaking, pushing, yelling, or simply breathing, we create space for something new: regulation, clarity, connection. These practices don't require perfection. They just ask for presence.

PRACTICE
GLIMMERS AND THE FELT SENSE OF SAFETY

Just as triggers activate our survival states, glimmers allow us to access safety. A *glimmer* is a term (coined by Deb Dana) from Polyvagal Theory describing the micro-moments when our nervous system detects cues of safety and connection. These can be as small as sunlight filtering through trees, the sound of a kind voice, or the comfort of a familiar smell. In this next practice, we'll actively look for the subtle signals of safety, especially the moments of warmth, calm, and connection that your nervous system already knows, even if they're fleeting.

1. **Make a list of what characterizes the "glimmer" moments when you felt safe, comforted, or at peace.** Examples might include:

   ◁ The sound of rain
   ◁ A pet curled beside you
   ◁ A warm drink in your hands
   ◁ Soft music
   ◁ A kind glance or encouraging word

2. **Choose one glimmer to focus on and close your eyes to fully recall the experience.** Reflect and explore by asking yourself the following:

   ◁ Where do I feel this in my body?
   ◁ What helps me relax or slow down?

3. **Create a "Glimmer Kit" with tools that evoke these feelings.** It might include a calming playlist, a scented oil, a comforting photo, or a soft blanket. When activated or dysregulated, return to one of these items to support co-regulation.

The more you practice noticing glimmers, the more you begin to teach your nervous system that safety can exist in everyday experiences of calm. These small sparks of connection or ease may seem subtle, but they matter. They help rebuild your sense of wholeness. Let them be a place you regularly return.

TYPES OF INNER CHILD WOUNDS

Many of our emotional reactions in adulthood, especially the ones that feel confusing, disproportionate, or hard to control, can be traced back to unresolved experiences from childhood. These are often referred to as our *inner child wounds*: deep emotional imprints shaped by how we were parented and what our nervous systems learned about safety, love, and connection. These wounds are learned adaptations, and they often resurface in our closest relationships, where vulnerability runs deepest. To help you explore how these patterns might show up in your own life, let's look at a couple of real-life examples.

Let's start with Yelena. She's married to Mark, a gentle and dependable partner. On most days, Yelena is home from work around seven. One evening, when she still isn't home by eight, Mark sends her a quick text: "Hey, I'm at home, just checking in, are you okay?" She doesn't respond. Thirty minutes later, he sends another message. Still no answer. Finally, Mark calls her, but by now Yelena is irritated.

"What's going on?" she asks, sounding defensive.

"Nothing," Mark replies. "I just hadn't heard from you and wanted to make sure everything was all right."

"I'm with my girlfriends. Why do you always have to make a big deal out of everything?"

They end the call, both feeling upset. Yelena later vents to her friends that Mark is being clingy and controlling. But what's actually happening beneath the surface is that Yelena carries a rebellion wound. She grew up with overly permissive parents who rarely set boundaries or followed through on consequences. This can lead in different directions for different people. One child might seek boundaries and safety to replace that which was missing, but in Yelena's case, being questioned by Mark felt controlling and threatened the tough façade of independence she'd developed to survive. Now, even a simple check-in from her husband registers as control. She continues to misread care as intrusion, without realizing that her reaction is rooted in the past, not the present.

Now consider Jemma. She's at the grocery store when she notices a man walk up to a young girl and speak to her. Jemma's body instantly tenses and her heart pounds. She feels a surge of protectiveness and moves quickly toward the pair, interrupting their conversation.

"Is he bothering you?" she asks the girl with urgency.

The young girl looks confused. "No, not at all. We know each other from church."

Jemma, still on edge, says, "Okay, I just wanted to make sure no one was bothering you without your consent."

The moment ends in an awkward silence. What Jemma doesn't realize right away is that her nervous system was reacting to an over-responsibility wound, the result of growing up in an environment where she had to step into adult roles far too early. Her body is conditioned to anticipate danger and intervene before anyone else can. Even when the situation doesn't call for it, her protector instinct kicks in without warning.

These are just two examples of how unresolved childhood experiences can shape our adult reactions. Sometimes our wound causes us to overreact. Other times, we feel nothing at all in moments that should register something.

By tuning in to your body's signals and emotional reactions, you can begin to explore the childhood wounds that are still asking for your attention to help you feel secure in yourself and your choices.

Below are some common types of emotional wounds, each shaped by specific parenting dynamics. As you read through them, you might recognize aspects of yourself in more than one pattern. The goal here is not to pathologize or assign blame but to bring compassionate awareness to the parts of you that adapted to stay safe and connected to your caregivers.

You can start by asking yourself:

- What kinds of moments cause me to "freak out," shut down, or feel unusually anxious or numb?
- What does my body feel like in those moments (e.g., tight chest, racing thoughts, numbness, tears)?
- Is this similar to anything I experienced earlier in life?

Let's begin with one of the most common wounds, shaped by unpredictability, emotional volatility, and the fear that safety could disappear at any moment.

Distrust Wound: Reactive Parent

A distrust wound develops when a parent is emotionally unpredictable, swinging between warmth and anger, calm and volatility. Their reactions may have felt random, disproportionate, or explosive. One moment, they were affectionate; the next, they were irritable or reactive. As a child, you never knew which version of them you'd get. That lack of consistency created a deep sense of emotional instability.

To cope, you became like an emotional guard dog, always scanning for tension and trying to anticipate threat before it appeared. Connection didn't feel comforting; it felt loaded. You learned to brace for impact, even in moments that were supposed to be safe. Staying on guard eventually hardened into a belief that people are unpredictable and safety can vanish at any moment. In adulthood, this often shows up as relationship anxiety, clinginess, or a constant need for reassurance. Without a foundation of safety, mistrust and hypervigilance become the default mode of protection.

Healing a distrust wound starts by noticing when your suspicion is more about the past than the present. You begin to tell the difference between old reflexes and current reality. You rebuild trust by keeping promises to yourself, respecting your boundaries, and paying attention to who shows up for you consistently. Instead of always scanning for danger, you start looking for signs of safety. You practice staying connected even when it feels unfamiliar, giving your nervous system time to adjust. The goal isn't to trust blindly; it's to feel safe through your own clarity and discernment. You start by noticing which relationships feel steady and mutual. Over time, you learn that trust grows slowly, moment by moment, in the presence of your own consistency and reliability.

Affirmation: *I can trust myself to know who is safe now.*

Abandonment Wound: Disconnected Parent

This wound forms in childhood when love and attention were inconsistent, often depending on your caregiver's mood or emotional availability. At times, they felt close and engaged; at others, withdrawn and unreachable. You learned to read subtle cues—changes in tone, energy, or silence—as signs of coming disconnection, so you did whatever you could to hold their attention. Their emotional unpredictability left you feeling destabilized and anxious, always bracing for the moment connection might fade.

The unpredictability of connection planted the belief that people eventually leave and that love cannot last. You began to doubt your worth and fear you were destined to be left behind. To cope, you learned to shrink your needs, quiet your voice, and make yourself easy to manage, hoping that would make people stay. Even when someone offered warmth, it might have felt suspicious or temporary, so your instinct was to pull away, question their motives, or leave before you could be left. As an adult, this can look like craving connection but sabotaging intimacy. Small changes—like a delayed text or a shift in tone—can trigger panic, shame, or the urge to shut down.

Healing an abandonment wound means becoming the steady, supportive presence you once needed. It starts by staying with your own painful feelings instead of distracting yourself or pushing them away, breathing through fear and uncertainty without falling apart or clinging to them. And when someone offers consistent care, you allow yourself, little by little, to actually receive it. Part of healing includes grieving the emotional unreliability of early caregivers, which helps you stop blaming yourself for their absence. As you practice emotional regulation and self-soothing, safety becomes something you can create from within rather than constantly seek from others.

Affirmation: *I am safe to stay, and I am safe to be stayed with.*

Rejection Wound: Status-Oriented Parent

This wound often forms in childhood when a parent values performance, appearance, or achievement more than genuine emotional connection. You may have been praised for looking the part, getting good grades, or being well-behaved, but when you showed sadness, made mistakes, or stepped outside their expectations, you were met with criticism, disappointment, or withdrawal. Their warmth and attention came in bursts—high when you impressed them, low or absent when you didn't. As a child, you learned to read every glance or shift in tone as a measure of how well you were doing. Connection felt like something you had to earn.

As time went on, you learned that love came through performance.

Showing your true feelings—being messy, emotional, or imperfect—didn't feel safe. To protect yourself, you put on a mask: performing, perfecting, and pleasing to secure acceptance, even while hiding your authentic Self. As an adult you still crave approval yet find it hollow, noticing that compliments land more on your achievements or appearance than on who you truly are. You might hold back your real thoughts or needs, fearing rejection if you step outside the image you've built. Deep down, love feels conditional, and belonging feels tied to performance rather than authenticity.

Healing a rejection wound means reclaiming your right to show up as your full, authentic Self. It begins by noticing the moments you hold back and self-censor or edit yourself to be more acceptable, and choosing, even in small ways, to express what's real. You start to understand that your worth isn't based on how much you achieve, and that you don't have to be perfect to be loved. As you learn to tolerate being seen in your imperfection, you start to trust that love can hold more than just the polished or seemingly perfect parts of you. Real belonging doesn't come from changing who you are to make others like you. It comes from being yourself and not hiding. Learning to like and accept yourself helps you feel grounded and secure, even when it's uncomfortable that others don't always understand you or agree with you.

Affirmation: *I am lovable exactly as I am.*

Humiliation Wound: Critical Parent

This wound often forms in childhood environments where criticism, mockery, or shaming were common and normalized. If your parent frequently belittled you, whether through harsh words, sarcastic jokes, or calling you out in front of others, you may have learned to associate attention with humiliation. Even if they claimed they were "just joking" or "trying to help," the repeated put-downs, ridicule, or emotional dismissal chipped away at your sense of safety. Being visible started to feel dangerous, so you began to scan for the next jab or cutting remark, bracing yourself for the moment when someone would point out your flaws or make you the punch line. Eventually, you learned to keep your guard up, hide your vulnerability, and avoid drawing too much attention, to protect yourself from the sting of judgment.

Being consistently watched or judged eventually created the belief that visibility leads to shame. To avoid criticism, you learned to be agreeable, stay quiet, or shrink yourself. Being seen felt risky, so you hid the parts of yourself you feared others would target. In adulthood, this wound often shows up as self-consciousness, overthinking, or fear of exposure. You may feel nervous speaking in front of others, worry constantly about saying the wrong thing, or avoid new experiences because you're afraid of being laughed at or dismissed. Sometimes you might even joke about yourself first, hoping that if you point out your flaws, it will hurt less if someone else does. In more subtle ways, you may hold back your truth or follow along with others, even when it feels wrong, because it feels safer than standing out or risking ridicule. Beneath these behaviors is often a deep belief that something is wrong with you, leaving you hesitant to show your real feelings or take up space.

Healing a humiliation wound means changing your relationship with being seen. It begins by offering compassion to the parts of you that learned to hide, shrink, or self-criticize in order to stay safe. You start to notice when you're silencing yourself to avoid embarrassment, and you gently practice speaking up even when your voice shakes. With time, your body learns that self-expression doesn't have to lead to harm and your urge to brace for judgment begins to soften. You allow yourself to take up space. When you're around people who treat you with respect and care, your nervous system begins to relax and shame begins to loosen its grip. Slowly but surely, you become more at home in your truth and begin to feel brave enough to show trusted others who you really are.

Affirmation: *I am safe to be seen with dignity and self-respect.*

Over-Responsibility Wound: Peer-like Parent

This wound often forms in childhood when caregiving roles become reversed and the parent relies on your bond for emotional stability, validation, or support. Sometimes the parent is overwhelmed by their own struggles—mental health, financial stress, loneliness—and sometimes they're emotionally immature, craving approval or closeness from you instead of providing it. In both cases, you're forced to become a confidant or caregiver. You may have been praised for being "mature" or "easy," but underneath that praise was pressure: to agree, to self-soothe, to always be available. Other people's moods, self-esteem, and sense of stability depended on how well you managed their emotions, so you learned to anticipate what they needed before they even asked, meeting those needs at the expense of your own.

Over time, you learned that saying no could upset people, and when you did share your needs, it often led to guilt, silence, or withdrawal. To avoid conflict, you stopped speaking up and paid closer attention to others than to yourself. Setting boundaries felt selfish, and acting independently felt like a betrayal. Being the one to hold everything together became your unspoken role, until eventually your own needs grew invisible—even to you. In adulthood, this survival strategy can look like over-functioning: always taking care of others but struggling to let anyone care for you. You might feel guilty when resting, anxious when you're not helping, or resentful when relationships feel one-sided. Deep down, you may believe your worth comes from what you do for others, not from who you are.

Healing an over-responsibility wound means reclaiming the right to exist beyond your usefulness. It begins by noticing when your actions are driven by guilt, fear, or the belief that love must be earned. You start to ask: *Am I choosing this, or am I afraid not to?* Slowly, you begin to set boundaries, unlearning the idea that saying no is unkind and beginning to see it as a way of respecting and honoring your own needs and limits without guilt. You practice saying no without apology and letting others carry what isn't yours to hold. As you resist your instinct to fix, manage, or absorb everyone else's emotions, something powerful begins to shift and rest no longer feels selfish. Receiving becomes a skill you practice. You may grieve the years you spent over-functioning, mistaking responsibility for love. But in that grief, you make space for something new. You begin to separate your identity from your role as helper. Your relationships shift from caretaking to connection.

Affirmation: *I am worthy of love, in rest and in action.*

Scarcity Wound: Uninvolved Parent

This wound forms in childhood when a parent is absent in ways that are deeply felt—physically, emotionally, or both. They may not have been abusive, but they were unavailable, distracted, or detached, lost in work, stress, or their own struggles. This wasn't a home where you were shaped to perform or please; it was a home where you were simply overlooked. You may have learned that asking for help was pointless, that comfort wasn't coming, and that it was safer to manage everything on your own. Whether the neglect was material, like hunger, housing instability, or lack of routine, or emotional, like being dismissed, forgotten, or treated like an afterthought, the feeling was the same: *I do not matter; no one is coming to help me.*

Gradually, this absence shaped your beliefs about yourself and the world. You began to expect that your needs would go unnoticed or unmet, and that there was never enough—care, attention, or stability—to feel secure. To protect yourself, you became hyper-independent: doing everything alone, keeping your needs hidden, and avoiding vulnerability to prevent disappointment. As an adult, this can look like discomfort with receiving care, reluctance to ask for help, or overextending yourself while neglecting your own needs. Even when support is offered, it can feel foreign or unsafe to accept. You may push yourself to exhaustion, compare yourself constantly, or feel like good things won't last. Relationships often swing between overextension and withdrawal, giving too much to feel secure or pulling away to avoid being let down.

Healing a scarcity wound means rewriting the belief that there's never enough—never enough care, attention, or space for you to exist as you are. It begins by acknowledging the pain of what was missing and allowing yourself to grieve the care, attention, or resources you didn't receive. You start to recognize when you minimize or dismiss your needs and slowly practice asking for and accepting help without guilt. You build safety by giving yourself consistent attention, checking in on how you feel, meeting small needs before they become big, and letting trusted people show up for you. As you build trust in your own enoughness, you stop measuring your value by what you produce or how much you give. You come to understand that needing care and support doesn't make you weak; it makes you human.

Affirmation: *There is enough for me, and I am enough for me.*

Rebellion Wound: Over-Permissive Parent

This wound often begins in childhood homes where boundaries were unclear or entirely absent. If your parents were overly permissive, emotionally disengaged, or avoided asserting authority, you may have grown up without the structure children need to feel secure. Rules may have been inconsistent, consequences unpredictable or nonexistent. On the surface, this lack of control can feel like freedom, like you were trusted to make your own choices. But beneath it was something far more destabilizing: a deep sense of chaos. No one told you where the edges were. Life wasn't predictable. Without someone to model boundaries or set consistent expectations to keep you safe, you were left to navigate the world without a map. Without external limits, you never learned to set internal ones, so freedom came with disorientation, not ease.

Over time, you started to think of rules imposed by others as limiting. You began to push back against structure, thinking it was just a way for others to control you and rob you of your agency. Because no one showed you how limits could be safe or helpful, you didn't learn how to build them for yourself. Instead, you started to believe that all rules and limits were unfair or meant to hurt you. As an adult, this often shows up as a push-pull dynamic in your relationship with freedom. You crave independence yet feel lost without direction. You might reject guidance, procrastinate on commitments, or rebel against structure even when it serves you. Even when someone offers help or healthy boundaries, you may instinctively resist, interpreting it as control. Cooperation can feel like submission.

Commitment, whether to a relationship, job, or personal goal, can feel suffocating, even when it's something you deeply want. Beneath the defiance is often a deeper mistrust, not only of others but of yourself. Without internal tools to navigate responsibility, freedom becomes overwhelming, and limits feel foreign or unsafe.

Healing a rebellion wound means redefining freedom as the ability to choose your own path. It begins by recognizing that not all structure is control, and not all guidance is a threat to your autonomy. You start to notice where your defiance was once protection, and where it may now be keeping you stuck or unsupported. Little by little, you learn to build internal boundaries that support you and see that discipline can be empowering, and you begin to feel more rooted in what's important to you. You stop seeing all commitments as traps and begin to recognize the value in relationships that feel supportive and aligned with who you are. As you practice sticking with something by choice, you start to see that freedom and safety can coexist. Structure can be something you create for yourself, to help you feel strong and better supported.

Affirmation: *I choose what grounds me and find freedom within structure.*

Powerless Wound: Helicopter Parent

This wound often develops in childhood homes where parents tried to protect against discomfort by managing everything themselves. Your caregivers may have had good intentions and wanted to keep you safe, help you succeed, or prevent you from failing. They made decisions for you, fixed problems before you could try to solve them independently, and stepped in before you had a chance to fall and recover. But in shielding you from challenge, they also shielded you from growth. These early experiences often lead to internalized beliefs about your own inadequacy. You may become dependent on external guidance while also resenting how reliant you feel.

As you grew, this overprotection sent a deeper message: You can't handle things on your own. Without chances to make choices or face natural consequences, you didn't build confidence, resilience, or trust in your instincts. You learned to look to others for direction, second-guess your gut, and avoid risks for fear of making the wrong move. Even small decisions began to feel overwhelming, each one carrying the pressure of "getting it right." In adulthood, this often shows up as chronic indecision, procrastination, or difficulty following through. You may feel paralyzed by everyday choices, abandon projects midway, or rely on reassurance before taking action. Taking initiative or asserting yourself can feel unfamiliar, even threatening, because underneath it all is the fear that if you try and fail, it will confirm your deepest worry—that you're not capable after all.

Healing a powerless wound means learning that your voice, choices, and actions matter. It starts by remembering all the times you were told what to do, how to feel, or who to be, and letting yourself feel the frustration or sadness those moments left behind. You may realize you've been waiting for someone else's permission to act, speak, or take the lead. Now, you begin to take your agency back by starting small: deciding what you want to eat, how you want to spend your time, or who you want to be around. Though these choices might feel scary at first, each one builds trust in yourself. You start to see even "failures" as feedback, allowing you to try new things, speak up when it matters, and remind yourself it's okay when things don't go as planned. Every time you follow your own voice or take action for yourself, you grow in self-trust.

Affirmation: *I trust my ability to choose, act, and begin again.*

Injustice Wound: Authoritarian Parent

In some homes, obedience is prioritized over connection. If you grew up with rigid, controlling parents who imposed harsh rules without space for emotion, individuality, or discussion, you likely learned that love was granted only when you met expectations. Mistakes weren't seen as learning opportunities but as moral failings. Expressing disagreement or emotion may have been punished, ignored, or labeled disrespectful. In this kind of environment, being "right" became your safest option. You learned to survive by following rules because structure gave you a sense of safety when love felt unpredictable. Being right made you feel safe, while being "wrong" made you feel exposed, ashamed, or unworthy.

To cope, certainty became your shield. You started to see the world in black and white—things were either good or bad, fair or unfair—and these rigid categories helped protect you from the unpredictability of your childhood. As this way of thinking grew stronger, it shaped how you saw others: People who didn't follow the rules or who disagreed with you felt unsafe or hard to trust. Forgiveness began to feel like betrayal, and letting go seemed impossible, so you held tightly to what felt fair as a way to survive. When you're an adult, this can show up as emotional reactivity to perceived injustice, feeling compelled to call out unfairness even when it damages relationships or drains your energy. Gray areas may feel intolerable, and you might retreat into moral superiority, guarding against vulnerability while appearing detached or critical. Beneath the righteousness, though, live unmet needs for compassion, flexibility, and repair. The very clarity that once gave you safety can harden into a barrier to connection.

Healing an injustice wound means letting go of the belief that being right is the only way to stay safe or in control. It begins by recognizing how rigidity, black-and-white thinking, or a need to correct others may have been protective, and then it continues by gently loosening your grip on those reflexes. You start to allow space for complexity: for people to be both flawed and good, for situations to be unfair without defining your worth. Over time, you allow yourself to be honest about what hurt you without being mean or harsh to others, quieting the voice of your own inner critic as a result. Little by little, you realize that fairness can come through setting clear boundaries, speaking up, and choosing compassion even when things are hard. You begin to understand that fairness and kindness can work together, side by side.

Affirmation: *I choose connection over control and can hold what's messy with care.*

These wounds don't define who we are, but they do influence how we respond to the world around us, especially when we're unaware of them. The good news is that awareness is powerful. When we begin to name what's wounded us, we give ourselves the opportunity to respond differently. We stop living on autopilot and begin to interrupt the habits and patterns that are keeping us stuck.

WOUND TYPE	PRIMARY CAREGIVER PATTERN	CORE CHILDHOOD EXPERIENCE	INTERNALIZED BELIEF	ADULT PATTERN
DISTRUST	Reactive Parent	Emotional volatility created hypervigilance	People are unsafe; trust leads to betrayal	Cling to or push away others; struggle with emotional regulation and reassurance
ABANDONMENT	Disconnected Parent	Inconsistent emotional presence; love felt conditional and unpredictable	Connection is fragile, people eventually pull away	Guardedness, suspicion, emotional distance or sabotage
REJECTION	Status-Oriented Parent	Praise for performance; rejection of emotional expression	Love is conditional; my real self is not acceptable	People-pleasing, perfectionism, hiding authenticity
HUMILIATION	Critical Parent	Criticism and mockery made visibility feel unsafe	There's something wrong with me; I must hide	Self-consciousness, avoidance, self-deprecation, or shame-driven behaviors
OVER-RESPONSIBILITY	Peer-like Parent	Parentification; love tied to usefulness and emotional caretaking	My worth depends on what I do for others	Compulsive caretaking, burnout, difficulty setting boundaries
SCARCITY	Uninvolved Parent	Needs ignored rather than met; emotional and material neglect	There isn't enough; I have to overperform to survive	Over-functioning, urgency, guilt with receiving, or emotional shutdown
REBELLION	Over-Permissive Parent	Lack of structure created a sense of chaos and mistrust in limits	Freedom means resisting structure; rules equal control	Rebellion against rules, struggle with consistency or follow-through
POWERLESS	Helicopter Parent	Overprotection blocked development of autonomy and self-trust	I can't trust myself to decide or act alone	Chronic indecision, passivity, anxiety around self-direction
INJUSTICE	Authoritarian Parent	Rigid rules without emotional attunement; obedience over connection	Being right keeps me safe; letting go feels unsafe	Moral rigidity, difficulty forgiving, emotional distancing

PRACTICE
SPACE FOR YOUR TRIGGERS

When our nervous system perceives danger, even unconsciously, it reacts based on past survival patterns. These responses are often rooted in unresolved childhood wounds. This practice helps you connect the dots between your body's responses and your emotional history so that you're not just managing triggers but understanding them.

1. **Think of a recent moment when you felt emotionally flooded, triggered, or unusually stressed.** What sensations arose in your body? Where did you feel them?

2. **Pause and breathe calmly.** Let the sensation rise and fall without trying to change anything; just practice witnessing.

3. **Reflect and explore by asking yourself the following:**
   - What memory, dynamic, or relationship does this remind me of?
   - What belief about myself gets activated here?

4. **Write down your reflections.** Is there a younger version of you showing up in this moment? What might they need to feel seen, soothed, or supported?

By connecting your body's signals to your past, you begin to meet yourself with understanding instead of shame. It's not about fixing or overriding these sensations; it's about witnessing them. Sometimes what your inner child needed wasn't advice or solutions but presence.

Remember, healing is not linear, and there is no finish line to cross. Each time you pause to breathe, to name what you're feeling, to choose a grounding action instead of an old survival response, you're rewriting your story. You're becoming the steady, safe presence your inner child never had. You are showing them, again and again: You are no longer alone.

As we begin to reconnect with those younger parts of ourselves, we may also come face-to-face with one of the most common and most misunderstood emotional wounds we carry: shame. Shame can be subtle or overwhelming, hidden in silence or expressed through self-criticism. In the next chapter, we'll explore where shame originates, how it shapes our identity, and what it takes to begin releasing its grip.

7

THE SHADOW OF SHAME

When we hear the word *shame*, we might picture moments of embarrassment, like blushing, wanting to hide, or feeling exposed. But the kind of shame that stems from childhood wounds runs much deeper than an awkward moment. It's about a persistent and pervasive belief: *There's something wrong with me.* This kind of shame is quiet but consuming. It's the invisible force whispering, *You're too much . . . you're not good enough . . . you're unlovable.* It's that internal alarm that goes off when you start to express yourself and are met with a rush of discomfort and a voice that says, *Don't do that. Don't be like that.*

At its core, shame is the internalization of rejection. Somewhere along the way, your authentic Self was met with disapproval, neglect, criticism, or punishment. A part of you learned it wasn't safe to be fully *you*. So you adapted. You became smaller, quieter, more agreeable. Or maybe you became a perfectionist, a high achiever, a people-pleaser, anything to avoid the sting of feeling unworthy. These adaptations were brilliant survival strategies at the time. But as we grow into adults, they often continue running in the background, unconsciously influencing our thoughts and behaviors. The tricky thing is these patterns become so ingrained and reflexive that we don't even recognize them as signs of shame. They just feel like *who we are.* But when we slow down and begin to look more closely, we start to see all the ways we silence ourselves, hide our needs, chase approval, or brace for rejection. And with that awareness, we can begin to loosen shame's grip.

PRACTICE
INTERVIEW OF YOUR INNER CRITIC

Shame often hides behind a critical inner voice that sounds harsh, judgmental, or demanding. This "inner critic" is usually trying to protect you—from rejection, embarrassment, or failure—but control isn't the same as care. By bringing curiosity to this voice, you can begin to understand its fears, trace its origins, and respond with compassion instead of letting it run the show.

1. **Introduce Yourself.** Open your notebook or journal and write: *Dear Inner Critic, I want to ask you some questions.* Imagine this part of you as a character or voice. You don't need to agree with it—just practice letting it speak.

2. **Ask Questions.** Write down three to five questions and let the critic "answer" in its own voice. Examples:
    - Why do you say these things to me?
    - What are you afraid will happen if you stop?
    - Where did you learn to talk to me like this?
    - Who are you trying to protect me from?

3. **Name Its Script.** Make a list of ten to fifteen phrases your critic repeats. Examples: *You're too much. You'll never get it right. If you rest, you're lazy.* Notice: Does this voice sound like someone you knew—parent, teacher, coach? Write it down.

4. **Respond Back.** Now write a short reply from your own wise, compassionate voice. Example: *Thank you for trying to protect me, but I don't need you to be so harsh anymore.* For each repeated phrase, offer a gentle reframe. Example:

    Old: *If I rest, I'm lazy.*
    New: *Rest replenishes me and helps me grow.*

5. **Create Counter-Affirmations.** Choose three to five affirmations to keep nearby. Examples: *I am worthy. My voice matters. I am allowed to be messy and am still lovable.*

Deepen Your Practice. In your notebook or journal, write a letter to your inner critic, thanking it for trying to protect you and letting it know it doesn't have to be in charge anymore; you've got this.

Your inner critic is a younger, protective part of you that doesn't realize you've grown. The more you listen and respond with care, the less power shame has to influence your choices. Compassion takes the edge off control. The more you approach yourself with gentleness, the less you feel the need to force, fix, or manage every part of you. What was once a harsh inner monologue can, with practice, become a kinder and more compassionate dialogue, and eventually, a supportive partnership with yourself.

THE FUNCTION OF SHAME

Many of us struggling with shame believe that we are somehow inherently damaged, but the truth is that shame is a fundamental part of the human experience, and its effects are not always negative. People everywhere, across cultures and societies, experience shame in similar ways. As social creatures, we connect with others to feel safe and secure, especially in moments of stress or threat. In its healthiest form, shame acts as an internal regulator that helps us navigate interactions by encouraging us to conform to shared norms and values. It heightens our sensitivity to social cues, protecting and strengthening our connections. For instance, if we're about to do something that could jeopardize a relationship, like betraying trust, acting selfishly, or deceiving someone, shame often steps in to course-correct. And if we go through with the action, the resulting embarrassment, guilt, or humiliation serves as a painful reminder of our misstep.

These dynamics begin early in life and are passed down through generations, embedded in family systems, where certain emotions, needs, or realities are punished, ignored, or silenced. Families may keep secrets to preserve appearances or hide stigmatized issues like addiction, mental illness, infidelity, or poverty, creating an emotional atmosphere where shame is absorbed if not always expressed. Even toddlers as young as eighteen months begin to show signs of self-consciousness. By ages two or three, they respond visibly to pride, disapproval, or failure. And by age three, many children have already begun to internalize their caregivers' reactions so deeply that they feel shame even when their caregiver is not actually disapproving, critical, or even present. This marks the beginning of shame's role as an emotional safeguard that helps preserve our sense of attachment and belonging.

How we experience shame is shaped by culture and social conditioning. Shame can arise through experiences like social exclusion, pressure to meet overwhelming expectations, or being subjected to abuse. In some cultures, one person's actions can bring shame to an entire family or community, which is why Romeo and Juliet had to keep their love secret from their warring families. Customs, traditions, and religious beliefs often intensify the pressure to preserve group honor. Gender socialization plays a role too: Women are more likely to internalize shame through self-criticism and self-doubt, while men may externalize it through anger, blame, or withdrawal. These patterns often operate beneath our awareness, shaping how we connect, cope, and see ourselves. While painful, shame can serve a purpose by motivating repair, accountability, and the preservation of relationships.

When shame becomes excessive or distorted—what's often called *toxic shame*—it stops serving its original purpose and can begin to have the opposite effect. Rather than helping us preserve our social bonds, it begins to erode them. This kind of shame doesn't guide us toward connection, empathy, or accountability; it isolates us. When we feel shame too often or when we absorb it from caregivers who carry their own unresolved pain, it can start to shape how we see everything. This happens when a caregiver, because of their own past hurt, reacts to us in ways that pass their shame on to us, like criticizing, ignoring, or over-controlling. This can make us start to believe the same negative things about ourselves that they believe about themselves. This kind of shame twists how we see ourselves and results in unhealthy patterns like perfectionism, people-pleasing, hiding our emotions, or punishing ourselves.

Social shame is a kind of toxic shame that happens when we feel the pressure to follow rules or expectations that go against who we are inside. Someone raised in a rigid or traditional community, for example, may feel deep shame for wanting something different, like staying single, choosing a nontraditional career, or expressing a nonconforming identity. Even if they later decide to live their own way, shame can still linger, causing them to believe that they're wrong or selfish for being different and creating a painful pull between being true to themselves and feeling like they belong.

Toxic shame can of course also result from direct harm, like emotional or physical abuse. When words, silence, or punishment repeatedly send the message that we are defective, unworthy, or too much, we begin to absorb it as truth. Over time, that shame becomes embedded in our identity. We don't just feel bad about something we've done; we feel bad about *who we are*. This kind of shame is especially harmful because it cuts us off from other people and from our own sense of worth. It fuels anxiety and hypervigilance, making us self-conscious and fearful of judgment, distorting how we see ourselves, and disconnecting us from our true Self. And it can make love, closeness, and joy feel far away, convincing us we must either hide who we are or work endlessly to prove we're worthy.

Ultimately, while shame can serve a functional role in guiding behavior and preserving relationships, it becomes destructive when it's chronic, misdirected, or rooted in experiences that were out of our control, especially those that occur in childhood.

A FRACTURED SELF

Shame is fundamentally relational. It emerges when our emotional connections are ruptured or nonexistent. When children reach out for attunement—wanting to be seen, comforted, or understood—and are met instead with disconnection or dismissal, they start to believe something is wrong with them. This can happen through hurtful words ("Why are you wasting my time?" "That's a stupid question"), dismissive actions (being ignored, brushed off, or met with distraction), or even absence. Because doubting a caregiver feels scary and unsafe, children rarely blame them, so instead, they turn the blame inward.

Over time, shame settles in. It becomes ingrained in our thoughts, our body, our emotions, and our identity. Shame doesn't require a dramatic event or a clear memory to take root. It often grows in homes marked by chronic misattunement, absence, or emotional neglect. You may not recall overt shaming, but you remember being overlooked. A parent who couldn't meet your emotional needs might not have meant harm, but their absence still impacted you. You learned that having needs was risky or that expressing yourself could lead to discomfort or silence. As an adult, you may feel guilty or ashamed for wanting basic things like rest, food, comfort, or moments of joy. This habit of pushing down your needs can even shape the way you see and talk to yourself. In fact, research has shown that emotional neglect and invalidation in childhood can also lead to the development of a critical inner voice tied to body image issues in young women.[1]

When our feelings were routinely dismissed or ridiculed, we started to feel shame about having those feelings at all. We didn't need anyone to criticize us anymore—simply feeling certain emotions, like anger, fear, desire, or even joy, could make us feel wrong inside. When shame sets in, even our most human needs—for closeness, comfort, connection—begin to feel unsafe. Without anyone to reflect our worth back to us, it's hard to believe in it ourselves. And without someone to help us carry our pain, we learn to carry it alone. The result is a fractured sense of self, often hidden behind coping mechanisms like perfectionism, avoidance, or chronic self-reliance. Beneath those patterns, we all carry parts of ourselves that feel uncertain, unworthy, or afraid.

Internal Family Systems (IFS), a therapeutic model developed by Richard Schwartz, helps us understand this idea. IFS suggests that we are composed of "parts," or inner subpersonalities shaped by early experiences. Some parts carry shame. Some carry protectiveness. Some learned to numb, others to achieve. These parts are adaptations. They arose in response to moments when our core self didn't feel safe, seen, or protected. And they continue to influence how we think, feel, and relate.

Healing happens when we listen to these parts and offer the validation they never received. By becoming the steady and compassionate presence they've always needed. Through this process of internal repair and integration, we begin to reclaim the parts of ourselves we once exiled. We learn to inhabit our wholeness as a lived, felt experience. We'll explore this process more deeply in chapter 9, but for now, it's enough to know that these parts of you are waiting to be understood, supported, and welcomed home.

WE ARE NOT OUR SHAME

While shame can seep into every part of our being and impact how we see ourselves, it is not an accurate reflection of who we truly are. The shame we internalized in childhood often came from misattunement in our relationships. This is especially true for children who were parentified or forced into adult roles before they were ready. When a child becomes the emotional caretaker of their caregiver, they silently absorb the belief: *If no one is here to take care of me, I must not be worth caring for.* Not only do they feel unseen but they also feel selfish or guilty for having needs of their own. Parentified children often grow into adults who struggle to accept support, rest, or gentleness—still carrying the message that their role is to serve, not to be served.

Take Rosa, for example. She grew up in a crowded household where her parents were overwhelmed and rarely intervened. Her older brother often took out his rage on her—name-calling, shoving, and sometimes worse. When she tried to tell her parents, they waved it off: *Go outside if you're going to fight.* Rosa learned early to keep quiet, to minimize the bruises and the fear, and to carry the shame alone. As an adult, Rosa found herself replaying that same silence in her relationships. When boundaries were crossed, she struggled to speak up, convinced she was "too sensitive." Shame accompanied every thought she had about asserting her needs, reminding her that conflict was dangerous and that her pain didn't count.

It wasn't until therapy that she began to name what had happened: abuse. The recognition didn't erase the past, but it loosened the grip of shame. Her healing came slowly through support groups, through naming the harm and building friendships where conflict didn't mean danger. For the first time, she experienced the process of repair: being hurt, speaking up, and being met with care. Every successful experience of repair helps rewire our brain, linking conflict not only to stress but also to resolution.[2] Repair teaches our nervous system that rupture doesn't equal abandonment, gradually expanding emotional tolerance and resilience.[3]

These repeated experiences of safety and repair form the foundation of self-esteem. We are less vulnerable to feelings of shame when we have a strong sense of who we are. This kind of self-esteem comes from having our needs met and being given the space to explore who we truly are. It develops when children can take pride in their accomplishments, share joy with others, and act with purpose, while parents set clear boundaries and limitations. In this balance, children learn how to adapt to societal expectations and how to tolerate frustration, disappointment, and rejection. Resilient individuals understand that mistakes are just experiences to acknowledge, repair, and move beyond. They know themselves well enough that external judgments or opinions carry less weight. Their confidence stems from their alignment with their own values, not from seeking constant validation from others. However, if we lacked the attunement we needed in childhood—whether due to emotionally immature, intrusive, or physically absent parents—our self-esteem suffers, making us more vulnerable to shame.

Our first experiences of shame often happened before we were even old enough to form long-term memories (usually before the age of two), typically in response to nonverbal cues that interrupted whatever we were doing. We might have been exploring something creatively or simply minding our own business when a caregiver's subtle disapproval—a scowl, a withdrawal of attention—sent the message that something about what we were doing or how we were being was wrong. In those moments, we blamed ourselves for their failure to attune to us, and we began to form a shame-based identity.

Shame can develop from many kinds of childhood experiences, including:

- **Unreciprocated Interest or Love:** When our bids for affection or attention go unanswered, especially by those we depend on, we may come to believe we're unworthy of love or connection.

- **Unwanted Exposure:** Being thrust into the spotlight before we're ready, whether through a public mistake, ridicule, or being singled out, can leave us feeling exposed and defective.

- **Disappointed Expectations:** Falling short of our own goals or others' expectations can spark shame, especially if we feel we've let someone down.

- **Disconnection or Exclusion:** Being left out or cut off from connection threatens our most basic need for belonging, reinforcing the belief that we are inadequate or unlovable.

- **Physical or Sexual Abuse:** Being subject to physical or sexual abuse can create deep shame, particularly when survival responses like freezing, complying, or staying silent are misinterpreted as consent.

Over time, these moments weave into false narratives about who we are. Because shame convinces us that these distortions are our truth when in reality they are by-products of our pain and misattunement—not reflections of our authentic Self.

THE FEAR OF BEING PERCEIVED

One of the most disorienting aspects of shame is the fear it creates around simply being seen. We expect to feel shame in moments of exposure, like taking a test when we're not confident we know the material, speaking in front of a group, walking into a party alone, or receiving negative feedback on our work. But shame also creeps into the most ordinary moments. You might be folding laundry, eating a snack, or tying your shoe when someone walks into the room. You weren't doing anything wrong, yet suddenly, something in you flinches, feeling exposed and self-conscious, as if you want to disappear. That reaction? That's shame. And it's far more common than we tend to admit.

Before going further, it's important to clarify the difference between shame and guilt. Though often used interchangeably, they originate in different beliefs.

Shame is the belief that something is wrong with *you*. Guilt is the recognition that something you *did* may have caused harm.

Here's how they differ:

SHAME	GUILT
I am bad or I am the mistake	I did something bad or I made a mistake
Focuses on who you are (your Self)	Focuses on what you *did* (your actions)
Feels like a personal flaw or defect	Feels like a poor decision or mistake
Leads to hiding, self-criticism, or withdrawal	Leads to accountability and repair
Often stems from early attachment wounds, societal pressure, or unmet emotional needs	Often arises from violating your own moral code
Can become toxic and long-lasting	Can be a healthy motivator for growth

Shame makes it hard to trust ourselves, leaving us unsure of what to do, always looking to others for answers, and stuck in ideas about who we think we "should" be. It can make us afraid of being seen for who we really are. Some people call this the *fear of being perceived*. It's the belief that if someone truly saw you, they would reject you. Deep down, it comes from the painful thought: *There's something wrong with me.* To protect ourselves from this fear, we often hide the parts we feel ashamed of and instead show a version of ourselves that we think others will accept.

This fear develops in overtly critical households, but it can also begin in families where unspoken pain lingers in the background. For many children, shame grows as a result of secrecy and survival, even more than moments of neglect or blame. For children raised by caregivers struggling with substance use, shame becomes a hidden thread running through everything. These children learned to stay quiet because often no one else is mentioning the truth of what is going on. On the outside, the home might have looked "normal," but the emotional cost of keeping it together was enormous.

Take Darren, for example. He stopped inviting friends to his home when he was eight years old because his dad drank most evenings—first wine, then vodka that he claimed was water. Nothing dramatic ever happened, but he never knew what version of his father he'd come home to. He might be slurring, sleeping, or short-tempered, so Darren learned to stay quiet, keep things light, and clean up before anyone noticed something was wrong. He didn't call it shame back then; he just knew he felt different. He watched other kids laugh freely and wondered what it was like to not feel responsible for his father's behavior.

Now in his thirties, Darren keeps his apartment spotless, fearful someone might drop by and see something that reflects badly on him. He's successful, funny, and charming but deeply uncomfortable receiving care, so when someone expresses concern, he deflects. When someone gets too close, he pulls back. He worries he's too much or not enough, never quite right, and love feels like a performance. Sometimes he feels flooded with emotion and doesn't know why. Other times, he feels nothing at all. He's spent so long managing others' comfort that his own needs feel indulgent, and he doesn't trust that someone would stay if they saw the full picture.

Darren's story illustrates what shame can build: a life that looks fine on the outside but is carefully curated to avoid being seen. And it's not just pain or conflict that stirs this fear. Even positive attention can trigger the same protective reflex.

Katie has a vibrant sense of style, mixing thrifted gems with designer pieces she finds on sale, and always looking effortlessly cool. One morning at a café, a stranger compliments her look:

"You look amazing. I wish I could put together outfits like that."

Katie's instinct? Deflect.

"Oh, this? I got it on sale. It's just a blazer and a skirt."

"Well, it really works," the woman says.

"I actually have no idea what I'm doing," Katie insists with a nervous laugh.

The woman laughs too but senses Katie's discomfort. The compliment was meant as a moment of connection, yet Katie couldn't take it in. Taking it in would mean being *seen*, but her shame tells her she's not allowed to stand out.

This fear of being seen can creep into the most ordinary corners of everyday life, including the clothes we choose, the way we speak, how much space we take up. As a child, I loved bright colors and bold prints, especially flowers. But over time, I started wearing muted tones, as if blending into the background could quiet my near-constant anxiety. Only recently have I begun reaching for color again, reclaiming that early spark of self-expression I had tucked away for safety. This fear shows up in many other small, seemingly insignificant ways:

- You're a guest at a wedding and a song you love comes on. You want to dance and start to stand up—but the idea of being seen stops you and you sit back down.

- You're staying with friends and hear someone say, "You went to bed early last night!" Suddenly, you feel embarrassed for simply taking care of yourself.

- A coworker says, "I saw you running the other day!" and your first reaction is humiliation, even though you have nothing to feel embarrassed about.

These moments might not register as *shame* at first. You might label them embarrassment, awkwardness, or "just a weird feeling." But if you find yourself replaying the moment in your mind, feeling exposed, and wondering if you should have done something differently, there's a good chance shame is at the root. At the heart of these experiences is the belief:

- If people see the real me, they won't accept me.
- I'm only worthy if I perform, hide, or conform.
- In order to be lovable, I have to manage how I'm perceived.

The truth is shame *tricks* us into believing that we can earn love by fixing ourselves. That if we just hide our flaws, meet the expectations of others, or present only our "good" parts, we'll finally be accepted. But this only deepens the disconnection from our authentic Self as we become fragmented—partially visible, partially hidden—always afraid that the wrong part of us will slip through and be "found out."

This fear of being exposed seeps into our bodies and relationships, especially our most intimate ones. Shame can profoundly affect our physical and sexual lives, reducing desire, inhibiting pleasure, and fueling anxiety that turns sex into performance rather than connection. It can cause us to detach from sensation or become consumed by fear of failure, while others, especially men, may depersonalize sex or objectify partners to avoid vulnerability. In some cases, sex becomes a substitute for emotional intimacy, a way to soothe anxiety or escape pain, leading to addictive patterns that further isolate and disconnect us from ourselves and others.

This fear of being perceived or exposed is a natural by-product of shame. And like all shame responses, it developed as a way to *protect* us. At some point, being seen was met with judgment, rejection, or ridicule, and our nervous system learned that visibility was dangerous. To survive, we layer coping strategies on top: roles, behaviors, and masks that once shielded us but aren't an authentic reflection of who we really are.

HOW WE COPE WITH SHAME

Even when we don't realize it or name it directly, shame shows itself in the ways we cope. These coping patterns often become second nature, formed to protect us in moments when being ourselves felt unsafe.

- **People-Pleasing.** We can become chronic people-pleasers in an effort to escape the painful feeling that something is fundamentally wrong with us. We try to be agreeable and accommodating, supportive and helpful, hoping that if everyone around us is happy, we might finally feel worthy of love and belonging. But in constantly attending to others' needs and approval, we lose sight of our own needs, abandoning or betraying ourselves in the very pursuit of being accepted. We see this often in teenagers, who easily shape themselves to others' opinions and tastes, as well as in romantic relationships, when we try to shape ourselves into what we think the other person wants.

- **Avoidance or Denial.** Shame is such an overwhelming emotion that sometimes we cope by denying it exists or pretending not to care about the simmering pain. Procrastination can become a shield, and acting out a preemptive strike, both ways we try to manage shame before it can catch us off guard. Others avoid vulnerable situations altogether, sidestepping the risk of painful interactions but also bypassing the chance to be truly seen and known. But often that avoidance can come with a cost, as was the case with Arthur. A talented writer in college, in later years, Arthur grew inhibited by a crushing fear of failure. When he graduated, he took an office job and continued to write in private, but he never showed his work to anyone else. If he wasn't a bestselling genius, he didn't want to be seen at all.

- **Isolation and Withdrawal.** For some, shame leads beyond detachment to a full retreat. We pull away from others, avoid eye contact, and move through the world in a muted, robotic way, hoping not to be seen. Emotional intimacy feels threatening, and the closer someone gets, the more exposed we feel. It becomes easier to disappear than to risk being truly known. Over time, hiding becomes a habit and connection begins to feel like a danger, not a lifeline.

- **Projection or Deflection.** Another unconscious strategy to lessen shame is to disown it and project it onto others. This can show up as arrogance, blame, judgment, or self-righteousness. Though it's hard to admit to ourselves, when we act this way, we are often fueled by an internal sense of inadequacy—we shame others in order to avoid feeling ashamed ourselves. Deflection works in a similar way: Instead of acknowledging our own discomfort, we turn our attention outward, focusing on others' flaws or mistakes to avoid confronting our own. Sometimes deflection slips into our relationships in subtle but corrosive ways, as it did for Quinn. She is a witty and charismatic gossip. She has a sly dig to offer about any one of her friends, and this often happens behind their backs. Her friends see right through this behavior—they know she tries to boost her self-worth by putting others down.

◁ **Body consciousness.** When shame is too painful or abstract to fully feel, we sometimes fixate on the physical—our weight, our appearance, our health, or symptoms in our body. The self-blame we carry becomes easier to manage when it has a visible form. We may chase physical perfection, constantly checking how we look, and struggle with a persistent sense that our bodies aren't good enough. Our self-critical voice may become fixated on features like our skin, hair, or body shape—trying endless exercises to change how we look, accumulating products or procedures in hopes of perfecting our appearance, or obsessing over weight and perceived flaws. Our physical form becomes the battleground where unspoken emotions wage their war, carrying the weight of wounds we haven't yet put into words.

◁ **Overcompensation.** Another common defense is overcompensating by becoming an idealized version of ourselves: the perfect parent, the tireless volunteer, the always-smiling achiever. We project an image of goodness or righteousness to distance ourselves from the shame of feeling not good enough. But sometimes that projection becomes a role we feel trapped in, as Danny did. He had an incredibly difficult childhood in the foster care system, and his response was to be a hero. His entire life is devoted to helping foster kids. He is always on, always there, but he never gives himself time to recover or think about what he needs. This kind of performance is exhausting, and it disconnects us from our authentic Self.

◁ **Secrecy or Dishonesty.** Shame thrives in silence. To avoid rejection, we hide parts of ourselves, tell half-truths, or lie—both to others and to ourselves. Anyone who has falsified a résumé or hidden a mistake from their past is hoping that by creating a false self, they can overcome the shame of who they really are. When we fear that if people really knew us, they wouldn't accept us, we edit ourselves to fit what we believe is acceptable.

◁ **Controlling Behavior.** When we grow up believing our worth is tied to meeting impossible standards, we may try to control ourselves and those around us. Micromanaging, hypervigilance, and rigid routines are all ways we try to prove our worth when we're afraid we're not enough. Micromanaging looks like controlling others step by step so things go "our way"; hypervigilance keeps us on constant alert for what might go wrong; and rigid routines offer an illusion of safety by making life predictable. Sometimes this constant monitoring shows up as warnings, like "That lake might have toxic bloom" or "Are you sure that lettuce has been fully washed?" While these behaviors can make us feel safer in the moment, they can also keep us stuck in cycles of anxiety, pressure, and ultimately self-doubt.

◁ **Defensiveness or Aggression.** Anger is often a cover for shame. When we feel powerless, weak, or inferior, we may lash out in an attempt to regain control. This is especially common in family dynamics, where underlying shame can fuel explosive or abusive behavior. Anger protects the wounded self by creating distance and fear. But in protecting ourselves through anger, we often push others away, sacrificing connection to preserve control.

◁ **Self-Harm.** Some of us try to control shame by turning it inward. Self-pity, self-loathing, self-deprecation, masochism, and emotional self-sabotage are all ways we "get there first," inflicting shame on ourselves so others don't have the chance to. We all know people who bring up ideas at work by saying, "This is probably stupid, but..." In more extreme cases, people may redirect shame into physical pain by harming themselves or sabotaging themselves before they can make a mistake they didn't control. When we put ourselves down, we feel a sense of control over something that once felt unbearable. But while we may protect ourselves from external judgment, we end up becoming the ones who wound ourselves most.

Each of these responses made sense at the time because they were survival strategies. That awareness is the first step toward healing and reconnecting with the parts of ourselves we once felt we had to hide.

THE EMBODIED IMPACT OF SHAME

Shame is a full-body experience that leaves us emotionally immobilized and psychologically fragmented. When we feel shame, our nervous system undergoes a powerful shift. At first, we may enter a state of high arousal as our body interprets judgment, criticism, or rejection as a threat. In a heightened stress response, our thoughts race, our muscles tense, and our heart pounds as heat floods our face. But when the threat feels overwhelming or unescapable, our body often shifts into collapse, our dorsal vagal response, a survival shutdown. We grow quiet, our shoulders round, our eyes drop, and our voice fades to a whisper. Our body's message is clear: hide, shrink, vanish.

In this state, we lose access to our ventral vagal pathways, which support our social engagement and emotional safety. This makes it harder to feel present, read social cues, or regulate our emotions. While we still may be able to plan, analyze, and perform, we often do so in a detached or robotic way. We may appear composed to others, but inside we feel fragmented—like pieces of ourselves don't fit together, foggy in our thinking and disconnected from our emotions or from those around us. In more severe cases, this disconnection deepens into dissociation, a numbing or split from both our body and identity. This pattern is especially common in those who experienced chronic early shame in their earliest relationships, the ones where a foundation of safety should have been built. When our nervous system is overwhelmed again and again, it learns to protect itself by blunting emotional signals and limiting our ability to respond. This protective blunting creates an embodied sense of emptiness, confusion, or wrongness, intensifying the very shame that caused the shutdown in the first place.

This sets the stage for a painful cycle. Our body gets caught in a shame loop, swinging between hyperarousal (panic, dread, overthinking) and hypo-arousal (numbness, withdrawal, collapse). In this back-and-forth, we lose access to the steady energy we need to act, connect, and feel like ourselves. Even when energy surges through us, we can remain frozen and powerless. Meanwhile, our mind races into overdrive, building defenses to keep us safe. But beneath those defenses lies one driving fear: being exposed. This is how shame sustains itself. It's reinforced through a repeating pattern that begins with a trigger, moves through reactive behaviors, and ends with even harsher self-judgment. Unless we learn to recognize the cycle, we remain trapped inside it.

THE SHAME CYCLE

The shame cycle is a repeating pattern in which shame-driven reactions deepen and reinforce the very shame that triggered them. Most of us experience this loop without realizing it. Over time, it becomes an ingrained emotional reflex that feels nearly impossible to interrupt. Here's how it typically unfolds:

1. **Triggering Event:** Something happens, whether it's making a mistake, receiving criticism, or feeling rejected, that activates shame in our body. The trigger may seem small, like being interrupted or overlooked, or more significant, like failing at a task or feeling abandoned.

2. **Activation of Shame:** The trigger ignites an intense emotional response where we feel exposed, inadequate, humiliated, or unworthy. Shame floods our body and mind with the old belief: *I'm not good enough*, *I'm a fraud*, or *There's something wrong with me*.

3. **Coping Mechanisms:** To attempt to manage this overwhelming emotion, we may unconsciously turn to coping behaviors. Some people numb out with overworking, shopping, drinking, or doomscrolling. Others withdraw, lash out, or get defensive, or find other ways to escape the discomfort of being seen or judged.

4. **Increased Isolation:** Sadly, these coping strategies often lead to more disconnection, not less. Instead of soothing shame, they deepen it. We end up feeling misunderstood, unseen, and alone, further confirming the belief that we're unworthy of acceptance or love.

5. **Cycle Repeats:** The longer this loop continues, the more entrenched it becomes. Each round reinforces shame-based beliefs and keeps us stuck in emotional survival mode and trapped by the very strategies we once developed to feel safe.

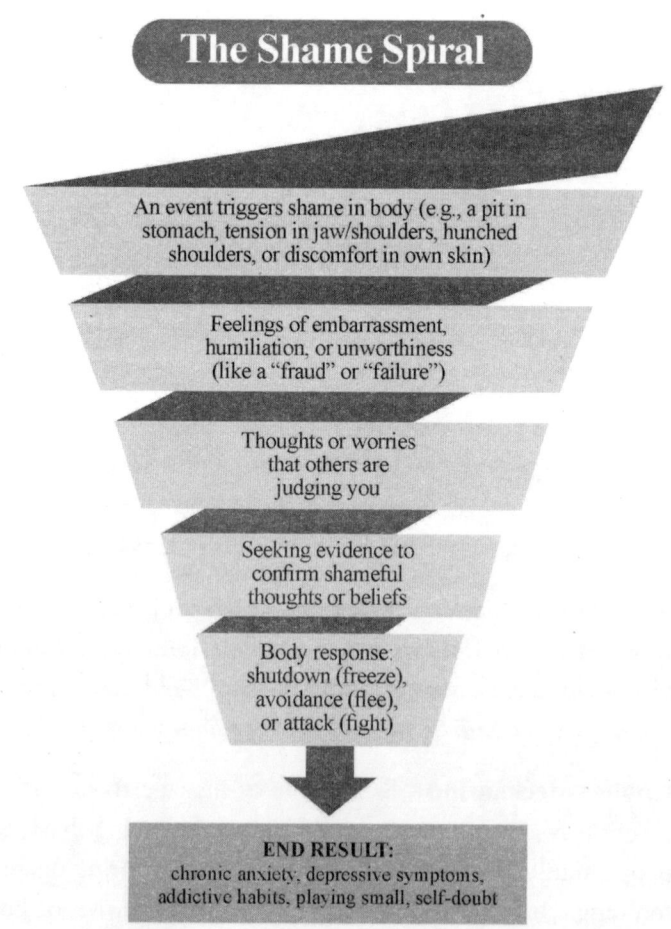

Being caught in this cycle can feel like being caught in emotional quicksand. If you don't recognize your shame, you may feel discomfort or distress, try to suppress it, and inevitably find yourself in the same place again. Over time, this loop can fuel anxiety, depression, perfectionism, addiction, chronic self-doubt, and a tendency to play small in life.

In many cases, this pattern reflects the emotional dysregulation that we see when children experience prolonged, repeated trauma early in life (which can lead to complex PTSD). The highs and lows can be exhausting. We lash out, collapse inward, or numb ourselves entirely in response to perceived threats to our worth. Here's how we can interrupt a shame cycle when it starts.

PRACTICE
YOUR SHAME CYCLE

Shame rarely shows up directly. Instead of saying, *I feel ashamed*, it tends to disguise itself as self-criticism, the urge to hide, or the thought *What's wrong with me?* This practice helps you witness your shame by mapping how it moves through your body, thoughts, and behaviors. Once you can see the cycle, you can begin to interrupt it and create new patterns.

1. **Draw Your Map.** Take a blank sheet of paper, draw a large circle, and divide it into four equal sections. Label each section: *Trigger* → *Feelings* → *Behaviors* → *Beliefs*.

2. **Pick a Moment.** Think of a recent time you felt small, unworthy, or convinced you had done something "wrong." Example: *I made a mistake at work.* Write this situation in the *Trigger* section.

3. **Notice Feelings.** Ask yourself: *What emotions came up for me in that moment (sadness, fear, anger, embarrassment, numbness)?* Write these in the *Feelings* section.

4. **Notice Behaviors.** Ask yourself: *How did I react? Did I hide, lash out, shut down, overexplain, or people-please?* Write your responses in the *Behaviors* section.

5. **Identify Beliefs.** Ask yourself: *What story did shame tell me here?* Examples: *I'm not enough. I always mess up. I'm unlovable.* Write these in the *Beliefs* section.

6. **Step Back and Reflect.** Look at your circle as a whole and notice how one part leads into the next. Ask yourself:

   ◁ Does this loop feel familiar?
   ◁ Do I see the same pattern repeating in different situations?
   ◁ Can I give my cycle a name that captures its energy—like *The Spiral, Storm Mode,* or *Freeze and Hide*. Naming helps you recognize it sooner the next time it begins.

Each time you map your shame cycle, you practice creating distance between your Self and the story shame tells. With awareness, you can interrupt the loop, respond with more compassion, and slowly replace old reactions with new, supportive ones.

PRACTICE
HOW TO STOP A SHAME CYCLE

1. **Empower a Pause:** Instead of reacting impulsively, take a moment to pause and reset. Avoid the urge to immediately fire off texts and emails or try to explain your emotions to others. By taking a brief pause, you allow your mind and body a chance to calm down, preventing knee-jerk reactions that you may later regret.

2. **Move Quickly to Release Energy:** Physical movement can be a quick and effective way to release built-up emotional energy. Try engaging in some form of exercise like power walking, jumping jacks, or squats. This helps to dissipate sympathetic energy and regulate your nervous system, giving you a sense of calm and control.

3. **Name the Emotion:** Identifying and labeling the emotion you're experiencing can be a powerful tool for emotional regulation. When you feel

intense emotions rising up, whether it's anger, sadness, or frustration, take a moment to say, "I feel angry right now." Acknowledge the physical sensations in your body, like a racing heart or a tight throat. Remind yourself that emotions are temporary, and while they're real right now, they don't define you. This mental shift can create some distance between you and the emotion.

4. **Let It Out:** Journaling is an excellent way to release pent-up emotions, but it's important to do so without self-censorship. Write freely, without worrying about grammar, structure, or how it sounds. This practice allows you to vent safely, expressing raw emotions that may feel too overwhelming or complex to share with others. (Note: This is not the same as emotional dumping on others, which involves unloading on someone else without regard for their emotional state or availability.)

Practicing these steps consistently will help you gain more control over your intense and shameful emotions, helping you navigate difficult moments with greater self-awareness and resilience.

Being trapped in the shame cycle can feel exhausting, repetitive, and impossible to escape. Each loop deepens the belief that something is wrong with us, even when the cycle itself is only a survival strategy. And when shame feels unbearable or relentless, many of us turn to coping strategies that become even more entrenched.

SHAME AND ADDICTION

For some, especially those living with chronic shame, coping results in habits that are harder to break. Addiction is one of the most common examples. At its core, addiction is a repeated behavior we feel driven to engage in even when we know it causes harm. We repeat these behaviors compulsively in order to escape, numb, or soothe ourselves, even as it begins to hurt our health, relationships, or sense of self. But addiction is not just about the substances or habits we develop; it's about the pain we're trying to outrun.

Unfortunately, the traditional "disease model" of addiction overlooks the role shame plays in driving these behaviors. Addiction goes beyond chemical dependency; it's a way of coping with the unbearable weight of shame. When we understand addiction as an attempt to manage deep emotional pain and unworthiness, we can begin to see the person beneath the behavior. Substances or compulsive behaviors may bring brief relief—a pause from self-criticism, loneliness, or grief—but that relief is temporary. Once it fades, the shame that fueled the cycle often returns even stronger, now layered with guilt or regret about the addictive behavior itself. This creates a painful loop: Shame leads to coping through addiction, addiction reinforces more shame, and each round deepens the sense of isolation. What began as a survival strategy becomes a trap, pulling people further from connection, self-worth, and the possibility of healing.

When we look deeper, we see that shame actually grows out of early attachment wounds. If love felt conditional, if comfort was absent, or if we had to hide parts of ourselves to be accepted, shame took root. Addiction then becomes less about the substance or behavior itself, and more about the attempt to soothe the ache of unmet attachment needs.

PRACTICE
DISTRACTION, DISCONNECTION, AND THE PRICE OF PROTECTION

Addiction and compulsive distractions are often misunderstood as weakness or lack of willpower. In reality, they're survival strategies, or ways our body and mind have learned to cope with the pain of shame and unmet needs. This practice helps you notice those patterns, uncover the emotions they've been guarding, and experiment with staying present with yourself instead of disconnecting.

1. **Track Your Protective Patterns (One Week, Minimum).** Each day, pause and write a few notes about where you notice these behaviors:

- **Avoidance:** When did I avoid a person, a situation, or a conversation because I was afraid of being judged or misunderstood?
- **Distraction/Addiction:** What did I reach for when I felt empty or anxious, like my phone, food, work, shopping, alcohol, caretaking?
- **Underlying Emotion:** What might I have been trying to avoid—fear, shame, sadness, anger, loneliness?

2. **Slow Down One Moment.** Choose one situation where you normally disconnect or overperform. This time, experiment with staying present for at least sixty seconds:

   - **Pause:** Place a hand on your chest and take a few slow, deep breaths.
   - **Affirm:** Whisper to yourself: *I can be here with myself, however it looks.*
   - **Notice:** What happens in my body when I pause instead of avoiding or reaching for distraction?

3. **Explore What's Beneath.** Take a few moments to explore the prompts below, writing your responses in a notebook or journal.

   - **Before the behavior:** What emotions or fears came up right before I acted? What was I hoping to avoid or get away from?
   - **After the behavior:** Once I acted, did I actually feel relief, or did the same need or feeling remain underneath?
   - **Impact:** What benefit does this pattern give me in the short term (comfort, distraction, control)? And what are the longer-term costs (exhaustion, shame, distance from myself or others)?

4. **Dialogue with Your Protective Part(s).** This step is about giving voice to the part of you that uses distraction or numbing to keep you safe and then letting your steadier Self respond with compassion.

   - **Write as the Protector.** Imagine this part is speaking directly to you. Example: *I scroll on my phone for hours because I'm afraid of feeling lonely.*
   - **Write as the Compassionate Self.** Now, let your wiser part respond with care. Example: *I see how you've been trying to protect me from loneliness. Thank you. What I actually need right now is rest and a call with someone I trust.*

◁ **Reflect.** Ask yourself:
- What does this protective part truly want for me?
- How can I give myself safety and care without abandoning myself in the process?

Avoidance, distraction, even addiction were strategies your body once relied on to keep you safe. They were never weakness; they were protection. But presence is what allows you to move forward. When you meet these shields with compassion instead of shame, you start to see the tender feelings they've been guarding and open space to respond differently.

Attachment and Addiction

Addictive behaviors are often rooted in the unmet attachment needs of childhood. When early relationships were marked by misattunement—caregivers who were inconsistent, emotionally unavailable, or unable to meet a child's needs—we are left with what has been described as *father hunger* (Margo Main) or *mother hunger* (Kelly McDaniel). These terms capture the deep longing created when love, validation, and nurturing were absent or conditional.

Attempts to self-medicate can become one way of trying to fill the shame that arises from unmet needs for love and care. Substances or compulsive behaviors might numb the pain of shame, fear, or feeling unworthy. Sometimes that pain feels so heavy that instead of going numb, we look for a rush of stimulation just to feel alive. That rush can trick our brain into feeling like it's experiencing connection, especially when it happens in a group or shared ritual. In these moments, the substance is no longer just about the high; it's about the bond. But while addiction may soothe for a moment, it ultimately deepens the wound, offering artificial connection at the cost of real well-being.

Whether through drugs, alcohol, gambling, overeating, shopping, hoarding, pornography, or sex, addictive behaviors all stimulate the same parts of our brain that are activated by love and connection. This helps explain why people who struggle with addiction may experience a temporary "rush" of love or satisfaction while engaged in addictive behavior, or conversely, the numbing relief that quiets a desperate hunger for attachment. While these activities may offer a momentary illusion of connection, they simultaneously harm the individual's body, mind, and relationships. The addiction then becomes a vicious cycle: The need for love and validation is temporarily satisfied, but the person continues to hurt themselves and those they care about.

The Purpose of Our Addictions

Addictive behaviors are often destructive, but at the same time they're rooted in our body's natural attempts to regulate overwhelming emotional states. At their core, these behaviors are attempts to self-soothe or to quiet anxiety, numb pain, and create a fleeting sense of control or relief. Whether it's alcohol, food, gambling, or compulsive patterns, addiction often begins as a strategy to survive emotional chaos, not as a deliberate choice to self-destruct.

Substances like alcohol, for example, calm our nervous system by releasing endogenous opioids, natural chemicals that relieve both physical and emotional pain. This release also boosts dopamine, creating a temporary sense of pleasure and well-being. For someone who grew up emotionally neglected or without healthy co-regulation, this rush of comfort can feel like a lifeline.

Research shows that our brain's reward system, especially the dopamine circuit, is deeply involved in addiction.[4] Addictive substances hijack this system, rewiring our brain to crave repeated hits of the same relief. Areas like our prefrontal cortex and amygdala—responsible for decision-making, impulse control, and emotional regulation—are gradually altered.[5] What begins as soothing eventually becomes a trap. Alcohol, for example, may lower stress in the short term, but with continued use, our nervous system becomes more reactive. Withdrawal increases anxiety, cravings intensify, and the stress response worsens, creating a vicious loop of short-term comfort and long-term dysregulation.[6]

Yet addiction is shaped by more than just brain chemistry. As Bruce Alexander's 1978 Rat Park study famously demonstrated, it's also about context. In sterile, isolated cages, rats drank morphine-laced water obsessively, sometimes to death. But rats placed in enriched environments with other rats, toys, and space to explore rejected the drugged water almost entirely. What the study showed was clear: Connection made the difference.

When safety, stimulation, and social bonds were present, the pull of addiction weakened, showing that addiction isn't simply about chasing a high. More often, it's a desperate attempt to fill the void left by disconnection.

Types of Addictions

Addiction often becomes the place we turn to when sitting with emotional pain feels like too much because many of us were never taught how to soothe ourselves, regulate overwhelming emotions, or feel safe in our own bodies. When connection feels out of reach and our nervous system is left without tools for calming ourselves, addiction can become our go-to coping mechanism.

Understanding the different ways addiction shows up helps us break free from the limited view that it's only about substances. In truth, addiction can show up in countless everyday behaviors that were once survival strategies. Alcohol addiction is one of the most familiar and deeply rooted forms of addiction, and for many, alcohol becomes a way to numb emotional pain or disconnect from unresolved inner turmoil, and this pattern often repeats across generations. In families where alcohol misuse is present, the entire system is affected as denial, enabling, and minimization become common. Caregivers may hide the extent of the problem or pressure the person to stop, all while avoiding the deeper emotional dysfunction underneath, creating an atmosphere of inconsistency, chaos, mistrust, and low self-worth. And in homes where drinking was present, children often begin to believe that they're to blame because they're not enough, or that if they were different, drinking wouldn't be necessary.

Because of its widespread impact, substance abuse is often what comes to mind when we think of addiction, though it's far from the only form. Here are just a few other ways addiction can manifest:

- **Overeating:** Soothes emotional distress, loneliness, or a sense of emptiness.

- **Gambling:** Distracts from pain through the adrenaline rush of risk and reward.

- **Shopping:** Offers a temporary sense of control, comfort, or worth.

- **Sex or pornography:** Seeks physical release to avoid emotional vulnerability.

- **Overexercising:** Channels pain into control, punishment, or distraction.

- **Hoarding:** Creates the illusion of safety and control through accumulation.

Another often-overlooked form is addiction to external validation. This can look like constantly seeking approval, overperforming at work, or curating a particular image on social media. These behaviors often stem from childhood environments where love felt conditional, based on performance, perfection, or pleasing others. Over time, we learn to mold ourselves into what others approve of, losing sight of our true needs and values. External validation becomes the only way we know how to feel worthy.

Sensation-seeking and self-harming behaviors are also common forms of emotional escape. When numbness becomes unbearable, we may turn to intense experiences—physical pain, adrenaline rushes, or high-stakes situations—to feel something. These behaviors are often misunderstood, but they arise from a nervous system stuck in survival mode, trying desperately to break through emotional disconnection.

Even chronic pain can result in hidden addiction. Chronic pain can create deep emotional and physical suffering, and without support, some people may turn to substances as a way to cope. My mom lived with chronic pain for much of her life, and over time, she developed an addiction to powerful painkillers. Her struggle taught me how, without adequate care and emotional support, pain can shape every part of a person's life and push them to seek relief wherever they can find it. In many cases, dependency isn't only about physical relief; it reflects a deeper longing for the relational comfort that comes from being cared for, seen, or needed.

For many children in emotionally unstable homes, food is often the first addiction. It's accessible, legal, and socially accepted. When a child is upset, a well-meaning adult might offer ice cream instead of comfort. Over time, food becomes a substitute for emotional processing. As adults, this may evolve into emotional eating, our go-to strategy for soothing stress, anxiety, or grief. Food addiction is not just emotional; it's also neurobiological. Research shows that eating, particularly eating foods high in sugar, fat, or salt, triggers our brain's pleasure centers, releasing feel-good chemicals like dopamine. This creates a sense of temporary relief from emotional discomfort. For many people, this pattern of eating becomes a way to distract from negative emotions, such as anger, guilt, shame, and fear. In some cases, eating offers relief from any feeling. For others, eating becomes a way to bond, avoid, or protect. In survivors of trauma, particularly sexual abuse, food may even become a form of self-protection, with weight gain acting as a subconscious barrier against further harm.

At their core, all these behaviors, whether they involve substances, control, performance, or disconnection, are attempts to soothe pain, regulate an overwhelmed nervous system, and cope with emotional wounds. They are adaptations. But while they may offer short-term relief, they block us from addressing the roots of our pain: unmet needs, emotional neglect, disconnection from our authentic Self.

While addictive habits may provide a fleeting sense of control, they eventually erode our ability to self-regulate, deepen our shame, and pull us away from what we truly need: emotional presence, relational safety, and internal steadiness. Once we understand the emotional roots of addiction, we can begin to regulate our nervous system through breath, movement, co-regulation, and somatic practices, and we can reparent ourselves by offering the comfort, attunement, and presence we once needed.

PRACTICE
RELATIONSHIP REPAIR WITH YOURSELF

Shame often makes us turn against ourselves, replaying mistakes or criticizing choices until we feel split from who we really are. This practice helps you interrupt shame's cycle and begin to meet yourself with compassion, creating repair where self-attack once lived.

1. **Name the Moment.** Think of a recent mistake or time you judged yourself harshly. Write it down in your notebook or journal as honestly as you can.

2. **Shift Perspective.** Ask yourself: *If a close friend told me this same story, how would I respond?* Write down the words of kindness and understanding you would offer them.

3. **Speak It Back.** Read those words aloud to yourself. Place a hand over your heart and whisper: "I deserve the same kindness I give others."

4. **Daily Practice.** Each night before bed, write down three things you're proud of. These can be small: telling the truth when it was hard, resting when you needed it, or showing kindness to a stranger. Then add one thing you like about yourself. If that feels difficult, imagine what your inner child would admire about you now.

5. **Future Self Check-In.** Close with this prompt: *If I fully believed I was worthy, how would I show up tomorrow—in my relationships, my choices, and my beliefs?* Let the answer guide one small choice the next day.

Deepen Your Practice. In your notebook or journal, reflect on:

- How does it feel to hear kind words spoken back to me?
- What changes when I respond with compassion instead of criticism?
- How does daily repair affect the way I see myself over time?

Healing shame is about returning to who you were before shame told you to hide. Meeting the needs of your inner child happens in small, repeated acts of recognition. The more you practice, the more your nervous system learns, *I am learning to feel safe in who I am.*

Our shame can lead us to dark, difficult places. Part of healing is remembering that it once served a purpose: It helped us survive. By staying small, hiding our needs, or striving for perfection, we protected ourselves from rejection, judgment, or loss of love. Shame kept us scanning for danger, trying to stay acceptable, or clinging to control—strategies that made sense when we were little and vulnerable. But what once kept us safe can begin to confine us. The very walls that shielded us become the barriers that keep us from intimacy, freedom, and self-trust.

Reparenting offers a way back to ourselves. It's the process of returning to the core spheres of development—Safety and Security, Individuation, Agency and Empathy, Authenticity, and Transcendence—and meeting the places where our needs went unmet. In this work, we begin to listen for the voice that was silenced, to honor the truths that were hidden, and to offer comfort to the younger parts of us that are still waiting to feel safe. Reparenting is not about erasing the past but about creating a new relationship with ourselves built on compassion, consistency, and care. It is through this practice that the shame we once carried as protection can finally begin to loosen, making space for authenticity, connection, and growth.

PART FOUR

REPARENTING AND INTEGRATION

8

THE TOTAL HEALING TOOL

By now, I hope you have a new appreciation for how your early experiences shaped you—how your caregivers, your culture, even the biology you inherited influenced the person you have become, including how you relate to your emotions, stress, and shame.

Over time, we all develop behaviors to cope with the circumstances we face, like shutting down, getting angry, working too hard, or avoiding feelings altogether. These responses are your nervous system's way of protecting you. But these habits are not the full truth of who you are. They're just ways you learned to stay safe when you didn't feel understood or protected. Recognizing where these patterns started can bring up sadness, frustration, even anger, which is all a natural part of the healing process. It shows you're beginning to acknowledge your inner child's needs and waking up to what was missing from their experience.

There are two steps to healing: first, becoming aware. That's what you've been doing. Once you're aware, you can begin to make new choices so that you can offer yourself the care and support you've always deserved. This is reparenting: noticing what no longer serves us and choosing something that does. Reparenting is a total tool for healing because it engages the body and mind together to revisit and rewire the patterns from our past.

Let's begin.

THE HABIT LOOP

We all have habits or behaviors we engage in without thinking. Some are small, like brushing our teeth or putting in our contact lenses. Others are big, like withdrawing when we feel hurt or lashing out when something feels too hard.

Some habits help us stay connected to our authentic Self. We may automatically offer gratitude for a gift, take a moment each morning to set an intention, or participate in weekly religious gatherings. These are habits that keep us rooted in our values. Other habits may keep us stuck and drive us to repeat things that don't feel right or true to us, like downplaying our accomplishments, apologizing when we're not sorry, or avoiding conflict. These habits are built from repetition. And they're shaped by our past.

Your "habit self"—or the part that's on autopilot, doing what it's always done—is years in the making. Every time you repeat a behavior, whether helpful or harmful, your brain strengthens the neural pathways that make it easier to do again. You may have heard the phrase *Neurons that fire together, wire together*. It's more than a catchy saying; it reflects how your brain forms habits and stores patterns. This idea comes from Hebb's law, a foundational principle in neuroscience. It explains how repeated activity between brain cells reinforces their connection, creating the basis for learning and memory. And here's the hopeful part: If your brain can wire itself into old, unhelpful patterns, it can just as powerfully rewire itself into new, supportive ones. That means you are *never* stuck. You can change your habits, and when you do, you're literally changing your brain. With small, consistent steps and new choices, you can create your future in ways your past never allowed.

On a basic level, habits are created through something called the *habit loop*. This loop has three parts: cue, action, and reward. The cue is a prompt that tells your brain it's time to do something. The action is the behavior you carry out in response to that cue. And the reward is the benefit your brain receives from your action, or the part that feels good and tells your body, "Do that again."

Here's a simple example: Let's say you feed your cat dinner every day at 5 p.m. As you might have experienced, it doesn't take long before they know your routine better than you do. Give your cat enough five o'clock dinners and it catches on—by five, it's hungry, waiting by the bowl, meowing until food shows up. If the food doesn't appear, the cat turns up the volume, wailing louder or trailing behind you, until you give in. Their brain locks the successful strategy in place, and the loop is repeated the next day.

This loop is facilitated by the release of the feel-good neurotransmitter dopamine. Dopamine doesn't just offer immediate satisfaction, it also tells your brain, "Remember this. It's important." When you do something that feels good, whether it's hugging a friend or eating a favorite food, the resultant release of dopamine reinforces the habit. Eventually, our brain begins to anticipate dopamine even before we engage in the behavior. And that's why some habits feel so hard to break—they're wired to expectation.

Think of it like walking through a dense forest. The first time you try, it's difficult as branches slap your face, tall weeds block your way. But if you keep walking that same trail day after day, it starts to clear. The branches bend aside, the weeds get trampled down, and the path becomes easier to follow. Eventually, it feels like the only way forward. Even if someone shows you a faster shortcut, you'll probably keep using the old trail because your brain favors what's familiar and predictable. Over time, your brain starts to say, "This is normal, so let's keep doing it." This is how behaviors, good or bad, become automatic. Even if a habit isn't helpful anymore, your brain defaults to it because it's familiar, and familiar feels safe.

In addition to storing actions, your brain is also mapping sensations, emotions, and a sense of safety. This is called the *brain-body map*, and it's centered in the somatosensory cortex, the part of our brain that continuously tracks our physical sensations, links them with our emotions, and helps determine how we react.

Beginning when we are infants, our brain assesses how each part of our body feels, especially during emotional moments. If you tensed your shoulders every time you felt afraid or curled into yourself when you were sad, those patterns became part of your body's emotional memory. Over time, your brain links physical sensations to emotional cues, shaping how you move, feel, and respond to the world. In this way, our inner child lives not just in our thoughts but in our muscles, breath, posture, and gut instincts.

Thankfully, through safety, movement, and new emotional experiences, we can rewire our relationship with our body, teaching it, over time, that we are safe now. When you choose a new action and repeat it, you start forming a new trail in the forest. At first, it's clumsy, awkward, and even uncomfortable, but over time, it becomes your new go-to path. And the old trail? Without regular use, it will fade back into the wild, overtaken by weeds. In the same way, your brain forms new pathways while gradually pruning the ones you no longer use, making room for the connections you're actively reinforcing.

Your brain is always listening and always watching. It learns not through what you *intend* but through what you *repeat*. This is the power of neuroplasticity: Your brain changes based on how you use it. So, when you start showing up in new ways—speaking your truth, setting boundaries, regulating your nervous system—you're not just "trying" to change. You're literally rewiring the neural pathways that control the action. And the more you practice behaviors that align with who you want to be, the more natural they become.

Repetition is how the unfamiliar becomes familiar, how the conditioned self gives way to the authentic one. So, if you've been stuck in habits that feel hard to break, know this: Your brain is not against you. It's just been doing what it was taught to do. And now, with awareness and repetition, you can teach it something new.

PRACTICE
A DAILY MINI-RITUAL

Rituals are more than habits. They are intentional acts of self-care—small, grounding practices that anchor your nervous system in safety and trust. This practice helps you create or strengthen rituals that help you rebuild self-trust. When life feels chaotic or overwhelming, even a few minutes of ritual can bring you back home to yourself.

1. **Choose a Specific Habit or Ritual You Want to Build.** Get clear and start simple, making it short and doable. Most important, make it real

for you. Instead of saying, "I want to be better," try something more specific, like "I want to be kind to myself in the morning." A small habit could look like:

- Stretching for one minute
- Drinking sixty-four ounces of water a day
- Writing down one thing you did well each evening
- Saying "thank you" to your body out loud

2. **Connect It to Something You Already Do.** Habits are easier to remember when they're linked to something that happens every day. Pick something simple and regular, like:

    - Brushing your teeth
    - Waking up or going to sleep
    - Making your morning coffee or tea
    - Checking your phone (before you scroll)

3. **Keep It Short and Kind.** Set a three-minute timer. This isn't about doing it perfectly; it's about showing up to care for yourself. Even if it feels silly or like "not enough," trust that small signals of consistency matter deeply to your brain and body.

4. **Celebrate the Act, Not the Outcome.** Smile, say, "I did it," or simply place a hand on your heart. These small internal rewards help your brain remember: *This matters.*

5. **Track It.** You can use a habit tracker or reflect at the end of each day: *Did I show up for myself today?* Remind yourself, there is not punishment if you missed, only an invitation to return tomorrow.

Remember, this isn't about fixing anything. It's about consistently nurturing yourself, in ways that feel safe, doable, and real. These daily rituals become small declarations: *I matter. I am safe. I am learning to trust myself.* Try it for a few days. Notice what shifts in your breath, your body, your energy, your heart. A new habit isn't just something you do; it's something you become.

REPARENTING IS REWIRING

In earlier chapters, we explored the different ways your caregivers, intentionally or not, may have overlooked or dismissed your emotional needs. They may have struggled to notice your feelings, to set boundaries with consistency, or to guide you in navigating your inner world. At the same time, you were quietly learning from how they treated themselves—how they coped, what they avoided, and where they fell short. These early impressions influenced how you relate to your body, your emotions, and the associated habits you carry today.

Now, with growing compassion for and awareness of why you are who you are, it's time to take the next step: consciously create the care, connection, and support you may not have received as a child. This is the work of reparenting. To reparent yourself means becoming the wise, loving inner parent you needed. It's how we tend to the younger parts of us that were neglected, wounded, or never fully seen. It's how we build the emotional scaffolding for growth: safety, regulation, empathy, and consistency. Every nurturing choice—every act of self-compassion, boundary-setting, and emotional regulation—helps rewire your brain. Through repetition, you carve new pathways of safety and connection. What begins as effort slowly becomes your embodied truth.

Below are five core practices that support the reparenting process. These are ongoing habits that nurture your healing and emotional stability over time:

1. **Acknowledge and Accept the Past.** We can't rewrite what happened, but we can stop abandoning or betraying ourselves because of it. Acceptance means making space for the truth of what hurt and what was missing. This is how we begin to meet the needs that went unmet, on our terms, in our time.

2. **Quiet Your Inner Critic.** The critical voice that shames or belittles you often echoes what you once heard or felt in childhood. Instead of arguing with it, begin to notice it and practice redirecting your attention toward a kinder response. Choose one phrase of

compassion—"I'm learning" or "I'm safe now"—and repeat it. Each time you do, you build an inner dialogue rooted in care.

3. **Validate Your Experience.** Your feelings are real, even if someone else once dismissed them. Practice naming your emotions, when you can, without judgment. "I feel sad." "I feel overwhelmed." "This was hard for me." Validation signals to your nervous system, *I matter and am worth listening to*, making us feel seen, which is the foundation of safety.

4. **Practice Compassion and Patience.** Self-compassion is essential. It calms our nervous system, releases oxytocin, and helps us feel safe in our own skin. Patience means honoring your pace even and especially when it's messy because healing is about presence, not perfection.

5. **Nurture Yourself.** Nurturing yourself teaches your nervous system that care is safe to receive. Peter Levine, a pioneering trauma therapist, identifies several forms of nurturance essential to healing. These small, consistent acts in each area help rewire your sense of worth:

    ◃ Physical Nurturance: Adequate rest, nourishment, and joyful movement

    ◃ Emotional Nurturance: Tenderness, empathy, and permission to feel

    ◃ Verbal Nurturance: Encouraging inner dialogue, reading, storytelling

    ◃ Spiritual Nurturance: Creative expression, awe, connection to something greater

Reparenting is about returning to yourself with more safety and care than you once had. Each choice to pause, soothe, or honor your needs is a step toward rewriting the old story. And just like any skill, reparenting grows stronger with practice.

REPARENTING ACROSS THE DEVELOPMENTAL SPHERES

Now, we'll explore how you can reparent yourself across the five Developmental Spheres: Safety and Security, Agency and Empathy, Individuation, Authenticity, and Transcendence. Each sphere offers a range of reparenting practices. While each sphere offers unique practices, Sphere One—Safety and Security—serves as the foundation. Without a sense of safety, it can be difficult to access or sustain growth in the others. What matters most is doing these practices consistently, since repeating them over time helps create new habits and rewires old patterns. There is no "right" way to use these practices. In fact, discovering how they best work for you is, in itself, a great way to tune in to your own needs and preferences.

Think of these practices as tools you can return to, again and again, as your needs evolve. Let this be your guiding reframe: You don't have to want to do the hard things (the dishes, the email, the difficult conversation), but you can stop resisting them. You can soften into them, reminding yourself, *This is how I care for me.*

SPHERE ONE: CREATE SAFETY AND SECURITY THROUGH SELF-CARE

Sphere One is rooted in our nervous system's need for safety. True self-care goes deeper than indulgence or surface rituals; it's actually a practice of self-regulation. It's the daily practice of building a secure home within yourself where you can feel at ease. Self-care means taking time to do things that make you feel good and looking after yourself physically and emotionally. This could be as simple as getting enough rest, eating nutritious foods, doing something you enjoy, or just taking a break when you need it. As easy as this sounds, many of us do not consistently give ourselves time and attention. Sphere One invites us to treat ourselves with kindness and develop a series of daily habits that empower us to cope, feel rested, and be present in our body.

Your body is meant to be a home, a place of presence, power, and peace. When your nervous system feels safe, your body becomes a steady anchor rather than a battlefield. You breathe more deeply. Emotions move through you without fear, allowing you to respond to life from a grounded, centered place.

And it's from this felt sense of safety that trust begins to grow. When your body consistently registers safety, it sends signals to your brain that say: You can rest, connect, digest, and heal. With repetition over time, these messages become familiar and reliable. This is how self-trust is built, not just through thoughts but through repeated experiences of inner steadiness. This calm baseline supports our emotional resilience, clearer intuition, and healthier relationships. It helps you live from your body rather than in your head, responding with confidence instead of reactivity.

And yet, presence alone isn't the full story. In a fast-paced, thought-driven world, it's easy to lose touch with our inner guidance. But your body is always speaking. It knows what you need before your mind can name it. To truly return to your body, you must learn to listen to it by attuning to your breath, heartbeat, tension, ease, hunger, excitement, exhaustion. Developing interoception, this ability to sense your internal world, allows you to navigate life with presence instead of running on autopilot, guided by curiosity instead of control.

This process is about building a relationship—moment by moment, sensation by sensation—with the world within you. Each time you connect to your breath or track a subtle sensation, you're reminding your body that it's safe to be here now. You're teaching your nervous system that presence is possible. That you can listen without judgment and that your body is not a threat; it's a guide.

Reparenting builds trust. Trust in your sensations, trust in your intuition, and ultimately trust in yourself. And from that trust comes a sense of grounded power that allows you to move through life with clarity, resilience, and deeper connection to what matters.

Let this be your invitation: to return to your body not as a project to fix but as a place to come home to.

Caring for Your Body

Your body is where healing begins. Nourishing food, deep sleep, intentional movement, and true rest are necessary for a regulated nervous system, grounded emotions, and lasting resilience. True rest isn't limited to sleep; it also lives in the moments we pause, breathe, or take a break from constant doing—small signals to the body that it's safe to relax. The following practices offer opportunities to take small, intentional steps to support your nervous system and make it easier to stay present, responsive, and grounded throughout the day.

When we care for our body in small, loving ways, we remind ourselves: *I am worthy of care, I am safe to rest,* and *I belong in my body.*

SPHERE ONE EXERCISES

Create Safety and Security

Let's learn how to take care of your body, mind, and emotions, so you can feel safer and more supported. When we practice these simple actions every day, we build a strong, steady place where we can rest, feel protected, and just be ourselves.

You don't have to do every practice listed here. Try them on for yourself and see what feels helpful. Try one for a week or two; then try something different. Come back to the activities that resonate. Slowly land on new habits that help you feel safe and secure.

> **QUICK CHECK-IN: HOW SAFE DOES MY BODY FEEL RIGHT NOW?**
>
> Pause and try to stop moving for just a moment. You can sit or stand, whatever you're already doing is fine. Let your hands rest and take a few slow, deep breaths as you ask:
>
> ◁ Do I feel tight or tense—like I'm bracing, clenching, or holding on?
>
> ◁ Do I feel heavy or distant—like I'm numb, shut down, or far away?
>
> ◁ Do I feel steady and relaxed—present and calm without gripping?
>
> Just notice. If you feel tense, heavy, or far away, that's a sign your body might not feel fully safe right now. That's okay. It simply means

creating safety and regulation in Sphere One might be a good place to start.

PRACTICE
RETURN TO WHERE YOU BELONG

Your body is more than muscle and bone; it's your first home. When life has been stressful or unsafe, it can feel hard to rest inside yourself. This practice helps you reconnect with your body as a safe place to return to, step by step. Practice for three to five minutes daily. Over time, these small returns build trust with your nervous system: You always have a place to come back to—yourself.

1. **Settle In.** Find a quiet space where you won't be interrupted. Sit with both feet flat on the ground or lie down with a pillow under your knees. Close your eyes if it feels safe or keep them soft and unfocused. Take three slow, deep breaths and remind yourself: *I am here. This is my body.*

2. **Anchor with Touch and Breath.** Place one hand on your chest and the other on your belly. Feel your breath rise and fall under your hands. Whisper or think: *This is my body. I live here. I belong here.*

3. **Move Slowly and Ground.** Rock side to side or forward and back. Notice the weight of your body shifting and then returning. Imagine roots growing from your feet or spine, steadying you. Say quietly: *I am supported. I am safe.*

4. **Scan Your Body.** Slowly move your attention from your head down to your toes. Pause at each area—jaw, shoulders, arms, belly, hips, legs, feet. If you feel tension, breathe into that spot and say: *This is part of my home too.* If you feel comfort, pause and savor it.

5. **Close with Belonging.** Place both hands over your heart or belly. Take one last slow, steady breath. Say to yourself: *This is my home. I am safe here. I belong here.*

PRACTICE
WHAT GROUNDS AND DISCONNECTS YOU

Once you've experienced what it feels like to come home to your body, you'll want to explore what nurtures—or interrupts—that sense of connection. This practice helps you reflect on the experiences, environments, and supports that influence how "at home" you feel in your body. By mapping them out, you create more awareness of what strengthens safety and what pulls you away from yourself.

1. **Reflect on Safety.** In your notebook or journal, write about specific people, places, objects, or practices that help your body feel calm, safe, or at ease. Examples: *Being in nature, hearing a trusted voice, wrapping yourself in a blanket, moving slowly.*

2. **Reflect on Disconnection.** Write about moments or environments that cause you to tighten up, shut down, or feel like you want to leave your body. Examples: *Being interrupted, loud conflict, overstimulation, criticism.*

3. **Identify What Brings You Back.** Think of times when life felt hard. What helped you return to yourself? Examples: *A grounding object, a simple routine, a movement, or a kind phrase.*

4. **Name Your Needs.** Ask yourself: *What does my body need when I feel overwhelmed—softness, quiet, movement, or something else?* Write whatever comes to mind without censoring or editing yourself.

5. **Capture Belonging.** Close by writing a short description of what it feels like to truly be "at home" in your body. Recall a time you felt relaxed, open, and fully yourself. What sensations, thoughts, or emotions were present?

PRACTICE
SOOTHING TOUCH: SCRATCH THERAPY FOR CALM

Once you begin noticing what naturally soothes you, you can start to offer that comfort to yourself on purpose. Gentle touch is one of the simplest ways to signal safety to your nervous system. Scratching, rubbing, or stroking your skin creates sensory input that can calm your body, quiet your thoughts, and help you feel more at home in yourself.

1. **Settle In.** Find a comfortable position in a quiet, cozy space. Place your feet on the ground or curl up somewhere you feel supported. Take a few slow breaths.
2. **Choose an Area.** Pick one spot on your body to start—your forearm, upper back, legs, or scalp.
3. **Apply Gentle Touch.** Using your fingertips, slowly scratch, rub, or stroke that area in small, steady motions. Move gently for thirty to sixty seconds.
4. **Add Reassurance.** As you do this, say to yourself: *It's safe to feel comfort in my own body. I don't have to be on guard right now.*
5. **Notice the Shift.** Pause and tune in to your body. Has your breathing slowed? Do your muscles feel looser? Do your thoughts feel less loud?

You can repeat this on another area of your body or return to the place that feels most soothing.

PRACTICE
PERMISSION TO REST

Many of us feel like we have to stay busy all the time. Productivity, perfectionism, or constant doing can act like shields against uncomfortable feelings. But true healing requires rest. Rest signals to your nervous system that you're safe. This practice uses Yoga Nidra, or "yogic sleep," to guide your body into deep relaxation while your mind stays gently aware. It's a form of waking rest that helps your system release tension and reset. Research shows that Yoga Nidra can calm the nervous system by activating the vagus nerve, lowering heart rate and blood pressure, reducing cortisol, and even strengthening brain regions involved in emotional regulation[1] and reward. Just forty-five minutes of practice can feel like the equivalent of three to four hours of deep sleep. If practiced consistently, Yoga Nidra can build emotional resilience, making it a powerful tool for healing from stress, trauma, and burnout.[2]

1. **Prepare Your Space.** Pick a quiet time each day (before bed works well). Find a comfortable place where you won't be disturbed. Gather what helps you feel safe and comfortable: a blanket, pillow, stuffed animal, even your pet. Set a timer for ten to thirty minutes.

2. **Settle In.** Lie down or sit with full support behind you. Let your arms rest by your sides, palms open if that feels comfortable. Close your eyes or keep them soft. Place one hand on your heart or belly.

3. **Begin with Your Breath.** Take a few slow, deep breaths in through your nose and out through your mouth. Say silently or aloud: *I deserve rest. I'm allowed to have it.*

4. **Rest in Awareness.** Let your body grow heavy into the support beneath you. Notice the gentle rhythm of your breath. If thoughts drift in, don't push them away; just let them pass like clouds in the sky, returning always to your breath. Stay here for ten to thirty minutes.

5. **Return Slowly.** When your timer rings, take a few full, deep breaths. Wiggle your fingers and toes. Roll to one side or sit up slowly. Notice how your body feels now compared to when you began.

PRACTICE
NOURISHMENT CHECK-IN: WHAT DOES YOUR BODY REALLY NEED?

Once you've reconnected to your body's sense of home, it's important to care for it with the nourishment it needs from a place of listening and trust. Food is more than fuel; it helps your body feel steady, strong, and calm. The goal isn't to be rigid with your food choices. It's to learn what helps you feel more grounded and stronger.

Try This Before Meals:

1. **Pause.** Before eating, take a breath and ask yourself: *What does my body need right now?*
2. **Choose Intentionally.** Pick something that supports how you want to feel—maybe warm and grounding, maybe light and energizing.
3. **Check In Afterward.** Notice: *How does my body feel now—calm, strong, tired, jittery, foggy?*

Deepen Your Practice. Take a few moments to explore the prompts below, writing your responses in a notebook or journal:

- What foods help me feel calm, clear, or strong?
- Which foods leave me drained, restless, or heavy?

Over time, these small moments of checking in teach your body it can trust you to listen. Every meal becomes a chance to rebuild safety, steadiness, and connection within yourself.

DEVELOPMENTAL MOVEMENT: YIELD

Yield is the very first movement pattern we learn as babies, resting into the ground, a caregiver's arms, or any surface that holds us. It builds the foundation for trust, safety, and nervous system regulation. Without yield, every later movement—rolling, crawling, walking, even speaking up—can carry tension or guardedness.

This practice teaches your nervous system that rest is safe. Yielding is a return to your first experience of being held. From this steadiness, every other movement—physical or emotional—can grow with more ease.

1. **Settle into Position.** Choose a comfortable place: a yoga mat, bed, couch, or carpeted floor. Lie on your back or side. If lying down isn't possible, stand with your back against a wall. Let your arms rest at your sides and close your eyes if it feels safe.

2. **Feel Gravity.** Notice the points of your body touching the surface beneath you—heels, calves, hips, shoulders, head. Imagine the floor is holding you completely. Whisper quietly: *I am supported. I can release what I'm carrying right now.*

3. **Notice Your Breath.** Without changing anything, feel your breath moving in and out. Notice where it flows—into your chest, belly, or back. With each exhale, let your body soften a little more into the surface.

4. **Explore Yielding Deeper.** Ask yourself: *Where am I still holding tension?*—maybe in your jaw, shoulders, or belly. See if you can release even 5-10 percent of that effort, letting gravity carry it. If nothing shifts, that's okay. Yield is about allowing, not forcing.

5. **Add Gentle Support.** If it feels comfortable, place one hand on your chest and the other on your belly. Feel your breath rise and fall under your hands. *Optional:* Invite a trusted partner to place a steady, light hand on your back or shoulder while you rest, practicing what it's like to be held in connection.

Deepen Your Practice. After five to ten minutes, slowly open your eyes. Wiggle your fingers and toes. Sit up gently. In your notebook or journal, take a few moments to explore:

- How did my body feel when I began?
- How does it feel now?
- What was it like to let myself be fully supported?
- Where in my life do I resist yielding, trying to hold it all together instead of trusting support?

Each of these practices—resting in your body, noticing what grounds you, offering comfort—teaches your system that safety can be rebuilt. Over time, small, steady actions reestablish trust, helping you feel secure enough to grow.

With this foundation of safety in place, you can begin to explore your edges—your desires, preferences, and boundaries—as you step into Sphere Two: loving discipline and healthy individuality.

SPHERE TWO: EXPLORE YOUR WORLD THROUGH LOVING DISCIPLINE AND HEALTHY BOUNDARIES

This sphere is all about discovering who you are—what you like, what you need, and where your boundaries live. It's about building autonomy through consistent actions that support your freedom, creativity, and truth. Loving discipline and clear boundaries give these practices the structure they need to create a stable foundation.

Loving discipline is the act of returning to yourself, over and over again through small, aligned actions that support who you're becoming. It is the ability to follow through on what matters to us with care, integrity, and flexibility. It helps us stay aligned with our values, meet our commitments, and move through life with a steady internal compass.

For many of us, the word *discipline* can bring up memories of control, shame, or rigidity. Especially if we grew up in authoritarian homes, discipline may have felt like something done *to* us rather than something practiced *for* us. But true discipline isn't about punishment or perfection. When rooted in love, *discipline* means committing to what matters and building habits that reflect that commitment. It heals the self-betrayal that happens when our actions don't match our values.

Loving discipline allows for imperfection. We all slip back into old habits, skipping the closet cleanout or scrolling on our phones past bedtime. That doesn't mean we're moving backward; it means we're human. What matters is that we keep returning, again and again, to the intention beneath our actions.

We can start to practice loving discipline by making doable commitments so simple they're difficult to break. Saying no to one request that drains your energy. Closing the laptop at the time you promised yourself. Following through on the bedtime you set even when the next episode of your favorite show is available to watch. These small acts lay the foundation for self-trust. With repetition, they reshape how we show up for ourselves, turning intention into lived experience.

And just as discipline creates steadiness within, boundaries create steadiness between. Healthy boundaries are the internal limits we set to protect our well-being, honor our values, and stay connected to our truth. At their core, boundaries are a way of communicating: *This is who I am. This is what I need. This is what I'm willing to offer.* They allow us to connect in ways that feels good and sustainable. Boundaries create a container for safety and self-trust, allowing you to choose relationships, experiences, and energies that align with your wholeness.

Boundaries aren't walls; they're bridges that allow us to stay connected to others and the world around us without losing ourselves. They help us define where we end and others begin, emotionally, physically, mentally, and energetically. They support us in honoring our energy and protecting our emotional space. With strong boundaries, we feel safe saying no without guilt and yes with confidence. We know what's ours to carry and what isn't.

Without boundaries, we can lose our sense of identity, overextend our energy, or absorb other people's emotions and responsibilities, leading to resentment, burnout, and disconnection. But when we set boundaries, we reclaim autonomy and are able to show up more honestly in our relationships, as we invite others to do the same. Boundaries teach people how to treat us, and they establish mutual respect, accountability, and care.

Boundaries come in many forms:

- **Physical Boundaries** protect your personal space and comfort with touch or proximity. They honor your body's signals and limits.
- **Emotional Boundaries** help you stay connected to your feelings without taking on someone else's. They protect your emotional well-being.
- **Mental Boundaries** affirm your right to your own thoughts, beliefs, and values even when they differ from those around you. They protect your mental space and help you stay grounded in your own perspective.
- **Time/Energy Boundaries** ensure you use your time and energy intentionally. They help you say yes with clarity and no with confidence.
- **Material Boundaries** allow you to decide when, how, and with whom to share what you have. They reinforce your right to manage what you've earned or created with discernment.

Together, loving discipline and healthy boundaries strengthen our sense of Self. When we practice them consistently, they create space for both stability and freedom for our inner child. They anchor us in our truth, build confidence in our choices, and help us move through the world with self-respect and compassion. This work of reparenting enables us to develop inner clarity and consistency, building the foundation that allows us to grow, explore, and remain rooted in who we truly are.

SPHERE TWO EXERCISES

Develop Loving Discipline and Autonomy

Exploration is how we discover who we are. It starts with small choices—learning what we like, what we need, and when we want to say no. Each time we practice honoring our preferences, boundaries, and desires, we strengthen our confidence and clarity.

Remember, you don't have to do all these practices at once. Try one at a time and notice what feels supportive. Come back to the ones that resonate and let them grow with you. Over time, these small choices add up to something powerful: the freedom to show up as your authentic Self.

> **QUICK CHECK-IN: HOW FREE DO I FEEL TO MOVE?**
>
> Pause for a moment, letting your body come to stillness either sitting, standing, or lying down. Let your hands rest by your sides or on your lap and take a few slow, deep breaths. Now bring to mind something you were asked to do that you didn't want to do, or something coming up that you'd rather not do. Without overthinking it, just notice what shows up. As you hold that image, turn your attention inward and ask yourself:
>
> ◁ Do I feel free to move away from something when I need to? Or do I freeze, fawn, or feel stuck even when something feels wrong?
>
> ◁ Do I have the space to change, grow, speak up, and make my own choice? Or do I feel rigid, like I always have to hold my ground or defend myself?
>
> ◁ When someone gets too close (emotionally or physically), do I notice it right away? Or does their closeness prevent me from speaking up, changing course, or making my own decision?

Just notice what comes up in your body, like sensations of tension, tightness, or the urge to move. There's nothing to fix or change. This is about noticing your personal patterns around space, separation, and saying no. If you feel stuck, rigid, or unsure how to move or respond in moments like these, that's a sign Sphere Two is a good place for you to do some work.

One of the most powerful ways to begin is by noticing what feels good.

PRACTICE
WHAT BRINGS YOU PLEASURE

The things that bring you pleasure offer important clues about who you are. Pleasure is a compass. When something soothes your senses, softens your body, or sparks delight, that's your nervous system saying: *More of this, please*. This practice of noticing helps you reconnect with what makes you feel alive, safe, and at home in yourself. It helps you build trust in your own preferences.

1. **Get something to write with.** Grab your notebook, journal, or a piece of paper and a pen to jot down your thoughts and ideas.

2. **Make a "Pleasure List."** Write down ten small things that bring you pleasure—moments that feel good in your body or spark sensory delight. Examples:

    - The first sip of morning coffee or tea
    - Sunlight on your face
    - Sliding into clean sheets
    - The smell of fresh bread or flowers
    - Warm water in the shower
    - Swaying or dancing to music
    - Laughing with someone you love
    - The sound of birds outside your window

- A cozy blanket and a good book
- Taking a slow walk in nature

3. **Circle your top three.** Which ones feel most nourishing to you right now? Which ones make your body soften just imagining them?

4. **Choose one to do today.** Pick one of those three and actually give yourself the experience today, even for just a few minutes. Let yourself fully receive it without multitasking.

5. **Savor it.** While doing it, pause and notice: What sensations arise in your body? What emotions come with it? What happens when you allow yourself to take this in? Silently say: *Pleasure is safe. I am allowed to feel good.*

Deepen Your Practice. In your notebook or journal, take a few moments to explore:

- What did I feel in my body before, during, and after?
- Did any resistance or guilt come up?
- Did I notice shifts in my mood or energy?
- How might I allow myself more of this each day?

PRACTICE
YOUR PERSONAL SPACE

Just as pleasure shows us what feels nourishing, boundaries show us what feels like too much. We each have something like an invisible bubble around us—our personal space. This bubble helps protect us. Where pleasure says, *More of this, please,* boundaries say, *This is enough.* Both are ways your body communicates safety, guiding you when to lean in and when to step back. This practice helps you notice, trust, and honor that boundary. This practice has two parts: a guided visualization to explore your personal space and a daily noticing practice to help you track your boundaries in real life.

Part One: Visualizing Your Boundary

1. **Get Quiet.** Find a calm spot where you can sit or stand without distractions. Close your eyes if it feels safe.

2. **Imagine Your Bubble.** Picture a soft bubble of light surrounding your whole body, from your head to your feet. This is your personal space. You get to decide who and what comes into it.

3. **Feel into It.** Imagine someone walking slowly toward you (this could be someone real or imagined). Notice how your body feels as they approach. Do you tense up? Want to step back? Stay relaxed?

4. **Test It with Movement.** Stretch your arms out wide like a starfish. Slowly draw them in until you have the sense, *This feels just right.* That's your personal boundary line—where your yes turns into a no.

Deepen Your Practice. In your notebook or journal, take a few moments to explore:

- How did my body tell me I needed space?
- What sensations came up—tightness, calm, or the urge to step away?
- Have I ignored that signal before? What happened?

Part Two: Daily Noticing Practice

1. **Track Your Body's Signals.** Over the next few days, notice what moments feel expanding (open, safe, connected) and what moments feel contracting (tight, withdrawn, unsafe). Example:

    Expanded → laughing with a friend.
    Contracted → someone standing too close in line.

2. **Quick Daily Check-In.** Write down:

    - One moment I felt expanded today: _____
    - One moment I felt contracted today: _____
    - What did I need in those moments?

3. **Practice a Small Boundary.** This week, try setting one small boundary: saying no, asking for space, changing your mind, or waiting before replying.

4. **Reflect.** Notice how it felt in your body *before, during,* and *after.* Did emotions like guilt, relief, anxiety, or empowerment come up?

PRACTICE
A LOVING "NO"

Boundaries don't end with noticing them, they grow stronger when you express them. Now, let's honor your space with your voice. Boundaries aren't about pushing others away; they're about respecting your own needs, feelings, and limits. The practice of the loving no turns your inner signals into clear, caring words. Many of us say yes when we really mean no. Saying no to others is a way of saying yes to yourself. This practice helps you notice when your body is signaling "enough," and gives you the words to respond with clarity and care.

1. **Recall a recent moment.** Think of a recent time when you said yes to someone or something, but deep down, you wanted to say no. This could be something small, like agreeing to a plan you didn't want to do or not speaking up when something didn't feel okay.

2. **Get grounded in your space.** Stand in front of a mirror or sit comfortably with your feet planted. Hold your hands a few inches away from your body, palms facing inward.

3. **Speak your truth aloud.** Say a simple sentence that you wish you had said in that past moment. Start small and speak kindly. Examples: *No, thank you. That doesn't feel right for me. I need a little more space.*

4. **Repeat with intention.** Practice your sentence a few times, using a calm, steady tone. Let yourself feel what it's like to speak from your truth, even if your voice shakes.

Deepen Your Practice. In your notebook or journal, take a few moments to explore:

- How does my body tell me when a boundary is being crossed?
- Where do I feel it—tightness, heat, a knot in my stomach?
- What thoughts or emotions show up when I imagine saying no?

PRACTICE
YOUR PHYSICAL AND EMOTIONAL SPACE

Boundaries live in your physical environment. Our surroundings shape how we feel, think, and show up in the world. The environments we inhabit either shrink us or invite us to expand. Where do you feel like *you*? Where do you feel like you're shrinking or hiding? This practice helps you become aware of how your environment influences you and invites small shifts so your space reflects who you are and what you need.

1. **Move through your space with awareness.** Take a walk through your room, house, school, or another place where you spend time. You don't need to change anything yet, just observe.

2. **Slow down or stop for a moment and notice how your body feels as you move.** Notice any shifts in energy, or places where you feel open, grounded, or tense. Do you stand taller, breathe deeper, or feel more open in one place? Do you tense, shrink, or feel uneasy in another? Let yourself feel the difference. Ask yourself: *Where do I feel most like myself? Where do I feel small, uncomfortable, or like I need to hide?*

3. **Make one small change.** Choose a space you want to feel more like you. Think of one small thing you can do to make it feel more safe, inspiring, or grounded. Examples: Move your chair to face a window. Hang up a favorite drawing or quote. Add a plant or object that brings you comfort. Clean up a cluttered corner so it feels calmer.

4. **Reflect on the change.** As you make this shift, notice how your body feels. Do you stand a little taller? Breathe a little deeper? Feel more at ease?

5. **Anchor the feeling.** Stand or sit in the updated space. Say to yourself (or out loud): *I belong here. I am allowed to take up space. This space reflects who I am becoming.*

PRACTICE
THE EDGE OF RESISTANCE

Now let's go even deeper. Environments don't just exist around us; they live inside us too. These inner environments are the places where old fears, beliefs, or survival patterns still echo. They show up as hesitation, resistance, or the urge to hold back, even when nothing outside is threatening. Resistance is feedback. It often shows up when we're getting close to something meaningful or vulnerable. This practice helps you gently meet those edges, where one part of you wants to grow and another part wants to hide.

1. **Choose one small action you've been avoiding.** Pick something simple that would support your well-being or bring relief. Examples: *Cleaning a corner of your space; journaling a few honest thoughts; stretching or breathing for a few minutes; finishing a task you've been putting off.*

2. **Set a timer for three minutes.** Begin the action with no pressure to complete it. Just show up and start.

3. **When the timer sounds, pause and reflect:**
   ◁ What did I feel when I started?
   ◁ What thoughts or stories came up in my mind?
   ◁ Did anything shift once I was in motion?

Deepen Your Practice. In your notebook or journal, take a few moments to explore:

◁ What do I tell myself in moments of resistance?
◁ Whose voice is that? Whose words? Are they authentically mine?
◁ What truth is trying to break through beneath the resistance?

DEVELOPMENTAL MOVEMENT: PUSH

Learning to push against something is another one of the earliest movement patterns we develop. It's how we learn to push as we roll, crawl, and eventually stand. On a deeper level, "push" teaches our body that it can create space, set boundaries, and move into independence. Without this pattern, we may hesitate to separate, struggle to assert ourselves, or feel unclear about where we end and others begin. Practicing push helps reawaken a felt sense of autonomy and strength. It reminds your body and mind that you can claim space safely, strengthening the foundation for both physical independence and emotional boundaries.

1. **Find Your Surface.** Choose a stable surface like a wall, the floor, or the seat of a sturdy chair. Place your palms or the soles of your feet firmly against it. Close your eyes if it feels safe.

2. **Feel the Contact.** Notice where your hands or feet meet the surface. Sense its solidity beneath you. Whisper quietly: *I can press. I can create space.*

3. **Activate Your Push.** Slowly press into the surface until your muscles engage. Notice how the effort travels through your arms, legs, and core. Hold for a few breaths, then gently release.

4. **Explore Different Directions.** Try pushing in a few ways: palms against a wall (standing), feet pressing into the floor (sitting or lying), or hands pressing into the seat of a chair (seated). With each variation, notice how your body organizes around the push and how your stability changes.

5. **Add Breath and Awareness.** Inhale as you prepare. Exhale slowly as you press. With each exhale, notice what it feels like to claim space with steadiness.

Deepen Your Practice. After five to ten minutes, release the movement gently. Wiggle your fingers and toes. Sit or stand slowly. In your notebook or journal, take a few moments to explore:

- How did my body feel when I first began to push?
- Did I feel strong, grounded, resistant, or something else?
- What emotions came up—relief, empowerment, fear?
- How does this practice mirror the way I set (or don't set) boundaries in my life?

Each of these practices—naming your needs, setting boundaries, and honoring your limits—teaches your system that self-knowledge and self-respect grow together. The more clearly you know yourself, the more capable you become of relating openly and authentically with others.

With this grounded sense of self in place, you're ready to explore Sphere Three: empathy—the capacity to stay present with your own emotions while understanding and attuning to the emotions of those around you.

SPHERE THREE: CULTIVATE EMOTIONAL MATURITY AND EMOTIONAL INTIMACY

In this sphere we develop emotional maturity so that we can more deeply connect with others. Emotional maturity is the ability to feel and manage your own emotions while also honoring the emotional experiences of others. It means staying grounded during moments of stress, taking responsibility for your behavior, and being willing to repair when there's a relational rupture. By tuning in to our body's signals, like tension, stillness, the urge to speak up or step back, we deepen our capacity for emotional responsibility and authentic connection. As we become more emotionally present with ourselves, we learn to meet others with greater clarity, compassion, and attunement.

For the many different reasons we explored in chapter 1, most of us didn't have emotionally mature role models growing up. Instead, we learned from parents who were reactive, avoidant, or emotionally unavailable. Emotional immaturity isn't about age; it's about development. I've worked with many people who are deeply self-aware. They've read the books, listened to the podcasts, and can name what isn't working for them. But without the tools to create change, they spiral into helplessness and hopelessness. Through daily practice, we learn to identify, name, and regulate our emotions. We stop abandoning ourselves in moments of discomfort. Over time, we develop emotional maturity: grounded, accountable, and capable of deep, safe connection.

From this maturity, we gain the capacity to practice empathy. Empathy isn't absorbing someone else's pain; it's the capacity to sense their experience while staying anchored in our own. It's about asking: *How does my behavior affect those around me?* This question marks a powerful shift from self-focus to relational awareness, allowing us to take responsibility for the tone we set, the energy we bring, the choices we make, and the impact those choices have on others.

When we cultivate empathy, we deepen our capacity for emotional intimacy. When two people feel seen, respected, and emotionally safe in each other's presence, trust can grow. Empathy opens the door to that trust. It helps us stay attuned in relationships, offer repair when harm is done, and create space where both people feel heard and valued. Empathy, in this way, becomes more than just a feeling—it's an embodied skill. Together, the empathy and emotional maturity you cultivate through reparenting enable you to build caring, accountable, and deeply connected relationships.

Exploring Your Emotions

Emotions are internal signals, like weather systems, that arise in response to our experiences, thoughts, and memories. They are physiological and psychological responses that give us information about what's happening inside and around us. Emotions are part of being alive, wired into our nervous systems as a tool for survival, connection, and meaning. They let us know when something feels safe or threatening, aligned or off, wanted or uncomfortable. Each emotion carries a message if we're willing to listen. Anger, for instance, signals a boundary has been crossed. Joy reminds us of what we love. Fear alerts us to potential danger. Sadness asks us to slow down and grieve a perceived loss. Our emotions offer us data to help us understand ourselves and our experiences. And yet, many of us were taught to suppress, ignore, or over-identify with them, which distorts their function. Healthy emotional awareness means noticing them, staying curious, and learning what they're trying to communicate without letting them hijack your behavior or define your identity.

The ability to recognize what we feel is essential because emotions carry clues about our needs, boundaries, and desires. When we name them accurately, we access deeper self-awareness and gain the ability to respond with intention rather than react from habit. Without this skill, we risk falling into cycles of avoidance, emotional shutdown, or reactivity. In fact, research shows that people who regularly suppress emotions are more than 30 percent more likely to develop depressive symptoms than those who express them.[3]

Understanding our own emotions strengthens our relationships. When we can name our feelings, we communicate more honestly, set clearer boundaries, and stay grounded while holding space for others. Many of us didn't grow up with emotional modeling or caregivers who could help us make sense of what we were feeling. As adults, learning to name and regulate our emotions is a vital part of healing and developing emotional maturity. This awareness not only reshapes our inner world but also deepens our connections with others, helping us stay resilient through stress, uncertainty, and overwhelm.

Emotional Resilience and Connection

Emotional resilience begins with self-regulation, or the capacity to notice what you feel, track changes in your nervous system, and respond with care. This means learning to pause, check in with your body, and use tools like breathing, movement, or creative expression to return to balance. When your body becomes dysregulated—whether you feel anxious, numb, reactive, or shut down—these tools help you come back home to yourself.

Resilience is about expanding your window of tolerance, the range of emotional and physiological states you can safely experience without becoming overwhelmed. This expansion happens when you challenge yourself to try new things, feel uncomfortable feelings, or engage in honest conversations while staying present and compassionate. And sometimes, that process includes getting upset, lashing out, or shutting down. These moments are part of resilience too. They show you where your edge is, and with awareness, they become opportunities to repair, reflect, and grow. Over time, your capacity for discomfort deepens, and so does your internalized sense of emotional strength.

True resilience also requires letting go. Letting go of chronic tension, past hurts, rigid expectations, or the need for constant control. Whether through journaling, stretching, shaking, or meditative reflection, release is how we make space for healing and new possibilities.

Emotional well-being doesn't end with our own emotional regulation. We are wired for connection and attunement, the subtle back-and-forth that builds trust, empathy, and intimacy. This attunement is expressed not only through our words but also through our posture, tone, and presence. It means creating space for others to authentically express themselves without rushing to fix them and allowing them to do the same for us. From this foundation, emotionally mature relationships become possible. They are relationships built on mutual respect, clear boundaries, and the willingness to repair after conflict, misunderstanding, or disconnection. We don't avoid hard conversations; we engage with humility. We don't expect perfection; we show up with accountability. And in moments of distress, we allow ourselves to be supported. This is the essence of co-regulation, or our nervous system's way of finding calm through safe connection with others, including loved ones, animals, and even nature.

SPHERE THREE EXERCISES

Cultivate Emotional Maturity and Intimacy

Empathy is how we learn to connect with others. It begins with noticing what we feel inside, what others might be feeling, and how our actions ripple out into the space between us. Each time we slow down and tune in, we grow the capacity to understand, to care, and to stay present even when things feel uncomfortable.

> **QUICK CHECK-IN: HOW WILLING AM I TO REACH OUT AND CONNECT?**
>
> Pause for a moment and let your body settle, whether you're sitting, standing, or lying down, letting your hands relax at your sides or in your lap. Take a few slow, deep breaths, bringing your awareness inward and asking yourself:
>
> ◁ Do I feel open and willing to reach toward others when I want connection or support? Or do I hesitate, disconnect, or feel too tired to try?
>
> ◁ Do I tend to overextend, always reaching, fixing, or caring for others before myself? Or do I pull back completely, unsure how or why to connect at all?
>
> ◁ Does reaching out feel energizing and mutual or draining and one-sided? What do I feel in my body when I imagine asking for help or expressing a need?
>
> Just notice any sensations that arise, like tightness in the chest, collapse in the shoulders, or a pull to lean forward or back. This check-in is about recognizing how your body has learned to reach or retreat in response to connection. If you often feel overextended, emotionally numb, or unsure how to show up for yourself and others without burning out, that's a sign this sphere—where we cultivate empathy and emotional maturity—is a good place to find the support you need.

Remember, you don't have to master empathy overnight. Try one practice at a time and see what helps you feel more connected. Return to the ones that resonate. These small acts of awareness build something powerful: the ability to make others feel seen, safe, and understood while staying true to yourself.

PRACTICE
EMOTIONAL ATTUNEMENT

Let's begin with the most important connection of all: the one you have with yourself. Your body has its own way of talking to you. Emotions show up in your breath, your posture, your voice, how you move, and how your body feels. This practice helps you tune in and learn how to listen. Learning how to feel your emotions in the body helps you care for yourself in a deeper way.

1. **Settle In.** Sit quietly or lie down in a comfortable spot. Close your eyes if it feels safe. Take a few slow, deep breaths, letting your body begin to relax.

2. **Scan Your Body.** Slowly bring your attention from the top of your head down to your feet. As you do, ask:
   - Is my breath tight, shallow, shaky, or calm?
   - Do I notice heat, fluttering, tension, or heaviness anywhere?
   - How am I sitting or lying—curled in, stiff, frozen, or at ease?
   - Is there a sound wanting to come out, like a sigh, hum, laugh, cry, or scream?
   - Does my body want to move by stretching, stomping, curling, or staying still?

3. **Name What You Feel.** Naming gives your body a voice. Try simple, kind statements like:
   - My shoulders feel tight.
   - There's a lump in my throat.
   - My legs feel restless.
   - My breath is calm and slow.

4. **Offer Yourself Compassion.** Place a hand on your heart or belly. Say quietly: *All of me is welcome here.* Notice if your body relaxes when you allow instead of judge.

PRACTICE
EMOTIONAL MATURITY

Conflict and disconnection will happen in every relationship. What's most important is how we reconnect, or repair, those disruptions when they do occur. That is where true trust and intimacy grows. By slowing down, naming what's happening, and choosing presence over reactivity, you begin to show up with emotional maturity for yourself and for the people you care about. This practice will help you develop the ability to repair within your relationships.

1. **Recall a Moment That Felt "Off."** Think of a time when something didn't go well in a relationship. Maybe you snapped at someone, shut down, or avoided telling the truth. Choose a moment where you wish you had responded differently.

2. **Step into Their Shoes.** Close your eyes for a moment and imagine the other person during that experience. What might they have felt in their body? What emotions might have come up for them—confusion, hurt, fear, disappointment? This step isn't about blaming yourself; it's about building empathy.

3. **Craft a Repair Statement.** Now write or say a statement that expresses care, responsibility, or understanding. Keep it simple, sincere, and emotionally attuned. Examples: *I care how that landed, even if it wasn't my intention. I was overwhelmed, and your feelings matter to me. I see how that may have felt, and I want to show up differently moving forward.*

4. **Visualize the Repair.** Imagine saying these words directly to the person. Picture their face. Imagine speaking calmly, with your body grounded and your voice soft but steady. Notice what happens inside you as you imagine this moment—do you feel more open, vulnerable, relieved?

5. **Anchor the Experience in Your Body.** Place a hand on your heart or belly if it feels comfortable to do so. Read your repair statement aloud, slowly and with intention. Let your nervous system *hear* your growth

and willingness to reconnect. Take a deep breath afterward and simply feel what arises.

6. **Reflect.** Ask yourself: *What shifts in me when I care more about connection than being right? What does it feel like in my body to imagine repair instead of regret?*

PRACTICE
RIGHT-BRAIN EMPATHY

Repair isn't just spoken; it's felt. Long before we developed language, our nervous systems learned safety through presence, breath, and eye contact. Connection lives in how we breathe, sit, listen, and show up as much as the words we say. Let's explore how to attune through presence. This practice shifts from words to attunement, helping you strengthen right-brain empathy: the ability to connect through how you *show up*, not just what you say. When we feel each other through breath, gaze, or stillness, we remember we're not alone.

Option A: Solo (Mirror Practice)

1. Sit in front of a mirror. Look into your own eyes softly.
2. Notice any emotions in your face—tension, softness, sadness.
3. Gently copy the expression with curiosity.
4. Say silently or aloud: "I see you. I'm here with you."

Option B: With a Partner

1. Sit across from someone you trust. Set a timer for two minutes.
2. Look at their face or eyes (or their cheek if direct eye contact is too much).

3. Breathe slowly and notice their breathing too.
4. Without talking, see if your bodies begin to relax together.
5. Afterward, share one word that describes how you feel.

PRACTICE
HOLDING SPACE

Sometimes being a good friend, partner, or human means resisting the urge to fix, explain, or rush. Holding space is the skill of staying present with difficult feelings, ours or someone else's, without needing to change them right away. It's how we build true emotional safety and empathy.

1. **Recall a Difficult Moment.** Think of a time when someone around you was hurting. They might have cried, shut down, got quiet, or seemed frustrated or overwhelmed. Choose a moment that left you unsure of what to say or do.

2. **Tune Inward.** Take a moment to explore how your body responded in that moment. Ask yourself the following questions and notice what comes up. There's no right or wrong, only awareness.
    - What did I feel in my body at that moment?
    - Was there a tightening in my chest? Did I start holding my breath?
    - Did I feel the urge to fix it, make it better, change the subject, or disappear?

3. **Reimagine the Moment with Presence.** Close your eyes and revisit the experience without trying to change or fix anything, picturing yourself there again and saying silently to yourself: *I can be with whatever is present.* Place a hand on your heart or belly and breathe slowly and deeply, softening any areas of tension. Visualize yourself offering steady presence—calm, warm, and grounded.

4. **Deepen Your Practice.** In your notebook or journal, take a few moments to explore:

    ◁ What makes it hard for me to stay with uncomfortable emotions—my own or someone else's?
    ◁ When do I tend to rescue, distract, or shut down?
    ◁ What helps me stay present, even when it's hard?
    ◁ What would it feel like to trust that presence is enough?

PRACTICE
FORGIVENESS AND SOFTENING

As you begin to hold space for others, it is still just as important to hold space for yourself. Forgiveness is one of the most powerful ways to do that. Let's practice softening, even when you feel unsure. Compassion means offering kindness, especially when it feels hard. You don't need to forget or pretend something didn't hurt. The goal is to soften your grip on the pain, so it doesn't keep holding you back. This practice helps you make space for healing, even when things feel messy, unresolved, or tender.

1. **Find a Quiet Space.** Sit comfortably in a space where you won't be interrupted. Let your hands rest on your heart, belly, or lap. Close your eyes if it feels safe.

2. **Bring Someone to Mind.** This could be someone who hurt you. It could also be you. Choose someone who still lives in your heart with a little bit of tension, regret, or heaviness.

3. **Offer Loving Wishes.** Either silently or softly out loud, begin by repeating a few simple phrases. Let each one land in your body. If emotions arise, allow them to be there without judgment. Repeat silently or aloud to yourself: *May you feel safe. May you feel loved. May you feel free.*

4. **Mirror Compassion.** Open your eyes and look gently into a mirror. If it feels difficult, start by gazing at your own cheek or eyes without judgment. Then say: *You're doing the best you can. You are still lovable, even when you mess up. You deserve gentleness and grace.*

5. **If You Feel Resistance or Shame.** That's normal. Instead of pushing it away, meet it with curiosity. Take a breath and allow the resistance to soften, even just a little. You might say: *I hear you. You're trying to protect me. It's okay to let go a little now.*

Deepen Your Practice. Sometimes, what needs to be said doesn't need to be spoken, it just needs to be felt and expressed. Take a piece of paper and write a short letter of forgiveness. You might write to yourself, to someone you're ready to release, or to a younger version of you. Be honest and kind, letting it flow from your heart. When you're ready, burn it safely, bury it, or tear it up, allowing yourself to soften and let go in whatever way is possible.

DEVELOPMENTAL MOVEMENT: REACH

Reaching is one of the earliest developmental movements. Babies instinctively extend their hands toward caregivers, toys, or anything that sparks curiosity. This movement lays the foundation for initiative, exploration, and connection. As adults, practicing reach helps reawaken safety in extending outward to people, opportunities, and desires. Without it, engagement with the world can feel unsafe, hesitant, or overly cautious. Each reach becomes a rehearsal for engaging more openly with life. This practice teaches your nervous system that it's safe to extend beyond yourself. Reaching builds trust in your ability to explore while staying grounded in your own body.

1. **Get Grounded.** Sit or stand with your feet steady on the ground. Take a few slow, deep breaths. Feel your spine tall and supported, your body rooted.

2. **Practice a Simple Reach.** Slowly extend one arm forward to an object in front of you—or toward empty space. Notice how your torso, spine,

and breath move with your arm. Allow your whole body to participate, not just your hand. Alternate sides, reaching with your right arm, then your left.

3. **Explore Directions.** Reach upward to the ceiling. Reach sideways, diagonally, or gently backward if it feels safe. Pay attention: Does your body feel energized, hesitant, playful, or uncertain?

4. **Add Meaning.** As you extend your arm, silently name what you are reaching for: *support, connection, joy, clarity, rest, opportunity.* Pause for a breath with your arm extended, imagining yourself receiving it.

Deepen Your Practice. After five to ten minutes, release the movement slowly. Wiggle your fingers and toes. Sit or stand gently. In your notebook or journal, take a few moments to explore:

- What sensations did I notice in my body while reaching?
- Did I feel excited, vulnerable, hesitant, or playful?
- Was there a difference between reaching in one direction versus another?
- What feelings arose when I imagined reaching for something I want?

Each of these practices—listening inwardly, softening judgment, and responding with care—teaches you to stay connected even when emotions are strong. Over time, empathy becomes both your anchor and your bridge, grounding you in self-trust while opening you to intimacy.

With this emotional balance in place, we turn to Sphere Four: authenticity, cultivating the freedom to express who you are through your words, creativity, and presence.

SPHERE FOUR: ACCESS SELF-EXPRESSION, IMAGINATION, CREATIVITY, PASSION, AND PURPOSE

To be authentic is to show up as your whole Self—unmasked, unfiltered, and fully alive. When we're around someone who feels inauthentic, whether they're hiding something, performing, or censoring their true nature, our body knows. Your stomach tightens, your breath becomes shallow, or you feel uneasy for reasons you can't name. That's your body detecting incongruence. Your nervous system is wired to recognize truth. It softens in the presence of authenticity and braces in its absence. This sphere invites you to reconnect with joy, imagination, and self-expression that come with being fully yourself. It is how you remember who you are beneath the roles, reactions, and expectations placed on you.

When we suppress our own truth—when we pretend, minimize, or perform—our body bears the cost. Kinesiologists, who use the relative strength of muscular responses to assess health issues, have observed that muscles weaken when we speak falsehoods and strengthen when we speak truths. In other words: Our body doesn't lie. So, when we abandon or betray ourselves, even in subtle ways like minimizing our needs or silencing our truth, our body registers it as stress, carrying the weight of what our mind tries to deny.

This is why healing requires a return to radical honesty. Not oversharing and not spilling every thought to every person but choosing to live in alignment with your truth. Radical honesty is having the courage to say, *This is who I am, even when it's uncomfortable*. It's being transparent with yourself about what you want, need, feel, and believe and allowing those truths to shape your choices and relationships.

Many of us learned early on that being ourselves wasn't safe. You may have been scolded for crying, laughed at for dreaming too big, or praised only when you performed a role others wanted you to play. You learned to edit yourself to stay connected, burying your joy, dimming your voice, or trading creativity for compliance. But what kept you safe back then is keeping you disconnected now.

This sphere of reparenting invites you to unlearn the lie that your authenticity is too much or not enough. It helps you reclaim your imagination, your creativity, your desires, and your voice, rebuilding trust with yourself and others. Because when your inner and outer Selves are aligned, your body relaxes, your mind clears, and your life begins to feel like your own, allowing your purpose to guide you.

Being Yourself: The Integration of Truth and Belonging

We are born curious, expressive, and wired for connection, with a natural sense of Self. As we grow, we pick up on cues about what's celebrated, what's ignored, and what earns us love or safety. From these cues, we begin to adapt and build important relational skills: how to listen, cooperate, and belong. But they can also lead us to temporarily set aside certain emotions, preferences, or traits that don't seem welcome. Gender norms often shape these adjustments: Girls may be praised for being agreeable and helpful, while boys may be rewarded for being strong and self-sufficient. These roles can offer structure and even safety in childhood, but over time, they can restrict our full self-expression.

Now, as adults, we have the chance to examine these patterns and choose how we want to show up. As we mature, we gain the capacity to reflect on our patterns and ask: *What's truly mine? What was learned? What still fits and what's ready to be reclaimed?* The goal isn't to reject the adaptive parts of us but to integrate them into a more complete, conscious version of who we are.

Reconnecting with our authenticity means tuning in to our real needs, values, and voice. When we live from a place of wholeness, we experience less internal friction, greater emotional clarity, and deeper, more honest relationships.

Being yourself and returning to your inner compass is a powerful act of coming home.

Igniting Imagination, Passion, and Purpose

Our imagination is an essential survival tool, one that can allow us to break free from the limits of what is and step into the possibilities of what could be. Through imagination, we glimpse a different future. Through creativity, we begin to build it.

Often seen as abstract or artistic, imagination and creativity serve deeply practical purposes. They help us problem-solve, express unspoken emotions, and process experiences that feel too complex for words. Whether through writing, painting, music, movement, or simply daydreaming, creative expression allows us to externalize what lives inside us. This process can be profoundly healing, especially when we've felt silenced, stuck, or disconnected.

Your imagination lights the path to your passion and ultimately purpose. Passion emerges when you engage with what inspires you, activities that bring joy, energy, or a deep sense of flow. In these moments, the usual barriers created by fear or conditioning begin to fall away. You feel most like yourself. Most alive.

This sense of flow often leads you toward your purpose, or your deeper "why." Purpose isn't just one grand mission; it's the meaning behind your actions, the way you want to show up in the world, and what you feel called to contribute. It's the fuel that keeps you going, even on the hard days.

When you give yourself permission to imagine, to create, to explore what brings you joy, you reconnect with your authentic self. And from that place of truth, passion and purpose are not things you find; they're things you remember.

SPHERE FOUR EXERCISES

Cultivate Self-Expression, Creativity, and Passion

Authenticity is how we learn to live as ourselves. It begins with listening and hearing the signals of our body, following the spark of our creativity, and speaking with honesty. Each time we honor what feels true for us, we build trust in our own voice and create space for joy to return.

These small acts of honesty—how you move, speak, or create—add up. They become reminders that authenticity is a way of living day by day. One of the most powerful ways to start is by noticing the difference between what feels true in your body and what doesn't.

> **QUICK CHECK-IN: HOW FREE DO I FEEL TO BE MYSELF?**
>
> Pause for a moment and allow your body to come to stillness. You can sit, lie down, or stand with ease, letting your hands rest by your sides or over your belly. Take a few slow, deep, grounding breaths, bringing your attention inward as you ask yourself:
>
> - Do I know what makes me happy, or do I feel unsure of what I need?
> - When I picture sharing a dream or idea, does my body feel excited or shut down?
> - Can I ask for and receive help without pretending, or do I keep trying and still feel unseen?
>
> Just notice what arises. Your throat may tighten, your chest may feel like it's rising or puffing up, and you may notice feelings of excitement or fear. These are clues to how safe it feels to be seen, heard, and expressed. If you often feel stuck, silenced, or unsure of who you are beneath it all, the work of Sphere Four—cultivating self-expression, creativity, and passion—is where you can cultivate authenticity.

PRACTICE
THE POWER OF YOUR TRUTH

When you hide parts of yourself, your body often feels like it's tightening, shrinking, or shutting down. When you tell the truth, something shifts. Your breath deepens. Your shoulders drop. You feel more like you. This practice helps you tune in to the difference between performance and authenticity in your body.

1. **Think of a Moment When You Weren't Fully Yourself.** Call to mind a time when you said or did something to please, hide, or avoid conflict. Maybe you said *I'm fine* when you weren't, or agreed to something that didn't feel right.

2. **Speak the Performative Statement Aloud.** Say the words you used in that moment. Examples: *I'm totally okay. I don't need help.* Pause and notice:
   - Is your jaw tight?
   - Are your shoulders slouched or tense?
   - Do you feel numb, flat, or disconnected?

3. **Now Speak the Truth Aloud.** Say what was really true in that moment. Speak it gently, as if you were talking to someone you trust. Examples: *I felt confused. I wanted to say no. I was scared to be honest.* Pause again and notice:
   - Does your breath deepen?
   - Does your posture shift?
   - Do you feel more open, lighter, or grounded?

4. **Place a Hand on Your Chest or Belly.** Take three slow, deep breaths, letting your nervous system register the safety of speaking truth.

5. **Reflect.** Take a few moments to explore the prompts below, writing your responses in a notebook or journal:

- What did I feel in my body when I was being inauthentic?
- What changed when I told the truth?
- What parts of me are still waiting to be heard?

PRACTICE
THE REAL YOU BENEATH THE ROLES

Authenticity often lives in our inner child—the one who dreamed freely before fear or performance took over. This practice helps you reconnect with that part of yourself and notice the difference between the roles you've played and the real you underneath.

1. **Call Your Inner Child to Mind.** Sit somewhere quiet and close your eyes. Picture a younger version of yourself. Notice their face, body, what they loved, and what they dreamed about. If it helps, imagine a specific age—your five-year-old self, your ten-year-old self, or another age that feels important.

2. **Write Them a Letter.** Open your notebook or journal and write directly to this younger version of you. Ask them:

   - What did you love?
   - What did you dream about?
   - What did you need to hear?

3. **Dialogue Between Your Parts.** Now write a short back-and-forth dialogue between two parts of you. Let each one speak in turn, without censoring or overthinking. Write down what each part wants, fears, or needs.

   - *The Performer*—the part that tries to fit in, please others, or "get it right."
   - *The Authentic Self*—the part that longs to be real, honest, and free.

EXAMPLE:
Performer: I do _____ when I want to fit in, please others, or "get it right."
Authentic Self: When you do that, I would rather be doing this: _____

Performer: I do it because I'm afraid if I don't, then _____.
Authentic Self: I understand that, but I feel like I've sacrificed my chance to _____.

4. **Ask What's Needed.** Once both voices have spoken, pause and ask: What does each part need from me right now? Notice any sensations in your body as you ask—tightness, softening, or release.

5. **Choose One Small Act.** Pick one thing you can do today that honors your authentic Self. Examples: *Saying no to something you don't want, doing something creative just for yourself, allowing time to rest.*

Deepen Your Practice. Take a few moments to explore the prompt below, writing your responses in a notebook or journal: *If I stopped trying to be who they wanted me to be, who would I become?*

PRACTICE
LET YOURSELF BE SEEN

Being authentic doesn't mean telling everyone everything. It means allowing at least one safe person to see something real about you, like your truth, your dreams, or your creative expression. Authenticity also grows when you allow it to be witnessed. The next practice invites you to gently let yourself be seen by someone safe.

1. **Choose Something True.** Think of something real for you right now. It could be a story, a boundary, a desire, a piece of art, or a truth you haven't spoken aloud.

2. **Share It Safely.** Choose someone who feels trustworthy and supportive. Share in a way that feels comfortable—speak it out loud, write it in a message, or express it through creativity.
3. **Check In with Your Body.** After sharing, pause and notice, placing a hand on your chest or belly and take a slow breath as you acknowledge what comes up:
   - Do I feel relief?
   - Do I feel fear?
   - Do I feel pride, lightness, or energy?

Deepen Your Practice. In your notebook or journal, take a few moments to explore:
   - What was it like to be seen in my truth?
   - What do I want to remember about this feeling?

PRACTICE
YOUR FLOW

Flow states occur when you're present, aligned, and expressing yourself without overthinking. You are fully connected to what feels most natural and true to you. In a flow state, you express yourself without effort or without trying to be anyone else. This practice helps you experiment, choosing small, steady ways to express yourself and noticing what activities or spaces allow your authentic Self to emerge naturally and effortlessly.

1. **Settle into Stillness.** Find a quiet spot and sit comfortably. Place one hand on your chest and one on your belly. Take a few slow, grounding breaths and remind yourself: *I am here. I can listen.*
2. **Recall Flow Moments.** Think of three to five times in your life when you felt fully immersed and free. It might have been painting, hiking, dancing, cooking, writing, building something, or having a deep conversation.

3. **Reflect in Writing.** In your notebook or journal, take a few moments to explore:

    ◁ What was I doing?
    ◁ How did my body feel—light, open, focused, free?
    ◁ What part of me felt expressed—creative, playful, wise, curious?

4. **Notice Patterns.** Look over your answers. Are there common threads—movement, nature, creativity, connection, play? Circle the ones that feel most alive for you right now.

5. **Choose One to Revisit.** Pick one flow activity and plan a time this week to return to it. Give yourself permission to do it without pressure or goals—just to feel alive in the process.

PRACTICE
CREATIVITY JUST FOR YOU

Creative engagement offers us an invitation to connect with our inner child. You don't have to be "good" at art to be creative. Drawing, dancing, writing, building, and storytelling are all ways your feelings and ideas can move through you without rules or expectations. This practice helps you feel free, playful, and connected to your true self.

1. **Pick a Fun Way to Create.** Choose something that feels fun or an activity you already enjoy even if you're not great at it. This isn't about being perfect; it's about having fun and letting your energy move as you express yourself. You could try:

    ◁ Drawing, painting, or coloring
    ◁ Dancing, singing, or acting something out
    ◁ Writing a blog, story, or poem
    ◁ Building or creating something with your hands (like sewing, crafts, or cooking)

2. **Set a Timer.** Choose how long you want to create, anywhere from ten to fifteen minutes is a great start. Set a timer so you don't have to keep checking the clock. Remember, this is your time to have fun and explore.

3. **Let It Out.** Start creating! Draw, dance, build, sing, or write; play with whatever you picked. Let your ideas flow, even if they feel silly or messy. You don't need to make it perfect and you don't even have to show anyone; this is just for you.

4. **Check In with Yourself.** When the timer goes off, take a moment to pause before cleaning up or moving on to your next activity. Place your hand on your heart or your belly and ask yourself:

   ◁ What did I enjoy or like about this?
   ◁ What surprised me or made me smile?
   ◁ What made me feel weird or awkward?
   ◁ What did I say or show with my creation that I didn't say with words?

5. **Do It Again Soon.** Pick another day this week or next to do it again. You can try the same creative activity or a new one. The goal is just to have fun and let yourself feel free.

DEVELOPMENTAL MOVEMENT: GRASP AND PULL

Grasp and pull is the natural partner to reaching. Once we extend toward something, the next step is to draw it closer. Babies instinctively grasp fingers, toys, or food and pull them toward themselves. This movement lays the foundation for intimacy, reciprocity, and the ability to receive. Many of us learned how to give, but not how to take in nourishment, care, or support. Without grasping and pulling, connection can feel one-sided or fleeting. This practice teaches your nervous system that receiving is safe and necessary. Grasping and pulling helps your body remember that taking in what's good for you is nourishing and vital for balanced connection.

1. **Get Grounded.** Sit or stand with your feet steady on the ground. Take a slow breath and notice the weight of your body supported.

2. **Begin with a Reach.** Extend one arm toward an object—real or imagined. Notice how your body lengthens as you reach outward.
3. **Practice Grasp and Pull.** Curl your fingers gently around the object or imagine holding it. Slowly draw your hand back toward your chest, letting your torso and breath move with it. Alternate sides, reaching outward and then pulling inward.
4. **Add Meaning.** As you pull the object toward your chest, silently say, *I allow myself to receive.* Pause and notice what it feels like to bring something good closer to you.

Deepen Your Practice. After five to ten minutes, release the object slowly. Wiggle your fingers and toes. In your notebook or journal, take a few moments to explore:

- How did it feel to receive instead of only give?
- Did I feel resistance, comfort, or longing in the act of pulling in?
- What might it mean to let myself accept more care, love, or support in my daily life?

Each of these practices—speaking truth, creating freely, and allowing yourself to be seen—strengthens your capacity to both reach and receive. They reinforce the inner knowing: *I am safe to receive what I need. I am worthy of nourishment and support.*

With this openness established, we move to Sphere Five: connecting with meaning, purpose, and something greater than yourself.

SPHERE FIVE: SEEK TRANSCENDENCE: SEEING BEYOND YOUR SELF

Transcendence is the ability to step outside the narrow lens of your conditioning to connect with something greater, whether that's nature, the collective human experience, or the vast mystery of the universe. It's a state of awe, wonder, and belonging that reminds us: We are not separate. We are not alone. We are part of something much larger, more intricate, and more meaningful than we often realize, whether that's spirit, beauty, play, or the living world around us. To transcend is to expand beyond the daily grind of "doing" and drop into the deeper rhythm of *being*. It's the quiet wonder in a sunrise, the thrill of laughter, the sacred stillness at the edge of something unknown. This sphere reminds us that we are already whole, always supported.

Our ego, or the part of us that seeks recognition, validation, and control, can make life feel one-dimensional and self-focused. Our ego is like a shield we built as kids to keep us safe—wanting to be liked, noticed, or in control. It pulls our attention toward wanting to win an argument, worrying about how we were perceived in the meeting, or dwelling on what we still haven't achieved. We'll explore the ego more deeply in the next chapter, but beneath it lies our inner child—the part of us that simply wants to be real, loved, and free. When we connect with beauty, vastness, or collective meaning, we loosen the ego's hold and tap into a deeper harmony.

We are not separate from nature; we *are* nature. Our well-being and our planet's health are intimately connected. Just as we impact the earth, the earth impacts us. A growing body of research reflects this truth. In the field of bioacoustics, the study of sound in ecological systems, scientists have found that sound, whether from rainfall, birdsong, or drumming, can influence both animal behavior and plant growth. Studies have even shown that drumlike frequencies can stimulate plant growth by enhancing vibrational energy in the environment. This suggests that ancient practices like communal drumming may have had subtle but meaningful effects on the living world around us.

Modern life teaches us to value productivity over presence, logic over wonder, and independence over interconnection. Transcendence invites us to remember what's been lost. It allows us to reclaim our capacity for reverence, stillness, and connection to something sacred, whether that's through nature, music, movement, prayer, or simply witnessing the stars.

Transcendence is about reconnecting with our wholeness. When we step beyond our ego, we meet a deeper Self that's grounded in connection, meaning, and trust in something larger. Reparenting helps us build this connection little by little, through consistent practice, until it becomes both our foundation and our freedom.

REDISCOVERING CURIOSITY, SPONTANEITY, AND PLAYFULNESS

Curiosity is the spark that drives us to explore, to wonder, and to seek understanding beyond what we already know. As children, we approach the world with openness, eager to touch, taste, and discover without fear of failure. This innate curiosity doesn't disappear with age, but many of us were conditioned to suppress it in favor of obedience, performance, or perfection. Reparenting allows us to reopen that door and let our inner child reclaim wonder, ask questions, make mistakes, and explore life with fresh eyes and an open heart. From this curious place, we can begin to ask: *What story does this memory carry? What am I most drawn to in this moment, and why? Is there a part of me that wants to speak but hasn't had the chance? If I could give this part of myself a voice, what would it say?* These explorations help us reconnect with aspects of ourselves that were once hidden or shut down and offer them room to breathe, move, and be known.

From this place of emotional freedom, playfulness and spontaneity begin to emerge, reminding us that life isn't meant to be rigid, overly serious, or entirely productive. In a culture that often equates play with immaturity, many adults lose touch with this essential part of themselves. But play is not frivolous. It brings us into the present moment, reconnects us to joy, and fosters emotional resilience. It can even be a portal to creativity, problem-solving, and self-expression.

Science validates the many benefits of play, including its role in emotional regulation and healing from trauma.[4] Research in the *American Journal of Play* suggests that adults who regularly engage in play, like hobbies, creative activities, or games, report lower stress and depression, with improved dopamine release. Neuroscientist Jaak Panksepp found that physical play enhances secure attachment and emotional regulation in both children and adults. Neuroplasticity research also shows that new forms of play can help rewire the brain, strengthening connections between emotional and executive centers like the amygdala and prefrontal cortex.

Beyond its psychological and physiological benefits, play helps us reach deeper truths that we can't always put into words. It connects us to the world inside—our feelings, memories, and imagination. When we play, we don't have to follow strict rules or stay in control. We can let go, be curious, and often discover new insights. Most important, play gives space for our inner child—the part of us that wants to laugh, explore, and create—to come alive again.

CULTIVATING WONDER AND AWE

Awe arises when we come face-to-face with something so vast it opens us up to the bigger picture of life and our place in it, like looking at the stars in the night sky, hearing the first cry of a newborn, or getting chills from music that moves us. It pulls us out of our own heads and opens us to something larger than ourselves, the way the awe that we feel when looking up at a night sky can lead us to wonder about its beauty or meaning. But wonder doesn't always need something vast to activate it; it can just as easily show up in the small things, like watching how a spider spins a web with such precision or pausing to notice how a plant slowly leans toward sunlight. Together, awe and wonder reconnect us to the magic of being alive.

You might have felt awe before, even if you didn't know what to call it. Unlike wonder, which can make us feel more curious, awe can take our breath away and touch us deeply. We experience awe when something feels magical or bigger than we can explain. Scientists have found that awe activates our vagus nerve, slowing down our heart rate, sharpening our focus, and connecting us more deeply to the world around us. It might even bring tears to our eyes or give us goose bumps as our body fully responds to the beauty of the moment.

Physiologically, awe is more than just a beautiful experience; it's healing. It reduces inflammation and stress hormones while increasing feelings of compassion, generosity, and creative openness. In a world obsessed with doing, awe reminds us to be. It helps us feel both smaller and more connected to the earth beneath us, the sky above, and the web of life into which we're woven.

Most of us felt these states naturally in childhood when we were gazing at a rainbow, asking endless questions, making worlds out of sticks and string. But many were taught to outgrow wonder when we were told to "get serious," to stop daydreaming, to value facts over feelings. Over time, we learned to mistrust what we couldn't explain.

As adults, whenever we let ourselves feel awe, we stop thinking only about ourselves and start to feel more connected to others and the world around us. Life becomes more than just getting through the day or trying to prove ourselves; it becomes something filled with wonder, connection, and new possibilities.

EXERCISES FOR SPHERE FIVE

Cultivate Curiosity, Awe, and Play

When we pause to feel wonder, follow our curiosity, or sit in quiet connection, we remember we're not alone. These practices help you awaken to something larger within and around you so you can live with more presence, play, and reverence and develop a sense of how you fit into the bigger picture.

> **QUICK CHECK-IN: HOW DO I FIT INTO THE BIGGER PICTURE?**
>
> Take a moment to pause and breathe. Let your body settle—standing, sitting, or lying down. Soften your gaze or close your eyes. Place one hand on your heart and one on your belly. Ask yourself:
>
> ◁ Do I feel connected to something larger than myself? Or do I often feel alone, stuck in my own story or stress?
>
> ◁ Do I still make space for wonder, curiosity, or joy? Or has life become all routine and responsibility?
>
> ◁ When I look at the stars or stand at the edge of the sea, what do I feel inside me?

Just notice what arises. Your chest may expand, your breath may catch, or a sense of awe might ripple through you. These are clues to how open you feel to connection, meaning, and wonder. If you often feel cut off, burdened, or small in the face of life, cultivating curiosity, awe, and play in Sphere Five can help you reconnect with something greater than yourself. One of the most powerful ways to begin is with stillness, learning to pause long enough to notice what is here.

PRACTICE
SACRED PAUSE

Stillness gives you space to connect with yourself more fully. The sacred pause is a ritual. It's intentional time to step out of the rush of life and return to what matters most. Practicing it daily—morning or evening—roots you in meaning and opens you to connection with something greater.

1. **Set the Scene.** Choose a consistent time either to begin or end your day. Create a simple ritual by lighting a candle, sitting quietly, or placing a meaningful object nearby.

2. **Come into Stillness.** Sit or stand comfortably. Place a hand over your heart or chest. Take three slow, deep breaths, letting your body relax into the moment.

3. **Ask and Listen.** Ask yourself, noticing what comes up: *What connects me to something greater than myself? Where do I feel that in my body?*

4. **Reflect.** Take a few moments to explore the prompts below, writing your responses in a notebook or journal: *What am I devoted to? When do I feel closest to spirit, nature, or meaning? What sustains me when life feels hard?*

MINI-PRACTICE
DAILY MICRO-PAUSE

Unlike the sacred pause, which is ritualized, the micro-pause is your quick, practical tool making something you can integrate into daily life whenever you feel pulled, pressured, or overwhelmed. It's about giving your nervous system a short reset right where you are.

1. **Pick a Moment.** Choose a natural pause point in your day: before answering your phone, opening your laptop, walking into a meeting, or starting your car.
2. **Stop for Thirty Seconds.** Let your body go still. Notice your feet pressing into the ground.
3. **Breathe.** Inhale slowly through your nose. Exhale fully through your mouth. Feel your body settle.
4. **Check In.** Ask yourself: *What do I need right now?* Don't force an answer—just listen.
5. **Return with Awareness.** Move into the next moment with a little more steadiness, as if you've pressed a reset button.

PRACTICE
GRATITUDE OFFERING

Gratitude grounds us in what *is* here, now. Practicing gratitude reminds your body and mind to see not only the threat but also the gifts in our breath, body, nature, and connections.

1. **Choose a Daily Moment.** Pick a consistent time—morning, evening, or before a meal.

2. **Name One Thing.** Say one thing you are grateful for. Keep it simple. It could be your body, a person, the air, or something ordinary that sustains you.

    ◁ Thank you to my breath.
    ◁ Thank you to the sun.
    ◁ Thank you to my ancestors.
    ◁ Thank you to my resilience.

3. **Offer It Outward.** Speak it aloud or whisper it into the earth, sky, air, or your own heart. Imagine the words as a small gift you're returning to life itself.

4. **Reflect.** Take a few moments to explore the prompts below, writing your responses in a notebook or journal.

    ◁ Who or what do I want to thank today?
    ◁ How can I honor the gifts I've been given?
    ◁ What shifts in me when I notice what's already here, instead of what's missing?

PRACTICE
WALK AND WONDER

When we pause to give thanks, our hearts open, and from that openness, wonder and awe become possible. Awe lifts us into what could be. It expands the nervous system, slows us down, and reminds us that we're not alone. This practice helps you reconnect with the part of you that can still be amazed by life.

1. **Go Outside.** Choose a safe place where you can walk for about ten minutes. This could be a park, your street, a garden, or even a balcony where you can look at the sky.

2. **Move Slowly.** Walk at half your usual pace. Let your senses, not your thoughts, guide you. Begin to notice small details:

- The pattern of shadows on the ground
- The shape of a leaf
- The color of the sky at this moment
- A birdcall or the hum of traffic
- The feel of the air on your skin

3. **Feel the Vastness.** Pause at least once to take in something larger than yourself—the horizon, the sky, a tall tree. Let yourself feel small in a good way, part of something mysterious and alive.

Deepen Your Practice. Take a few moments to explore the prompts below, writing your responses in a notebook or journal.

- Name three moments in your life when you felt awe or deep connection.
- What did those moments have in common?
- How can you invite more of them into your life this week?

PRACTICE
PLAY WITHOUT PURPOSE

Play helps regulate the nervous system, restore lightness, and remind us that joy doesn't need a reason. It doesn't have to be elaborate or productive—just free. This practice helps you reconnect with spontaneity and possibility by giving yourself permission to play without an outcome.

1. **Choose Your Play.** Think of something you enjoyed as a kid or something that feels silly and lighthearted now. Examples: *coloring, doodling, kicking a ball, blowing bubbles, dancing in the kitchen, jumping rope,* or *building something silly.*

2. **Set a Timer.** Start with five to fifteen minutes. Giving this practice a clear time frame helps your brain relax and treat this time as intentional.

3. **Play Freely.** Do the activity without worrying about being "good" at it. Let your body move, your hands create, or your imagination wander. Follow whatever feels fun or ridiculous.

4. **Notice Your Body.** While playing, pause briefly and ask: *How does my body feel right now? Lighter? Looser? Freer? More alive?*

5. **Reflect.** After you're done, in your notebook or journal take a few moments to explore:

    ◁ When I play, I feel . . .
    ◁ Play reminded me that . . .
    ◁ One area of my life that could use more lightness is . . .

PRACTICE
FOLLOW YOUR FASCINATION

Curiosity is how we keep growing. It wakes us up when life feels flat or repetitive. It pulls us toward the things that spark energy in our body or light up our mind. This practice helps you follow your natural curiosity to rediscover joy, exploration, and learning.

1. **Ask Yourself:** *What am I curious about right now?* This could be a question, a subject, a place, a story, or even something small in your surroundings.

2. **Follow the Thread.** Choose one thing and spend fifteen to twenty minutes exploring it. You might:

    ◁ Read an article or book
    ◁ Watch a video or listen to a podcast
    ◁ Go look at something in nature
    ◁ Stare, sketch, or daydream about it
    ◁ Ask someone about it

3. **Reflect.** Take a few moments to explore the prompts below, writing your responses in a notebook or journal:

- What felt fun, exciting, or interesting while I was exploring?
- Did I notice any new ideas, feelings, or surprises?
- What could this curiosity be showing me about what I like or want in my life?

DEVELOPMENTAL MOVEMENT: RELEASE

Release is the closing gesture in the cycle of connection. Just as babies learn to reach, grasp, and pull, they also learn to let go. Release allows us to metabolize experiences, end relationships with grace, and return to rest. Without it, we may grip too tightly to people, habits, or old pain. This practice reminds your body that letting go is not loss but space-making. Releasing creates room for new experiences, relationships, and growth. By practicing it physically, you strengthen your capacity to let go of what no longer serves you and return to rest with trust.

1. **Get Grounded.** Sit or stand with your feet flat on the floor. Take a breath and feel yourself supported by gravity. Close your eyes, if that feels safe.

2. **Practice Letting Go.** Hold a small object in your hand—a pen, a stone, anything small and sturdy. When you're ready, open your hand and let it drop or gently place it down. Notice the sensations as your arm relaxes by your side.

3. **Add Breath.** Inhale as if gathering energy. Exhale as you release, softening your shoulders, unclenching your jaw, or relaxing your belly. Silently say: *I release what I no longer need.*

4. **Explore the Cycle.** Try moving through the sequence: reach → grasp and pull → release. Notice how the cycle feels when you allow yourself to complete it.

Deepen Your Practice. After five to ten minutes, slowly open your eyes. Wiggle your fingers and toes. Sit up gently. In your notebook or journal, take a few moments to explore:

- What did it feel like in my body to let go?
- Did I notice resistance, relief, or both?
- What in my life might I be gripping too tightly?

Each of these practices—reflection, release, and surrender—teaches your body and mind that letting go creates space for what's next. This is the rhythm of transcendence: trusting flow, allowing renewal, and sensing your place within something larger than yourself.

DAILY REPARENTING CHECK-IN

Reparenting offers you a way of coming home to yourself again and again.

1. **Find a quiet space.** Sit or lie down in a way that feels comfortable. Take a few slow, deep breaths, placing one hand on your heart and one on your belly.

2. **Ask yourself:** *What do I need most today?* You can also think about the five spheres—Safety and Security, Individuation, Agency and Empathy, Authenticity, and Transcendence. Which one feels most important right now?

3. **Whisper these words to yourself:**

- I am listening.
- I am here.
- I am becoming who I was always meant to be.

Reparenting through these spheres builds the foundation for healing your inner child. You are creating safety in your body, establishing a new relationship with your emotions, and becoming your full, authentic Self. But there are still wounds to be healed because there are parts of you that were shamed and suppressed. These wounds cause those seemingly inexplicable moments when the nervous system is over- or underreactive. Even as you reparent yourself, those wounds can still be activated. Next, we're going to address how to witness these different parts of yourself and to integrate them into the whole of your being.

9

BECOMING WHOLE

You might remember the Hans Christian Andersen story "The Ugly Duckling." An unusual-looking hatchling amid baby ducks is mocked and rejected for being bigger, clumsier, and different from the rest. He spends seasons wandering alone, trying to belong, until one day he sees his reflection in the water and realizes he's not a duck. He's a swan. He didn't fit in because he wasn't meant to; he was becoming something else entirely.

This story mirrors the journey of integration. Many of us are still trying to shrink, edit, or hide the parts of ourselves that once felt rejected. The "ugly duckling" lives inside us as our wounded child who's still questioning their worth and still trying to earn belonging. But healing begins when we stop running from those vulnerable parts and turn toward them with compassion and nurturance. We were never broken; we were only disconnected from who we really are. We're all swans who've been misunderstood.

The reality is, keeping those parts hidden is exhausting, physically, emotionally, and spiritually. Even after we've left our old environment behind, we may still be trying to follow its rules, conforming ourselves to fit a place we've already outgrown. That disconnection drains us, sometimes resulting in burnout and other times numbness. Still, it can feel safer to repeat our past than to risk change.

Integration is the process of becoming whole again by reuniting with the child we once were and allowing the adult we are now to lead. This is the moment we stop performing and start living in truth as the resilient, nurtured, wise adult we are meant to be.

THE PATH TO WHOLENESS

Sasha grew up in a house where strength was survival. Her mother was a single mom who never asked for help, priding herself on doing everything alone. She was tough as nails, sharp-tongued, and fiercely independent. Vulnerability wasn't an option, and needing comfort was treated like weakness. Sasha absorbed the lesson early: Love was something you earned by being strong, competent, and low-maintenance. She became her mother's mirror—resilient, quick-witted, and armored.

In her twenties and thirties, she tore through relationships. She cheated, ghosted, and made dramatic exits, calling it freedom. She told herself she didn't believe in monogamy because she didn't need anyone. But deep down, a small part of her—the little girl who once longed for her mother's attention—was still screaming to be loved without having to earn it. That unhealed longing made closeness feel dangerous. Her inner child carried that fear into every relationship, sabotaging intimacy before it could form, never truly believing it would last.

Eventually, Sasha married Omari, a kind man who gave her space and loved her deeply. For a while, she thought she'd found the perfect balance. But eventually she became restless and started fantasizing about her exes, flirting too much, and distancing herself from her husband. When she had an affair with someone at work, Omari found out. It devastated him. As Sasha watched him sob on the couch, she saw, for the first time, the cost of the strategies she once relied on to survive.

A few days later, she began therapy to reconnect with the part of her that ran from intimacy. That part was still a girl who had learned love was always out of reach, so she stopped reaching. Instead of drowning in shame, Sasha began to understand the armor she'd built around her heart and grieved for the child who never felt safe enough to be vulnerable.

Healing wasn't linear. Sasha and Omari separated, then slowly found their way back together, not to what was, but to something new. Sasha still had wildness in her, but she no longer used it to destroy. Instead, she painted, traveled, and learned how to stay in hard conversations. The rebel in her didn't vanish; it softened, learning to use its fire to serve, to speak, and to stay. Omari eventually forgave her, because he could finally begin to connect with the real, imperfect human in front of him. Together, they began to rebuild a love she never thought she could keep.

Our personalities are like a mosaic made up of parts we've gathered and shaped over time. Each piece holds emotion, memory, and desire. But when certain parts are deemed unworthy, by us or by others, the whole can't function coherently. We become fragmented, people-pleasing, overperforming, trying to earn what we already are.

Carl Jung wrote, "Wholeness is not achieved by cutting off a portion of one's being, but by integration of the contraries." To put it simply, true healing comes not from becoming someone else but from welcoming every part of who we've been. Integration is a spiritual journey that allows us to meet all parts of ourselves with curiosity. It quiets our inner critic, inviting compassion and gradually transforming the way we see both ourselves and everyone around us.

When we don't do this work, our pain doesn't disappear; it leaks out in other ways. A harshly judgmental person often hasn't sat with their own wounds. They might shame others for being needy because they were punished for their own vulnerability. Or mock sensitivity because theirs was never welcomed. Or demand perfection because, deep down, they fear they'll be unlovable without it. A lack of integration can also show up as chronic indecision, with our inner parts pulling us in different directions, or as burnout, when our need for rest gets pushed aside. Or it may appear as codependency, when we silence our own needs to keep the peace or make another person's comfort our responsibility. As you've been learning, these patterns are adaptations, parts of us that learned to protect, perform, or disappear when safety wasn't there. Gaining this awareness helps us disrupt the shame cycle and cultivate the humility that comes from seeing both our strengths and our limitations without judgment. Because, ultimately, integration means acknowledging and accepting all our parts—the fearful, the reactive, the tender—and bringing ourselves into wholeness. This process shows us how messy and human we all are, and in that knowing, we begin to love ourselves and others more honestly and more wholly.

INTEGRATION AND OUR BRAIN

Our brain is made up of different areas, each with a unique role. Our right hemisphere develops first and is involved in emotion, nonverbal processing, and early attachment. It links experience with sensation, and relationship with meaning. Our left hemisphere develops later and specializes in language, logic, and sequential reasoning. It craves coherence—the sense that things fit together logically—and searches for clear causes and explanations. This is called *brain lateralization*, a process where the two hemispheres of our brain develop specialized, but interconnected, roles. When they work together, as an integrated and balanced system, we're better able to understand what we feel and find words for what our body is experiencing.

When all regions of our brain—left and right, top and bottom, front and back—are in communication, we gain coherence. In this state, we can think clearly, feel safely, and respond with awareness. When trauma occurs, especially in early life, our right brain's capacity to integrate emotion with narrative often goes offline. As a result, we may experience overwhelming feelings we can't explain or memories we can't access with words. When logic and emotion become disconnected, our thoughts and feelings no longer communicate effectively. We don't just remember the past; we relive it, reacting without knowing why, trapped in patterns we can't explain. Integration happens when we allow different parts of our experience—mind, body, memory, emotion—to speak to one another. This creates steadiness and builds self-understanding, helping create coherence. Then we can rewrite the narrative and rewire the neural pathways that carry it. A memory that once overwhelmed us can be remembered with less reactivity. A part of ourselves we once rejected becomes incorporated into our story with compassion instead of shame.

Because integration is an energetic process, coherence restores harmony across our entire being. This inner rhythm between logic and emotion and thought and sensation reflects a deeper polarity that lives within all of us. In Eastern philosophy, these are known as *yin* and *yang*, or complementary forces that influence our energy, nervous system, and way of being. Yin is the energy of rest, emotion, and receptivity. It aligns with softness, stillness, and our parasympathetic nervous system's capacity to restore, repair, and regulate ourselves. Yang is the energy of action, direction, and protection. It fuels boundary-setting, movement, and our sympathetic drive to assert or defend ourselves. When we grow up in environments where one of these energies is shamed, neglected, or overdeveloped, imbalance sets in. A child who is punished for needing rest may abandon yin. Another who is discouraged from speaking up may suppress yang. These are nervous system adaptations, survival strategies etched into our body.

Healing means more than processing our past. It means restoring an inner balance between our left and right brain, between doing and being, and between action and surrender. Integration invites us to rest without guilt and act without apology. To feel deeply and speak clearly. To receive love without shrinking. And to assert truth without aggression. This is wholeness—our capacity to notice, hold, and respond to our different parts with presence and compassion.

It is only when we begin to relate to our inner world with curiosity that we stop fighting ourselves. When we bring compassion to our pain, we can soften. And with clarity, we can finally make meaning from the things we've carried. Integration is how we return to ourselves, and to the world, whole.

Before we move on, let's take a moment to turn inward. Like any experience, integration begins in our body. This next practice invites you to explore your own energetic patterns through the lens of yin and yang. You'll begin to notice where old conditioning has shaped your inner rhythms and gently open space for a new kind of balance.

PRACTICE
ENERGY BALANCE

This guided reflection helps you look at how your balance of energy—between doing and being, strength and softness—was influenced by your past experiences. This practice will help you trace where your patterns began, so that you can better understand why you lean toward one side more than the other and take small steps to restore a sense of harmony within yourself.

1. **Tune In.** Find a quiet space where you can sit or lie comfortably. Take a few slow, grounding breaths. Place one hand on your chest and the other on your belly, noticing the rise and fall of your breath. Ask yourself:

    ◁ When do I feel most at ease—during stillness or in movement?
    ◁ Which energy do I tend to over-rely on: the *doing* (yang) or the *being* (yin)?
    ◁ Which energy feels harder to access, and what memories or beliefs might be connected to that?

2. **Trace the Roots.** Take a few moments to explore the prompts below, writing your responses in a notebook or journal:

    ◁ How were rest, softness, and emotion treated in my family when I was a child?
    ◁ How were action, anger, or assertiveness handled?
    ◁ Was there space for me to embody both vulnerability *and* strength?

3. **Embody the Opposite.** Choose one small act today that expresses the yin and yang energy you usually suppress. Examples: *If you tend to overdo (yang), take ten quiet minutes to rest, feel, or simply be. If you tend to over-yield (yin), speak a truth, set a boundary, or take a direct action you've been avoiding.*

4. **Notice What Arises.** As you move through this practice, pay attention to your sensations, emotions, and thoughts. Let your awareness be open and curious rather than controlling or judgmental. Ask yourself: *What does it feel like to touch the part of me I usually hide?*

Integration begins when we stop fighting against ourselves and start listening to the stories that shaped us. Once we can see the beliefs and narratives we've carried, we can begin to rewrite them with compassion and choice. To do that, we also need to understand how old wounds live in us today.

INTEGRATING THE WOUNDS OF THE PAST

Trauma overwhelms our nervous system's ability to cope with what we're experiencing. When we're unable to act, escape, or make sense of what's happening, our experience becomes fragmented. Instead of being stored as a coherent story, it's held in scattered pieces as sensory flashes, emotional surges, or bodily imprints. You may not recall what happened in detail, but your body remembers how it felt. And instead of forming a clear cause-and-effect story, our brain often builds protective patterns. Rather than thinking, *I was bullied in middle school, and that's why I fear rejection*, our trauma might show up more subtly: *I just don't like being around new people.* Our nervous system uses language, sensation, avoidance, and instinct. Left unprocessed, past pain doesn't stay in the past. It influences how we move through the present, how we protect ourselves, and what we believe we're capable of receiving.

To heal, we need to rebuild a sense of safety and agency, both internally and relationally. This means helping our body release stored tension, guiding our mind back into the present, and reclaiming our capacity to respond rather than react. These shifts can be subtle, and they unfold in three essential stages:

Somatic Work: Restoring Safety Through Our Body

Healing begins with our body. When we're overwhelmed, our nervous system can shift into survival states—fight, flight, freeze, fawn, or flop. Somatic practices teach us to recognize these states and gently guide our body back to regulation by developing tools for presence, safety, and grounded connection. This might mean learning to breathe more deeply, to track sensation, or to move in ways that release held tension. As our body becomes a safer place to inhabit, we expand our capacity to feel without being emotionally flooded.

Narrative Reframing: Making Sense of What Happened

Healing also requires us to understand our story in a new way. When we go through something scary or overwhelming, it can make us feel split into two, as though the thinking part of us and the feeling part of us aren't working together. The left side of our brain helps us tell stories and make sense of things. The right side holds our emotions, body feelings, and memories. But during trauma, those two parts stop sharing information. When that bridge breaks, the story of what happened becomes disjointed. We may feel strong emotions with no clear origin or recall events without any felt sense of their impact on us. To truly heal, we must reconnect these parts so that we can understand and feel at the same time.

When our earliest caregivers couldn't help us make sense of what we felt or experienced, our inner world became fragmented. The stories we tell ourselves, and later tell others, grow out of these early attachment patterns. Each attachment style shapes how coherent, emotional, or confusing our stories become. As a result:

- ⊲ People with dismissive attachment might tell stories that sound flat or dry, sharing the facts but with little emotion.

- ⊲ People with anxious attachment might tell stories that feel rushed or all over the place, with lots of details and intense emotions.

- ⊲ People with disorganized attachment might tell stories that come across as confusing or contradictory, with sudden shifts in feeling or thought.

These communication styles reflect how our brain attempted to organize our experience without the safety and co-regulation needed to do so effectively. Attachment research shows that coherent storytelling is a hallmark of secure connection. In healthy families, caregivers help children create internal narratives that weave together emotion, memory, and meaning. This co-constructed storytelling builds a stable sense of identity and fosters resilience. As Dan Siegel writes, narrative coherence is the foundation of psychological integration. And as Peter Levine reminds us, storytelling is more than insight; it's a biological process. When we name what we feel and place it in a meaningful timeline, we don't just understand ourselves better; we regulate our nervous system in the process. Research shows that attuned back-and-forth conversation—calm and steady tone,[1] feeling language, narrative,[2] and shared attention[3]—directly supports brain development,[4] emotional regulation, and secure connection.

Insight is only the beginning. Healing requires action through small, intentional steps that help us embody what we've remembered and begun to integrate.

BECOMING WHO WE WERE MEANT TO BE

Integration is about incorporating what we want to take back. As we face and process our pain and give it new meaning, we begin to live differently. This final stage involves taking action with intention, engaging in activities that reflect our truth, and building connections rooted in authenticity. Whether through creativity, movement, rest, or relationship, we reinhabit our life as a whole person who is not ruled by trauma but led by clarity. These small, embodied shifts are acts of reclamation.

Integration means weaving together insight and action, past and present, body and mind. It's an ongoing process that never really ends. It asks us not just to know our story but to meet it with compassion and rewrite it with intentional choice. The patterns we carry began somewhere. And when we trace them back with honesty and care, we create space for something new. This process begins by noticing the old stories as they arise and giving your body a new script to follow.

PRACTICE
REWIRING YOUR INNER NARRATIVE

The stories we carry show up in our bodies as reactions, defenses, and survival strategies. This practice is about noticing the moment your old story takes over and practicing a different way of responding so your body learns something new.

1. **Catch the Story in Motion.** Think of a recent time you felt triggered, reactive, or shut down. Instead of focusing only on the thought, remember what happened in your body: Did your chest tighten? Did your breath shorten? Did you feel frozen, restless, or like running away?

2. **Name the Old Narrative.** Ask yourself: *What story was I telling myself in that moment?* Examples: *I'm failing. No one cares. I have to handle this alone.* Write it down briefly.

3. **Pause and Regulate.** Place a hand on your chest or belly. Take three slow, deep breaths, lengthening the exhale. Let your shoulders soften. Remind your nervous system: *I am safe now.*

4. **Picture the New Possibility.** Without forcing words, imagine what it would look and feel like to respond differently next time.
    - If your old story made you shrink, picture yourself standing taller.
    - If it made you lash out, imagine yourself pausing, steady and grounded.
    - If it told you you're alone, imagine reaching for support and feeling met.

5. **Let Your Body Rehearse It.** Move into the posture of this new response—open your chest, stand firmly, or breathe deeply. Let your body try on the new story without needing to make it perfect.

6. **Affirm It with Your Words.** Repeat silently or aloud one simple phrase that fits this new posture. Examples: *I stand tall in who I am. I can pause and stay grounded. I welcome support.*

Each time you rehearse a new response in your body, you loosen the grip of the past and expand your freedom in the present. Next, we'll go deeper into this embodiment practice with a movement-based return to the body.

SOMATIC WORK

When trauma is repeated or overwhelming, our nervous system initiates survival responses. Without the chance to complete these responses, our nervous system can remain stuck in a state of activation. This unresolved energy gets stored in our body, often showing up as chronic anxiety, dissociation, tension, or emotional numbness.

Somatic Experiencing (SE), developed by Peter Levine, is a body-based trauma healing approach that helps our nervous system release this stored survival energy. Rather than revisiting traumatic memories, SE gently guides individuals to tune in to internal sensations, supporting our body in completing the defensive responses that were interrupted. Central to SE is the idea that trauma isn't just what happened but how our body experienced it and whether it had a chance to return to safety. By slowly reestablishing our body's natural rhythm and restoring regulation, SE can ease trauma-related symptoms and rebuild a felt sense of stability, self-trust, and resilience. The goal is embodied vitality, or a return to presence, choice, and ease in our body.

Somatic Healing and Attachment Repair

Somatic healing helps our body complete survival responses that were interrupted or suppressed during moments of overwhelm. These responses often mirror our attachment patterns because early relational wounds imprint directly into our nervous systems.

For example:

- **Anxious attachment** is often linked with a hypervigilant nervous system that's constantly scanning for signs of disconnection and tends toward overactivation and difficulty settling. As somatic release begins, your body may finally soften—breathing deepens, shoulders drop, and tears or yawns may arise as stored adrenaline releases and your system learns that calm can be safe.

- **Avoidant attachment** tends to involve a collapsed or frozen response, numbing sensation and emotion in an effort to stay self-reliant. As reactivation begins, your body may tremble, stretch, or feel emotion returning in waves—signs that your system is thawing and reconnecting with previously suppressed emotions like grief, longing, or need.

These physical signs—twitches, tears, shakes—are signs that your body is finishing what it couldn't before. This is how somatic healing works: It helps connect old pain with new safety, and it helps us move from survival alone into healthy connection with ourselves and others.

Somatic Activation and Flow Movement

While Somatic Experiencing focuses on resolving trauma by increasing our awareness of our internal sensations and completing our survival responses, Somatic Activation and Flow Movement offers a complementary approach. This practice uses mindful, fluid movement to deepen body awareness and support nervous system regulation not by revisiting past trauma but by inviting our body into present-moment coherence. Unlike exercise routines that focus on form or outcomes, somatic activation emphasizes how movement feels, not how it looks. Through slow, intentional motion, we learn to track breath, tension, and subtle shifts in sensation. This helps enhance our ability to sense what's happening inside our body, which is essential for self-regulation.

Somatic activation can help release chronic muscular tension, improve posture and alignment, and increase access to a "flow state," where our movement feels effortless and integrated. Research shows that body-based practices like this can reduce stress, enhance proprioception (body position awareness), and support emotional resilience.

But insight alone is not integration. To truly heal, we must fully return to our body—the place where our history is held and where transformation takes root.

PRACTICE
A RELATIONSHIP WITH YOUR BODY

When trauma fragments our sense of safety, our body often bears the weight of what our mind cannot hold. Integration is not a single moment; it's a series of returns. Breath by breath and step by step. You don't need to execute each movement perfectly; the goal is to notice how you feel while doing it so you can rebuild a relationship with your body in real time. These movements help restore your inner rhythm and awaken what has long been silenced.

Each practice in this series supports a different aspect of reintegration, calming your nervous system, building resilience, and reclaiming your right to move, feel, and exist in your body with safety and sovereignty.

The Butterfly Hug. After trauma, our nervous system becomes overprotective, wired for danger even in safe spaces. The Butterfly Hug, developed by EMDR pioneers Lucina Artigas and Ignacio Jarero, uses bilateral stimulation to regulate our nervous system and reintroduce the possibility of calm. In this practice, you gently signal to your body that it's safe to settle.

- Sit upright, grounding through your seat, letting your spine lengthen gently.
- Close your eyes or soften your gaze, taking three slow, deep belly breaths.
- Cross your arms so that each hand rests on the opposite collarbone, thumbs touching, fingers splayed like butterfly wings.
- Begin to slowly and gently tap: left, right, left, right, like a heartbeat.
- Continue for at least eight full rounds, letting your breath stay soft and even and noticing any sensations, emotions, or memories that arise.
- Pause and notice if anything has shifted. Continue tapping as needed.

As you reconnect with the rhythm of regulation, you may find yourself ready to move deeper in your exploration.

Thaw Your Freeze. Trauma is both the story of what happened, and what never finished. This somatic sequence invites your body back into motion, honoring what's been held and helping it gently let go and reawaken your body's natural flow. When your body regains full mobility, it sends a powerful signal of safety to your nervous system. The following practices can be done while standing, sitting, or lying down.

- **Circular Movements:** Begin by slowly circling your wrists. Then your shoulders, hips, ankles. Move at a slow pace without rushing, focusing on fluid motion, like you're gently stirring still water.
- **Pendulation:** Tune in to your body. Find a sensation of tension or activation. Then find one of ease or neutrality. Gently move your

attention back and forth between the two. This trains our nervous system in flexibility and resilience.

- ◁ **Orienting:** Let your eyes wander. Name three things you see. Then three sounds. Then three sensations. This grounds you in the here and now.
- ◁ **Bilateral Sound or Tap:** Listen to alternating audio tones or tap your thighs rhythmically, left then right. Just relax and let your mind drift, your thoughts floating like you're daydreaming.

Once you've reclaimed subtle movement, you may notice an urge to move more fully. The next practice invites you to embody what cannot be said, through dance and intuitive expression.

Moving What Words Can't Access. Some feelings are hard to explain with words. They live in our bodies. This practice helps you express those feelings through movement and breath. Remember, it doesn't matter what it looks like; what matters is how it feels.

- ◁ **Grounding Stomp:** Feel your feet land solidly on the ground with each stomp, reminding yourself: *I am here.*
- ◁ **Flowing Waves:** Let your arms move like waves in the ocean, smooth and gentle. Keep them moving without stopping. As you move, imagine your feelings riding on the waves and leaving your body.
- ◁ **Breath-Centered Dance:** Breathe in as you raise your arms or body up. Breathe out as you lower down. Keep moving with your breath, slowly and naturally, letting your breath lead the way.
- ◁ **Restorative Touch.** Move slowly and gently. Use your hands to touch parts of your body that you usually ignore, like your shoulders, belly, or legs. Imagine sending kindness and care to each place you touch.

Synchronizing Your Body and Brain. Integration happens in our bodies and our brains. When both sides of your brain work together, and your body moves across the middle (like reaching your left hand to your right side), your nervous system starts to feel more balanced. It's like the grown-up version of learning to crawl before you walk. These movements help your body and brain work as a team so you can feel more present.

- **Cross-Crawl March:** Stand up tall. Slowly march in place. Bring your left elbow to your right knee, then your right elbow to your left knee. Keep a steady rhythm. Breathe in and out as you move.
- **Add Music or Words:** Try doing the cross-crawl while listening to calm music or saying kind words to yourself, like "I am safe" or "I am strong." This can turn the movement into a calming routine.
- **Finish with Stillness:** Place your hands on your heart. Take a deep breath and say aloud or silently: *I am here. I am whole. I am home.*

Each of these practices is a way to come back to yourself. Some days, moving your body might feel easy. Other days, just showing up is more than enough. Trust your body's pace. It knows how to guide you home. Healing may not always feel like progress, but every step, even the messy ones, is part of the path forward.

These small rituals are reminders that you're learning to feel safe in your body again. Healing doesn't erase what happened in the past. But it can help you carry your story with less fear, more peace, and more trust in yourself.

FAMILY STORIES AND SECRETS

As we return to our bodies, we start to notice the stories we inherited. Family stories—communicated in words, actions, and even in the quiet moments when nothing was said at all—influence how we understand our past and anticipate our future. They guide how we relate, behave, and belong. Some families define themselves by what they've overcome. Others by how they innovate, create, or preserve what matters most. These stories, retold across holidays, hardships, or daily conversations, become the scaffolding for how we see ourselves. The story of a mother who left everything behind to create a new life in another country. The memory of siblings pulling together to keep the family afloat during scarce years. Over time, these narratives shape values, identity, and belonging. When we see where the story started, we can choose what we want to keep and what we want to let go.

But what happens when the most painful stories are silenced? When families experience trauma, especially interpersonal violence, abuse, or major loss, those events are often denied, minimized, or left untold. The result is a fragmented family history. Some children are given false explanations for a parent's absence. Others are left in silence, forced to make sense of what no one will explain. In both cases, secrets distort the family narratives, and silence speaks loudest. Children notice what isn't said. Even without words, trauma is felt in avoided glances, tense rooms, and subjects no one dares bring up. In these moments, they absorb the meaning: *We don't talk about hard things. The truth has no place here. It's safer to stay quiet.*

Over time, silence impacts our brain. When experiences can't be named, shared, or made sense of, they remain unprocessed. This lack of integration often leads to fragmented or repressed memories. When families deny, dismiss, or rewrite the truth to protect themselves, confusion deepens. Children absorb what's never spoken, carrying burdens without language or validation. As a result, patterns like scapegoating, emotional numbing, and disconnection emerge as adaptive strategies in unsafe environments that become costly over time. These distortions reshape our identity, narrow our emotional range, and define what we believe we're allowed to feel.

But when families can tell the truth—honestly, compassionately, and coherently—everything can change.

Family stories, when told truthfully, can become tools for resilience. Remember in chapter 4, when we talked about the stress response found in descendants of those who survived the Dutch Hunger Winter? Imagine growing up with a family story about how your ancestors had suffered but also summoned the resourcefulness to survive. These kinds of narratives create emotional continuity, allowing people to draw strength from shared experience when facing adversity. They offer a lifeline: *You're not alone. You're part of something greater. And this is how we survive.* Research even shows that adolescents who know the details of their family history, especially when those stories include struggle, tend to have higher self-esteem, stronger emotional regulation, and lower anxiety. When children understand where they come from, they feel more grounded in who they are.

Telling the truth, especially about painful histories, disrupts cycles of inherited shame, silence, and disconnection. When trauma is confronted rather than denied, families can build a more coherent narrative that fosters identity as well as connection to something larger than oneself.

Yet, trauma can make it hard to tell our story. In families where pain hasn't been shared or understood, stories are often incomplete or distorted. Some people talk about what happened with no feelings at all, while others share in a way that feels confusing or overwhelming. Our body and brain don't know how to tell the story. As trauma expert Bessel van der Kolk explains, when trauma isn't healed, people struggle to handle emotions, connect with others, or speak clearly about what they feel.[5] Our body holds on to what the family never says out loud. And when no one names the truth, families often create false stories to explain the pain—stories that blame, deny, or distract.

This creates generational patterns of avoidance and emotional disconnection. When family trauma is minimized or reframed to fit an idealized version of the family, it can prevent individuals from fully processing, understanding, and integrating their emotional experiences.[6]

Maya's story shows how these unspoken rules take root in a child's body and mind. Her mother was only a teenager when Maya was born, so Maya was primarily raised by her grandmother. She had vivid childhood memories of reaching for her grandmother's hand in the middle of crowded grocery stores, only to feel it subtly pull away. At night, when nightmares woke her, her grandmother told her to stop being so dramatic. Slowly, Maya came to the only conclusion that made sense to her young mind: She was too needy. So, she began to shrink herself, apologizing for her feelings, smiling even when she was hurting, and reaching out only when it felt "safe." It worked. Her grandmother's sharp reprimands faded, replaced by praise for her maturity. What Maya didn't know then was that she wasn't becoming mature; she was becoming invisible. She was confusing emotional suppression with strength.

As an adult, Maya repeated the same patterns. In relationships, she tried to be easy, low-maintenance, unbothered. When she needed comfort, she swallowed it down. And when someone pulled away, she assumed it was her fault for being too much, too emotional, too needy.

She thought this was just her personality. But it wasn't; it was a survival strategy learned in childhood. Her nervous system carried the lesson, shaping her thoughts: *You're too emotional. If you have needs, you'll be rejected. Don't get too close.*

Maya wasn't someone without needs; she was someone who had adapted when those needs weren't met. But now, it was time to find her voice. Maya's healing began when someone finally said, "That makes sense." It made sense that she feared being too much because as a child, her emotions made people pull away. Her therapist didn't pull away. She leaned in. Maya grieved the attunement she never had. Slowly, she reframed her fear. Her sensitivity was never the problem. The problem was no one taught her how to feel safe enough to feel. She started reparenting herself, journaling, crying without shame, surrounding herself with people who valued her depth. One day, she told a partner, "When there's silence a part of me feels like I upset you." And instead of rejection, she was met with care. Her nervous system calmed. A new narrative emerged: *My needs are valid. I am worthy of being heard and held. I can show up fully and still be loved.*

What Maya experienced in her own healing is what families, too, must face on a larger scale. When painful events are silenced, denied, or rewritten, families lose both a truthful account of what happened and their ability to feel honestly. These distortions set the rules of emotional life: what's acceptable, what's dangerous, and what must remain hidden. True healing begins when we name what was hidden, feel what was forbidden, and begin to rewrite the story on our own terms.

But healing doesn't stop there. To fully reclaim ourselves, we also have to look at who we became in response to these family rules—the parts of us that adapted, performed, and protected. This is where our ego comes in.

OUR EGO AND OUR IDENTITY

Our ego is our learned sense of self, created by our early experiences, emotional memories, and survival strategies. As children, we interpret everything through an egocentric lens—meaning we believe everything that happens is somehow about us. When a parent is irritable or emotionally unavailable, we don't yet understand context, so we assume we're to blame. This way of thinking is a normal part of development, and it makes us highly sensitive to relational cues. In these early years, our nervous systems are wiring themselves around one core question: *What do I need to be in order to stay connected to those around me?* We're not just learning rules; we're learning roles, and we begin to adapt based on the reactions of those we depend on. This is how our ego starts to form: as a bridge between our inner world and the outer demands of safety, approval, and belonging.

Ideally, caregivers help us navigate this growing tension between who we are and who we think we need to be. And this guidance doesn't happen through words alone; it's relational. When a child acts out or disrupts their connection, a secure caregiver responds not with shame but with regulation. They name the behavior while affirming the child's inherent worth. Over time, these moments of rupture and repair help the child feel safe enough to bring all parts of themselves into their relationships. They learn that their emotions are tolerable, their mistakes are workable, and all parts of them are welcome. But when that process is interrupted—when a child's feelings or self-expression are met with shame, dismissal, or punishment instead of understanding—the child often creates a rigid ego ideal to manage the discomfort. They develop an internal image of who they believe they *must* be to stay loved, accepted, or safe. Our ego, in this sense, is not vanity; it's armor.

As we grow, our ego attaches to values and identities that once made us feel secure, even if they were built on fear, rejection, or performance. Over time, this false self becomes a kind of cage. The more we identify with it, the more distant we feel from our authentic Self. What once helped us survive now keeps us from fully living.

THE EGO IN ACTION

Recognizing our ego is one thing. But when it gets activated—when we feel misunderstood, rejected, or challenged—it takes over. Suddenly, we're flooded with the urge to defend, withdraw, perform, or prove ourselves. Our nervous system mobilizes, our thoughts race, and old protective patterns take over. This is because our ego is shaped by our conditioning or the roles and defenses we built to stay safe.

Take, for example, someone who learned that expressing anger led to punishment or shame. They might grow up believing they're naturally easygoing or calm. But their composure may be a mask that hides resentment, unmet needs, or the fear of being too much. Similarly, a child who felt invisible may become the helper in every room, not because it brings joy but because their ego learned that being useful was the safest way to feel seen. Over time, these roles fuse with our identity. We forget they were once adaptations, mistaking them for our authentic way of being.

Ego reactivity arises when our conditioned self overrides our intuitive Self. It's the tug-of-war between who we had to become to survive and who we truly are beneath the surface. When our ego feels threatened, it overcompensates, rushing in to guard the most vulnerable parts of us, the ones that once didn't feel safe to be seen. This protection might look like people-pleasing, perfectionism, lashing out, shutting down, or needing constant validation. These are all practiced survival strategies, or ingrained responses to pain. Until we learn to recognize this dynamic, it will continue to impact our relationships, limit our choices, and drain our emotional energy.

These strategies influence how we act and how or what we think. Our ego becomes the voice in our head, repeating the messages we once absorbed as truth. Part of healing is noticing how this voice, formed in childhood, still affects how we see ourselves today. The words of caregivers, teachers, and peers often become our inner dialogue. A child who was told "You always mess things up" may grow into an adult who doubts every decision. While a child who was told "Mistakes are part of learning" grows into an adult whose ego carries a more supportive voice—one that allows room for error without collapsing into shame.

This is the work of integration. The journey back to authenticity is not about erasing our ego but about integrating it. When we stop identifying solely with the self we created to be loved, we begin to reconnect with the Self that was always worthy of love to begin with.

The next practice invites you to slow down, observe, and get curious to soften your ego's grip. When we witness the ego with compassion, we begin to loosen the old roles and reconnect with the being that's been there all along.

PRACTICE
UNHOOKING FROM YOUR FALSE SELF

Your ego is a loyal protector, shaped by fear and repetition. It formed in childhood to shield you from rejection, shame, or vulnerability. But what once protected you may now be limiting you. This practice helps you begin observing your ego with curiosity, creating a gentle separation between your awareness and the patterns that once kept you safe.

1. **Separate from your ego.** Take a moment to acknowledge yourself for showing up with self-awareness, not self-blame. Take a few slow, deep breaths, placing your feet firmly on the ground and feeling the weight of your body on the ground. Repeat aloud or internally: *I am safe, and I choose a new way to experience myself as separate from my ego.*

2. **Track your identity language.** Notice how you complete the sentence *I am . . .* throughout the day. This helps reveal where your ego subtly defines your sense of self.
    - What words, roles, or traits do I keep repeating?
    - Are these based on who I truly am or who I had to be to feel accepted?
    - What am I afraid will happen if I stop being this version of myself?

3. **When you feel triggered, pause and reflect.** Creating space between your reaction and your deeper truth loosens the grip of ego-driven responses. Let each answer come slowly and honestly; there's no rush.

Take a few moments to explore the prompts below, writing your responses in a notebook or journal:

- I am _____.
- I felt _____ when _____.
- My ego tried to protect me from _____.
- What I actually needed was _____.

The moment you see your ego is the moment you're no longer ruled by it. You become the witness, and the witness always has choice.

Deepen Your Practice

- **Somatic check-in.** After each journaling session, ask: *Where do I feel this in my body?*
- **Create a dialogue.** Write a conversation between your ego and your witness self. This builds empathy for the protective part without letting it lead.
- **Daily "ego spotting."** At the end of the day, note one or two moments when your ego showed up and how you responded differently or wish you had.

COMMON EGO SELVES

The ego takes form from deeply rooted stories about our worth, power, and place in the world. Many people carry an inner sense of unworthiness or unlovability, feeling undeserving of love, success, or happiness, or believing they are somehow inadequate compared to others. For some, their ego spins a narrative that they are inherently bad, flawed, or even dangerous, fueling chronic guilt and shame. Others may internalize a sense of powerlessness, feeling at the mercy of life's circumstances with no real agency. This can manifest as a deep mistrust of others, viewing the world through a lens of fear, suspicion, or isolation. On the opposite end, the ego may overcompensate with beliefs like "I have to do it all myself," creating pressure to appear strong, capable, and self-sufficient, often at the cost of vulnerability or receiving support. These beliefs, shaped by early experiences or trauma, function as defense mechanisms, and they shape how we see ourselves and move through the world.

We've talked about coping strategies, but over time, these strategies can solidify into full-blown identities. These *ego selves* are parts of us that stepped forward to manage our pain or keep us safe. Below are some of the most common ego identities and their traits:

The Perfectionist

The Perfectionist is driven by the need to create emotional stability in a tense or unpredictable family system. They discover, often unconsciously, that excelling in school, sports, or appearance earns praise and temporarily eases the tension. In doing so, they become a "trophy child," gaining approval while absorbing the message that performance is the path to peace. They internalize the belief that achievement, image, and constant busyness are what make them lovable. As adults, Perfectionists appear accomplished but feel depleted, struggling to rest or feel satisfied. They often equate self-worth with productivity, fearing failure or disapproval. They're hypersensitive to criticism, are driven to meet impossible standards, and berate themselves for every perceived flaw. They cope by overworking, overscheduling, and pushing themselves to excel across all areas of life to mask their inner self-doubt. To heal, the Perfectionist must separate their worth from performance, learning that love doesn't have to be earned and that honoring their own limits, desires, and truth is enough.

The Scapegoat

The Scapegoat is someone who is repeatedly blamed for problems, regardless of whether they are actually responsible. This identity forms when a child becomes the one who absorbs and reflects the family's unspoken dysfunction. The family projects discomfort, shame, and denied feelings onto them. They may be criticized, punished, or singled out more than their siblings, absorbing the pain others are unwilling to face. Over time, this child internalizes the belief that they are bad, defective, or unworthy of love. As they grow, the Scapegoat often acts out not from defiance but from a desire for truth, connection, and authenticity in a system that demands silence and conformity. Ironically, the Scapegoat is often the most emotionally honest person in the family, refusing to normalize dysfunction. In adulthood, they may feel misunderstood or excluded, drawn to honesty yet fearful of rejection. They may find themselves in relationships where they're blamed or misunderstood, replaying the roles they once held in their family. To heal, the Scapegoat must release the belief that they were the problem so they can begin to own their truth, validate their story, and step out of the family's narrative to reconnect with their authentic Self.

The Soldier

The Soldier develops in environments where emotional expression is discouraged or seen as weakness. This child learns to suppress vulnerability and adopt a mask of stoicism, becoming the strong and dependable one. This strategy helps them survive chaos or trauma, but at the cost of emotional connection. By equating control with safety, they survive chaos but lose connection to their emotional world. In adulthood, Soldiers pride themselves on reliability yet feel uneasy with stillness and fearful of dependence. Despite their outward toughness, they often feel lonely and disconnected. Their inner world is guarded, and asking for help may feel like failure. Suppressing emotions can take a toll in the long term, contributing to anxiety, depression, or burnout. The Soldier heals by redefining strength not as suppression but as the courage to feel, soften, and connect so they can begin to allow vulnerability to become a bridge back to themselves and others.

The Self-Saboteur

The Self-Saboteur emerges when a child learns, often without even realizing it, that success or visibility is unsafe. This identity may develop from early experiences of being unsupported, criticized, or emotionally abandoned. To protect themselves, they begin to associate achievement with exposure or disconnection. As adults, Self-Saboteurs often struggle with procrastination, self-doubt, and fear of success. They may abandon opportunities, deflect praise, or downplay their abilities to avoid disappointment or rejection. On the surface, this looks like self-destructiveness, but underneath, it's an attempt to stay safe from shame or rejection. They may fear that success will isolate them, or that they won't be able to maintain it. Deep down, they carry beliefs like "I don't deserve this" and "If I succeed, I'll lose connection." For the Self-Saboteur, healing begins with challenging those core beliefs, cultivating self-compassion, and building the capacity to tolerate the vulnerability of being seen, chosen, and capable so they can develop trust in their ability to be both visible and safe at the same time.

The Externalizer

The Externalizer copes with inner pain by projecting it outward. They may deflect blame, stir conflict, or dramatize situations as a defense against their own vulnerability. This identity often forms in families where emotions were dismissed, punished, or turned into weapons. By shifting focus to external problems, the Externalizer finds temporary relief from internal discomfort and a fleeting sense of power or validation. But over time, this strategy creates emotional disconnection, perpetuates conflict, and isolates them from true intimacy. Underneath the outward turmoil is often a deep longing to be understood, valued, and emotionally safe. As adults, they may re-create chaos in relationships, blame others when hurt, or overreact to small triggers as a way of managing deep emotional tension. These reactions often mask a fear of powerlessness or rejection. To heal, the Externalizer must redirect their attention inward, learning to sit with difficult emotions, take accountability without self-judgment, and form relationships grounded in empathy, honesty, and mutual care so they can reconnect with the power that this internal safety offers.

The Disconnector

The Disconnector emerges when a child learns that emotions are unsafe—too messy, overwhelming, or unwelcome. This identity often develops in families where feelings were ignored, invalidated, or left unsupported, teaching the child that shutting down was the safest option. To cope, they disconnect, appearing calm and capable on the outside while cutting themselves off from their inner world. Some do this by avoiding and staying busy, caretaking, or distracting themselves. Others by analyzing and retreating into their mind, treating emotions like problems to solve. Both strategies create distance from vulnerability, protecting them from pain but leaving them isolated. As adults, Disconnectors often appear composed and reliable but struggle to feel emotionally alive. They may overanalyze instead of feeling or withdraw when closeness feels unpredictable. Beneath the control is often loneliness and a longing for genuine connection. For the Disconnector, healing begins by turning back toward their emotions and body by slowing down, practicing emotional literacy, and allowing safe vulnerability until feelings shift from threats into gateways of intimacy and connection.

The Loner

Where the Disconnector is physically present but emotionally distant, the Loner chooses solitude as a way to protect themselves from pain. This identity often forms in response to abandonment, betrayal, or emotional inconsistency. They may withdraw as a form of safety, convincing themselves they don't need anyone. But beneath their detachment is a deep longing for connection. The Loner fears being hurt, misunderstood, or let down again, and so they keep their distance. Withdrawal becomes a shield against pain but also against love. In adulthood, Loners value independence yet feel uneasy with intimacy, convincing themselves they don't need anyone while craving closeness. To heal, the Loner must risk forming connections again, slowly and with discernment. They learn to be vulnerable without losing themselves so they can rebuild trust in themselves and others.

The Self-Blamer

The Self-Blamer internalizes everything that goes wrong. In chaotic or critical environments, they learn to take the fall, believing that if they're responsible, they can regain control or prevent further harm. This creates a fragile sense of safety but reinforces shame and self-doubt. The Self-Blamer may struggle to differentiate between healthy accountability and toxic over-responsibility. They become hypervigilant and self-sacrificing, anticipating others' needs to maintain peace. As adults, Self-Blamers often carry chronic guilt and anxiety, apologizing for things beyond their control and taking responsibility for others' moods or outcomes. They over-function in relationships, believing that keeping everyone else calm is the only way to stay safe. To heal, the Self-Blamer must challenge the belief that their worth is tied to fixing others or being responsible by practicing self-compassion, setting boundaries, and adopting a more balanced sense of responsibility.

The Rebel

The Rebel pushes against rules, roles, and expectations, especially when those structures once made them feel small, trapped, or invisible. This identity often forms in reaction to controlling or invalidating environments, where autonomy was not respected. Defiance becomes protection, a way to preserve autonomy when freedom wasn't respected. They may rebel not only against others but also against their own goals—starting strong and then abandoning efforts that feel restrictive. This defiance protects them from vulnerability but can leave them feeling directionless or misunderstood. While their resistance once protected them, it now keeps them stuck. Healing happens as the Rebel begins to differentiate between true autonomy and reactive defiance so they can reclaim their agency and channel their power into aligned, purposeful action.

We've now looked at several of the common ego identities—different masks we wear to stay safe in environments that once felt threatening or invalidating. You may see yourself in one, or a few, of the above examples. You may also notice other patterns or identities in yourself that weren't named here, since our egos can take many different shapes depending on our unique lived experiences. Each identity carries its own strengths and its own costs. But naming these patterns is only the beginning. The real shift happens when we learn how to work with them directly.

WORKING WITH THE EGO

Ego work is the practice of noticing, interrupting, and reshaping the patterns that once kept you safe but now keep you stuck. It's about realizing that the voice in your head—the one that doubts, criticizes, or always tries to keep control—isn't the real you. That voice is your *ego self*, the version of you that formed in childhood to help you survive.

Ego work is about coming home to who you really are. It means paying attention to the thoughts, feelings, and habits that have been running your life and letting go of the ones that no longer help you. Up until now, you've likely been living in ways shaped by your past, your family, or your experiences. You didn't consciously choose those patterns, and they aren't who you truly are because they formed as survival strategies. Ego work gives you the chance to choose differently.

Think of your ego like a guard dog. When you were little, this guard dog barked at every sound, ready to protect you when life felt unsafe. That barking helped you back then. But now, as an adult, you don't need the dog to bark at every noise anymore. If you let your ego run the show, it treats anything new, like setting a boundary, speaking your truth, or trying something different, as if it's dangerous. That's why you might feel defensive, shut down, or stuck in old habits. And when you recognize these reactions don't define you, a new question naturally emerges: *If I'm not just my ego, then who am I really?*

You are the part of yourself that can watch, reflect, and choose. That's your authentic Self, the part that is awake, aware, and capable of change.

So what do you do? You don't get rid of the dog; you train it by:

- **Noticing it:** Witness the voice when it shows up. What does it say? How do you feel in your body?

- **Pausing:** Instead of reacting on autopilot, take a slow, deep breath. Give yourself a moment before you act.

- **Choosing differently:** Ask yourself, *What would my authentic Self—my calm, aware self—want to do here?* Then try that, even in small ways.

Ego work isn't about fighting your ego or destroying it; it's about giving that guard dog a rest so you can live with more choice instead of fear, shifting your energy from guarding to growing.

PRACTICE
EGO WORK

As your body continues to release what it's carrying and relearn safety, the next step is to notice the inner guard—your ego's protective mechanisms formed in childhood to shield you from rejection, shame, or exposure. Back then, it helped you survive. But as adults, those same protective patterns can keep us stuck. This practice helps you notice your ego with curiosity—not blame—so you can separate from old roles and begin choosing who you want to become.

1. **Find a Quiet Space.** Sit comfortably with your feet on the ground. Rest your hands on your lap or over your heart. Close your eyes if it feels safe. Take three slow, deep breaths and silently remind yourself: *I am safe. I am more than my ego.*

2. **Name Your Ego.** Create distance by playfully naming your ego. You might call it *The Controller, The People-Pleaser, The Boss, The Protector,* or another name that fits. Imagine your ego as a character that shows up to keep you safe. Remember, it is only a part of you—not the whole of you.

3. **Notice the Protector.** Bring to mind a recent situation that activated defensiveness, withdrawal, or control. Ask yourself: *What was my ego trying to protect me from? How did it believe it was helping? What am I feeling underneath the reaction?*

4. **Thank and Retrain.** Acknowledge your ego's effort to keep you safe. Then gently remind it: *You helped me survive before. I don't need the same protection now.* Imagine reassuring this part with warmth rather than resistance.

Deepen Your Practice

- **Body Awareness:** Ask yourself, *Where do I sense this protective energy? What happens if I breathe into it?*
- **Reframe:** Replace one self-critical thought with a compassionate one.

The moment you can see your ego is the moment you're no longer ruled by it. You become the witness, and the witness always has choice. Each time you pause and meet your ego with curiosity, you loosen its grip and open space to live from your authentic Self.

PRACTICE
YOUR EGO SELVES

Each ego self was shaped by something real: an unmet need, a painful moment, a survival strategy. This practice helps you gently name the roles you've played, understand how they've tried to help, and begin to relate to them from your wise, grounded Self as parts of you that want care and clarity.

1. **Identify Your Top Three Ego Selves.** You may see parts of yourself in all the ego selves listed above, but start with the few that you relate to most. Read through the list again and ask yourself:

   - Which ones do I recognize most often in myself?
   - Which show up most often in my thoughts, behavior, or relationships?
   - Which feel the most exhausting or automatic?

2. **Map the Origin.** Understanding where these parts come from helps you meet them with compassion instead of shame. For each ego self, take a few moments to explore the prompts below, writing your responses in a notebook or journal:

   - When did this part first start showing up in my life?
   - What was happening in my environment at that time (home, school, relationships)?

- What was this part trying to help me avoid or gain?
- How did it help me survive, succeed, or stay connected?

3. **Name the Cost.** Explore how these ego roles affect your life today. This step helps you recognize the trade-offs of over-identifying with them as well as the ways they may keep you safe but also stuck. Take a few moments to explore the prompts below, writing your responses in a notebook or journal to explore the impact:

    - How does this part limit me today?
    - What does it cost me emotionally, physically, or relationally when it takes over?
    - What truths or parts of me get silenced when this role is in charge?
    - What does it need from me now—reassurance, rest, permission to stop striving?

Deepen Your Practice. Draw or Dialogue:

- Draw your ego self as a character. What does it look like? What's its mood, color, energy? If it had a shape, posture, or expression, what would that be? If it had a voice, what would it sound like? What would it say when it's afraid?
- Dialogue with it. Write a short conversation between your ego self and your wiser Self. Ask it what it's afraid of. Listen to its answers. Respond with kindness and truth.

Each time you meet an ego self with curiosity instead of judgment, you loosen its grip. Over time, these parts begin to soften, making more space for your authentic Self to lead with clarity and care.

OUR SHADOW AND OUR IDENTITY

Like our ego, our shadow is a part of our psyche that lives outside our conscious awareness. It holds all the traits, impulses, emotions, and desires we were told were "too much," "not enough," or simply unacceptable. We all have parts of ourselves we've learned to hide. Stories we think are too dark, too messy, too intense. These parts aren't shameful by nature, but at some point, expressing them made us feel unsafe or unlovable.

The parts we pushed away didn't disappear. They went underground into what psychologist Carl Jung called our *shadow*. Our shadow holds not only what we've been taught to fear or reject, like anger, selfishness, or envy, but also the bright parts we were discouraged from expressing, like creativity, boldness, or vulnerability. Assertiveness, too, often gets cast into the shadow. Especially for those who were praised for being agreeable, quiet, or easygoing, speaking up can feel like betrayal. But honoring your voice isn't selfish—it's an act of self-respect. Because integration also means making space for the part of you that no longer wants to be quiet just to keep the peace.

Many of us have been taught to be likable, to stay "kind," or to take the high road even when your boundaries are being crossed. And while we may have done that with incredible grace, it's come at the cost of self-abandonment. You may have learned to filter truth through softness just to be heard, or to avoid being labeled as "overly sensitive" or "falling short." The cost of silencing your needs is that eventually they return in the form of anger.

Anger, at its core, is simply your body's way of saying: enough. Not all anger is destructive because some can protect us, restoring agency and power by drawing a clear line against harm. It's the boundary that says: *No more, this ends here.* Anger is actually the protective energy that fuels healthy assertiveness, or your ability to express your needs, feelings, and boundaries clearly and respectfully, without silencing or dismissing others. But, for many of us, especially those raised in high-stress environments, anger often got tangled with survival itself. Expressing it threatened our connection or stability, so we either buried it or let it erupt in ways that felt out of our control. Instead of serving as a boundary, anger merged with our stress response, leaving us reactive or shut down rather than empowered.

When anger—or any instinct, like playfulness, sensitivity, or sexuality—gets shamed, punished, or simply ignored, it doesn't vanish. It gets buried, and we continue hiding it, even as adults. This is how the shadow is formed. Though buried, it shows up in our lives in disguised form: in our reactions, our resistance, and our patterns that make no logical sense but feel impossible to break.

You might recognize it in:

- Harsh judgments of others that mirror traits we've disowned
- Emotional reactions that feel out of proportion
- Relationship patterns that seem to repeat themselves
- Persistent feelings of shame, guilt, or self-sabotage
- A tendency to overperform or shrink to gain approval

When we're unaware of our shadow, we often project it onto others. We criticize someone for being arrogant or needy—traits we've rejected in ourselves. Or we might idolize others, placing them on a pedestal while losing touch with our own gifts and talents. This psychological defense, called *projection*, creates inner conflict and keeps us distant from our true Self. Integration begins when we take back these projections. When we stop seeing our reactions as enemies and start viewing them as mirrors.

Take Anna, for example. She's in a group chat with her friend Lexi, who often shares updates about her career success and recent engagement. Every time Lexi posts, Anna feels heat rise in her chest. She vents to another friend, calling Lexi a show-off. But Lexi isn't the real problem. Anna recently went through a painful breakup and feels stuck in her job. Lexi's confidence and milestones reflect the very things Anna longs for. Her irritation is a projection, or an unconscious reaction to parts of herself she hasn't fully acknowledged or allowed. In Anna's case, Lexi's visibility reveals her own hidden desire for connection, confidence, and momentum.

The shadow isn't just what we dislike; it's often what we've been too afraid to claim.

Anna's story is just one example of how the shadow shows up in daily life. Once we notice these reactions, the question becomes: What do we do with them? This is where shadow work comes in.

SHADOW WORK TO INTEGRATE

Shadow work is the practice of turning toward the parts of ourselves we once pushed away so we can finally understand and accept them. Our shadow holds the emotions, instincts, and traits we learned to hide in order to be loved, accepted, or safe, including feelings like anger, jealousy, grief, or even joy and creativity if they were judged or discouraged. These parts don't disappear just because we bury them. Instead, they find other way to express themselves—in our triggers, our overreactions, our judgments of others, or in habits we can't seem to break.

Doing shadow work means saying to these hidden parts: *You belong here too.* Instead of shaming or ignoring them, we listen for their original purpose, or how they once tried to protect us. Meeting these parts with compassion allows us to soften our defenses and see ourselves more clearly. This is integration: the process of weaving all parts of ourselves—light and dark, messy and beautiful—back together so we can live as whole, authentic individuals.

Because when we reject our shadow, we stay fragmented, stuck in cycles of shame and reactivity. But when we welcome it, we find freedom. We stop fighting with ourselves and begin to feel more grounded, more honest, and more able to show up in our relationships with openness and trust.

PRACTICE
SHADOW WORK

Your "shadow" is made of the parts of you that once had to be hidden in order to belong, be accepted, or stay safe. These might include feelings like shame, envy, anger, or grief—emotions that were too big for your environment to hold. So, you buried them. But what we suppress doesn't disappear; it often shows up in our reactions, projections, and patterns. Shadow work is the practice of turning toward those exiled parts with curiosity and compassion so that you can better understand their original purpose.

1. **Notice Your Triggers.** Pay attention to moments when you feel a strong reaction—jealousy, irritation, shame, or judgment. Pause and ask yourself: *What part of me might be getting activated here?*

2. **Identify the Projection.** When you feel critical of another, ask yourself: *Is this something I've disowned in myself?* Often, what we reject—or admire—most in others mirrors something buried within us.

3. **Tune in to Your Body.** Shadows live in your body as much as in your mind. Bring awareness to where your reaction lands—tight jaw, clenched stomach, burning chest. Breathe slowly into that space and notice what begins to shift.

4. **Name the Hidden Part.** Without judgment, give language to what you notice: anger, neediness, tenderness, playfulness, desire. Silently say to yourself: *This is part of me too.*

5. **Cultivate Compassion.** Place a hand on your heart or belly. Say softly: *It makes sense that you felt unsafe back then. I see you now.* Let your body register the safety of being acknowledged instead of exiled.

6. **Choose a New Response.** With awareness, interrupt the old pattern. Instead of snapping, numbing, or withdrawing, try a small new action:

    - Set a boundary.
    - Express a need.
    - Stay present instead of shutting down.

Deepen Your Practice. In your notebook or journal, take a few minutes to explore:

- What hidden part of me surfaced today?
- How has this part tried to protect me?
- In what new way can I meet it with care?

Each time you turn toward your shadow with curiosity and compassion, you transform what once felt dangerous into something you can hold. This is how fragmentation slowly becomes wholeness and exile into true belonging.

Like fitting the last jagged piece into a jigsaw puzzle, integration is about recognizing where the fragmented parts of us have always belonged. We don't become whole by cutting parts off; we become whole by welcoming them home. Integration doesn't erase the past; it changes your relationship to it. The ache becomes information. Our triggers become a doorway. The roles you played loosen their grip, and the Self that was always there steps forward with more clarity, warmth, and choice. From here, belonging is no longer something you earn; it's something you practice, inside your own skin and with the people who can meet you there.

In the next chapter, we'll build on this foundation. We'll explore resilience—how to keep your footing when life wobbles, how to repair when you rupture, and how to return to yourself again and again. Integration gives you your ground. And resilience teaches you how to stand, move, and keep choosing the life that fits the truth of who you are.

10

BUILDING RESILIENCE

Some experiences break us. Others build us. And sometimes, the same experience does both. What determines the outcome is how we meet the moment.

Resilience is our capacity to stay present in our emotions so we can adapt to our changing circumstances. Like the roots of a tree, resilience keeps us steady when life gets stormy. It allows us to stay grounded when we feel shaky. Sometimes resilience means taking the next step, and other times, it means remaining present when everything in us wants to run. It is both action and stillness. And life will always give us chances to practice it.

Elena's moment came when she was laid off without warning. It wasn't just the financial impact of losing her job that impacted Elena; it was that she was completely blindsided. She worked hard, followed the rules, and thought that meant her job was secure. Instead, one day she had a plan and a paycheck, and the next day, everything felt uncertain. Rent, groceries, health insurance—all the basic expenses of life suddenly felt out of reach. She lost her daily routine, her confidence, and her sense of identity. Suddenly, her days felt long and quiet. She felt embarrassed for not working, and every time someone asked what she did for a living, she felt even worse. She pretended everything was fine, but she stopped making plans, stopped texting people back, and gave a tight smile as she said, "I'm just figuring things out." She was still going through the motions, but inside, she felt worn down and lost.

Meanwhile, across town, there was Nina. Same year, same round of layoffs. She couldn't afford therapy at the time, so she checked out books from the library to try to get a handle on her state of mind. She found a podcast on trauma, scribbled her thoughts in a notebook, and joined an online support group. On nights when sleep wouldn't come, she sat with a warm mug cupped in her hands and pressed her feet to the floor, tuning in to simple cues that reminded her body she was safe. She focused on the things she could control—making healthier meals at home, taking walks and stretching her body, and getting the sleep she needed. Three years later, she found herself leading a community workshop on rebuilding after change. She still had bad days, but she was grounded and growing.

Elena and Nina managed the upsetting and often destabilizing experience of job loss very differently. Elena clenched her teeth and tried to power her way through the pain and fear—an understandable response. In Nina, however, we see the process of transformation that can emerge from deep pain. It's not about glorifying trauma or looking for the silver lining. It's about choosing, at our own pace, to build something meaningful from what's left. Trauma may crack us open, but growth is what we choose to create from those cracks. It begins when we stop bracing against life and start leaning into it and shift from asking, "Why did this happen to me?" to "Who do I want to become now?" Both healing and growth require presence, support, and a deep willingness to feel what once felt unbearable, so we can learn to carry it differently.

OUR ROOT SYSTEM

Resilience is shaped by our early experiences and genetic wiring, and, most important, by the meaning we make from what happens to us. Research shows it's a dynamic process, not a fixed trait: Secure attachment, neuroplasticity, spirituality, and belonging all contribute to our ability to adapt and transform through hardship.[1] Even when trauma has left its mark or safety has been scarce, resilience can still be nurtured at any point in life by regulating our nervous system, rebuilding trust in our capacity to cope, and building supportive relationships. In doing so, we remember a deeper truth: We were never meant to carry our struggles alone.

On a neurobiological level, resilience is supported by neuroplasticity. When we navigate manageable stress in a safe environment, our brain produces BDNF (brain-derived neurotrophic factor), which supports the growth and connection of new neurons. This process helps us become more adaptive, emotionally flexible, and better able to return to a regulated state.

When resilience is cultivated, we start to notice a shift. We become more present in our bodies and can feel our feelings without becoming overwhelmed. We begin to:

- Honor physical and emotional limits
- Set healthy boundaries to preserve energy
- Self-regulate and co-regulate when stress arises
- Respond to challenges with flexibility and clarity
- Reconnect to joy and purpose without bypassing pain

Some of us may have been able to build resilience in our attachment relationships, like Avery did. As a child, Avery came home from school in tears, heartbroken after her best friend ended their friendship via text. Her mother could have minimized the pain or jumped to fix it. Instead, she said, "It's okay to feel sad when you lose a friend. That feeling will pass, and we can figure out what to do next." In that moment, Avery was learning how to hold her emotions without collapsing or becoming overwhelmed. This is resilience in action, and this is what builds it. This is also what translates into our ability, as adults, to sit through a tough conversation with a partner without shutting down or running away. It's what allows us to feel hurt without losing our voice, and to keep showing up with honesty even when connection feels fragile.

Resilience isn't built by hardship alone. Joy, play, creativity, and rest are just as vital to our capacity to endure. Research shows that positive emotions lower cortisol levels, increase heart rate variability, and enhance immune function, all physiological signs of a body better equipped to regulate and recover. Psychologist Barbara Fredrickson calls this the "Broaden-and-Build" theory and found that when we feel good, like when we laugh, feel thankful, or experience something beautiful, our minds open. We think more clearly, connect more easily with others, and build inner reserves of strength. These uplifting moments aren't just pleasant; they're essential. They create a foundation of emotional strength we can turn to when challenges arise.

While resilience can grow from what we've overcome, it's also sustained by what restores us: connection, meaning, rest, and joy. It's what steadies us in the middle of a storm. Resilience doesn't erase what happened, but it helps us stay rooted as we face it. And over time, that steadiness creates space for something more. We don't just get through what happened; we become someone new because of it. This is the threshold where survival becomes transformation, and resilience begins to turn into growth.

GROWTH AFTER ADVERSITY

There's a common expression, "What doesn't kill you makes you stronger." And when we've been through something really hard, that can feel frustrating if not infuriating to hear. Our pain is deep and real, and many of us have gone through things we wish never happened. But they did, so the question becomes: What do we do with it now? When we heal from traumatic events, our goal isn't to minimize the pain or to deny the difficult aspects. Rather, we want to reframe the meaning in our lives and integrate these experiences into a future that we choose for ourselves.

Many Eastern traditions have long understood suffering as a potential gateway to awakening, healing, and growth. Modern psychology now supports this wisdom through the concept of Post-Traumatic Growth (PTG), a term coined by psychologists Richard Tedeschi and Lawrence Calhoun at the University of North Carolina at Charlotte. PTG describes the positive psychological changes that can emerge after struggling with trauma or overwhelming life events. In the mid-1990s, their research gave scientific language to what many cultures have known for centuries: that profound adversity, when integrated, can lead to deep inner transformation.

Growth after trauma isn't just an emotional shift; it's also a physiological and relational one. Research on post-traumatic growth highlights a key finding: Our ability to adapt or to stay flexible and emotionally responsive under stress is central to our healing. This kind of adaptability isn't just learned in hardship; it's nurtured through presence, safety, and support. That's why healing practices that center our body, like somatic awareness and nervous system regulation, matter. They give us the tools to stay with ourselves, even when things feel hard. And healing deepens when we're not alone in it. Whether through friendship, family, therapy, or community, we grow best in connection. When someone sees us, truly sees us, we begin to see ourselves differently too. And new versions of ourselves begin to emerge.

While growth might start small, like a feeling in your body or a change in how you connect with others, it can also be noticed, named, and understood. To better understand what this transformation looks like in real life, researchers have developed a framework to track the ways we grow after trauma. It's called the Post-Traumatic Growth Inventory.

POST-TRAUMATIC GROWTH INVENTORY

Studies show that up to 89 percent of trauma survivors report experiencing at least one aspect of growth following a traumatic event.[2] To measure this phenomenon, Tedeschi and Calhoun developed the Post-Traumatic Growth Inventory (PTGI), which researchers often use to assess the extent and nature of PTG. According to their foundational work, growth tends to emerge in five key domains:

- **Personal Strength.** You discover an inner toughness you may not have known you had. After facing something you thought would break you, you realize your own resilience. You become more confident in your ability to endure, adapt, and respond to future challenges.

- **New Possibilities.** Trauma can clear the way for something new. You may find yourself more open to change, more willing to explore different paths, or more curious about life outside the version you once clung to. New relationships, goals, or callings may emerge from the rubble.

- **Relating to Others.** Pain can deepen connection, making many more intentional about the relationships they choose. You might seek out safer, more supportive connections and show up more vulnerably, more honestly, because you know how much it matters.

- **Appreciation of Life.** When you've experienced suffering, small joys, like the sound of laughter, a warm mug, sunlight through leaves, can feel like miracles, helping you become more aware of what really matters and less willing to waste time on what doesn't.

- **Spiritual or Existential Growth.** After trauma, it's common to begin to ask the bigger questions: Who am I? Why am I here? What still matters, even after all I've lost? This kind of growth shows up when a shift in perspective allows you to feel more connected to your values, rooted in meaning beyond the past, and able to trust your own inner truth.

These five domains remind us that healing is about evolution. Growth after trauma often reshapes our values, our connections, and our sense of identity, but these changes rarely arrive with a bang. More often, they feel like small openings and subtle shifts, but are undeniable signs that something is different. These everyday moments matter deeply because they're the first signs that change is happening beneath the surface. Growth after trauma isn't about forgetting what happened or pretending we're "better." It's about allowing something new to emerge in the aftermath. Not in spite of our pain but through it. And it's in the smallest acts that this transformation becomes real:

- Saying, "I'm not ready yet" and meaning it
- Returning a call you've been avoiding
- Feeling anger and not apologizing for it
- Letting someone into your home before it's cleaned up
- Saying no without an explanation

◁ Leaving a text unread to protect your peace

◁ Asking for what you need without assuming it's too much

These seem like small moments, but they are milestones—steady signals that your nervous system is learning safety, your body is reclaiming choice, and your life is aligning with truth. We often overlook them because they don't look like transformation. But this is what real change looks like: a thousand small shifts that slowly stitch you back to yourself.

And beneath those quiet shifts, something even deeper is unfolding. Your brain is changing too. Healing is neurobiological. To understand how these small moments create a lasting transformation, we turn to our brain's remarkable role in making meaning, restoring coherence, and rebuilding our Self.

THE NEUROBIOLOGY OF MEANING-MAKING

Growth after trauma rewires our brain. When we begin to make meaning from what we've lived through, we're actually reorganizing the neural pathways that shape how we feel, think, and relate.

Throughout this book, you've seen how specific brain regions respond to trauma: how our amygdala signals threat, how our hippocampus sorts and stores memory, and how our prefrontal cortex helps us regulate emotion and make conscious choices. In the process of healing, these same areas become central to our growth. Meaning-making activates our Default Mode Network, a system involved in self-reflection, identity, and memory integration. It's what allows us to weave together fragmented experiences into a coherent narrative. When we say, "This is what I've been through, and this is who I'm becoming because of it," we're connecting neural dots between the past and the present. With time, safety, and support, our hippocampus begins to recontextualize trauma. Instead of getting stuck in survival mode based in our past experiences, our brain begins to signal: *That was then, this is now.* The past becomes part of our story, but it no longer defines us. Meanwhile, our prefrontal cortex—our brain's center of regulation and perspective—starts coming back online. As it strengthens, so does our capacity to hold complexity, to stay present with difficult emotions, and to respond instead of react. This is the essence of post-traumatic growth: the emotional and narrative parts of our brain working together again, left and right hemispheres in restored dialogue.

This is why telling the truth of what happened and reclaiming how we tell it can be profoundly healing. Some truths arrive suddenly, with no time to prepare. For Orion, that truth came when they lost their father in a car accident when they were just ten years old. Their whole family was heartbroken. Along with their mother and brothers, Orion had to adjust to life without the warm, steady man who had always been there. Though their mother grieved deeply, she also rose to the occasion by doing her best to help the family mourn and move forward. Still, Orion took it hard. They were anxious and had nightmares. Their mother noticed their moods shifting toward anger and withdrawal. And when Orion turned sixteen, they avoided driving altogether. Their mother suspected this fear was tied to the crash that took their father's life. They couldn't afford therapy, but their mother found a local support group for teens who had lost a parent. In the group, Orion learned mindfulness and meditation to calm their body and stay present. They spoke openly about their grief and started to feel less alone. They volunteered with a friend at a nearby trauma center. Eventually, they began to face their fear of driving by starting with short, supported steps. Over time, Orion's resilience surfaced. By their senior year, they made a promise to themself: They wanted to live a full life, to honor the years their father never got to have. They started asking big questions about life, like what really matters and who they wanted to be. They talked openly with friends and family about their feelings. After college, they traveled to new places, not just for fun but to learn and grow. Even though they still missed their dad terribly, their sadness became part of their strength, and from that pain, they found a new sense of purpose.

Orion's story reminds us that post-traumatic growth doesn't erase suffering. It gives suffering shape and helps us carry the past in ways that move us forward, rather than weighing us down. But growth isn't something we do alone or entirely from scratch. Just as trauma can be passed down, so can strength. Some of our resilience isn't self-made; it's inherited. It lives in the stories, rituals, and survival strategies of those who came before us.

THE STRENGTH WE INHERIT

Even if your family struggled, you inherited more than pain. You inherited power. Trauma may have been passed down like a family heirloom, but so was resilience. Resilience can look like many things:

- A grandmother's stubborn hope
- A song sung to calm babies
- The way someone created beauty with almost nothing
- A morning prayer

Even if you didn't grow up hearing the full stories of your ancestors, their strength is still in you. It might live in the way you hum while cooking, not knowing those same sounds once soothed others before you. The way your hands know how to calm a child, even if no one ever showed you. The way you light a candle when you need clarity. The way you gather people when things fall apart. These traces of strength passed down through time. Some resilience is learned, some is remembered, and some is carried faithfully across generations.

In our earlier discussion of epigenetics (chapter 4), we explored how stress and survival can imprint themselves biologically, shaping which genes are activated or silenced across generations. So, while trauma can be passed down the line, so can strength. Close relationships, cultural rituals, spiritual traditions all leave physiological footprints. When your ancestors danced, prayed, created, resisted, they weren't only surviving. They were shaping nervous system patterns, attachment patterns, and stress responses that you carry today.

Cultural neuroscience builds on this idea, showing that our brains don't develop in isolation. They're shaped by the languages we speak, the values we hold, the stories we're told, and the rituals we repeat. Identity, empathy, and morality are culturally wired patterns. Research confirms that brain processes—like how we see ourselves and how we see others—work differently depending on the culture we grow up in. In some cultures, *self* means mostly *me as an individual*—my goals, my feelings, my choices. In others, *self* means *me as part of a group*—my family, my community, my ancestors. What counts as *other* also changes accordingly. In a group-centered culture, "others" may not feel so separate, because belonging is part of identity. In this way, the world around us literally teaches our brain what *self* and *other* mean.

And because culture shapes how we see ourselves and others, it also shapes what makes us feel safe, connected, and strong. This helps explain why rituals, songs, and traditions hold such power. They regulate stress hormones like cortisol and help wire the brain for safety, empathy, and connection. And science shows us what many cultures have always known: Shared cultural practices like storytelling, music, and ceremony actively shape our brain's emotional circuitry and buffer us against stress.[3]

Seen this way, culture is a tool for healing, teaching us how to feel, how to belong, how to gather after loss, and how to begin again.

So, when you hum while stirring soup, or light a candle like your grandmother did, you're not just honoring memory. You're participating in the biology of resilience. You're reminding your nervous system what safety feels like. You're tapping into a resilience older than your wounds and a knowing deeper than memory. You are not starting from scratch; you are continuing something sacred.

PRACTICE
REMEMBERING WHO YOU ARE

Before we explore what can block our growth, let's first pause and anchor into what already lives within you. This practice is about remembering our power—the enduring strength that's been passed down through survival, creativity, love, and hope.

1. **Settle In.** Find a quiet space where you won't be interrupted. Sit or lie down in a comfortable position. Close your eyes if that feels safe or soften your gaze. Take three slow, deep breaths. Place one hand on your heart and one on your belly. Notice the gentle rise and fall of your breath. Let yourself feel your own presence—steady, warm, alive.

2. **Explore.** Once you feel grounded, bring these questions to mind. You may receive answers as memories, images, sensations, a song, a phrase, or simply a feeling in your body. Let whatever arises be enough:

   - What strength might I have inherited through someone else's survival?
   - Is there a ritual, phrase, instinct, or gesture I carry that echoes someone who came before me?
   - What is one thing, no matter how small, I want to carry forward?

3. **Speak It or Write It.** Let words emerge, either out loud or on paper. You might begin with:

   - I carry more than pain. I carry strength.
   - I carry more than fear. I carry the will to keep going.
   - I carry more than the past. I carry what I choose to plant next.

When you recognize that resilience isn't only something you build but also something you inherit, your story shifts. You begin to see yourself as the continuation of someone else's courage. Yet even with this strength running through us, growth isn't always easy. Old wounds, protective habits, and buried shame can rise up and block the path. To truly move forward, we need to name these barriers and understand how they keep us from trusting the very resilience we already carry.

BARRIERS TO GROWTH

Growth doesn't always follow pain. For many, trauma is followed by silence, shutdown, or self-blame. Understanding what blocks growth is just as vital as understanding what makes it possible. These barriers are signs that your body has been doing exactly what it needed to do to protect you. When we name them, we can begin to bring them into awareness, which makes change possible.

1. *Nervous System Dysregulation.* When your nervous system is stuck in survival mode, your body believes it's still in danger. You might feel constantly on edge, emotionally numb, or reactive without understanding why. In these states of stress response, our emotional brain takes over. Growth requires access to safety. When your body doesn't feel safe, imagining a different future or making meaning from the past becomes nearly impossible because your system is too busy protecting you to allow change.

2. *Lack of Safe Relationships.* Trauma often happens in relationships, and so does healing. If the people around you are emotionally unavailable, dismissive, or unsafe, you may learn to suppress your feelings, question your reality, or fear vulnerability. And when vulnerability feels risky, it's difficult to be honest, let alone heal. Without safe spaces to be seen, heard, and held, healing can feel out of reach. We grow best in secure connection, and when connection is absent, our growth can stall.

3. *Cultural Gaslighting and Toxic Positivity.* We live in a culture that glorifies grit, rushes healing, and romanticizes resilience. Instead of being encouraged to feel, we're told to stay grateful, be strong, or manifest something better. Phrases like "At least it wasn't worse" or "Look on the bright side" can sound like comfort, but they often ignore or minimize our feelings. This is cultural gaslighting, and it teaches us to *perform* strength instead of *build* it. As a result, we hide our sadness, feel bad for being angry, and keep our pain to ourselves. Real growth comes from being allowed to feel all of our emotions fully.

4. *Our Inner Critic and Internalized Shame.* One of the greatest barriers to growth is the deep-rooted belief that you don't deserve to heal. If you've internalized messages that you're too sensitive, too messy, or not enough, the possibility of change can feel out of reach for you. Shame convinces you that your pain is your fault, and your inner critic repeats what others once said, keeping you small, silent, and stuck. These voices often originate in childhood, but they aren't permanent. Healing begins when you question the story. When you remember that your pain is not proof of your brokenness; it's proof of your humanity. And it deserves care.

Naming what gets in the way of your growth honors your reality. The question isn't *Why haven't I healed yet?* It's *What might I need in order to take the next step?* Growth is always possible. When you begin to create safety in your body, surround yourself with people who truly see you, and soften the way you speak to yourself, something begins to shift. First subtly, then steadily, and eventually, unmistakably.

We can't be so focused on growth that we bypass pain in the name of enlightenment. Because sometimes, what looks like rising above is actually just a clever way of avoiding what we don't want to see.

WHEN GROWTH BECOMES ESCAPE

In the world of healing and self-development, some messages sound wise but actually silence our reality. Phrases like "Everything happens for a reason," "No regrets," or "Good vibes only" may come with good intentions, but they can dismiss our pain rather than honor it. This is what psychologists call *spiritual bypassing*: using spiritual ideas or wellness tools to avoid discomfort, grief, trauma, or truth.

Bypassing isn't always obvious. It can look like forgiving before you're ready, forcing gratitude when it doesn't feel real, or trying to meditate away what really needs to be mourned. It's positivity at the expense of honesty. And in trauma recovery, it can become a polished form of dissociation, floating above the wound rather than connecting with it.

Healing requires us to sit with our grief, not skip over it. It doesn't insist everything happens for a reason, holding space for the fact that some things just happen, and they hurt. Real healing requires presence with what is, not just hope for what could be. It is anchored in what psychologists call *radical acceptance*, or the ability to acknowledge reality without judgment, even when it's painful. Radical acceptance reminds us that healing doesn't require erasing the past. It sounds like:

- "This happened. I don't have to like it, but I can name it."
- "I can feel pain and still move forward."
- "Healing is possible even if closure never comes."

We see this in Mira. After leaving an emotionally abusive marriage, she did everything "right." She meditated, journaled, posted affirmations. Her coach encouraged her to "raise her vibration" and not "dwell" on the past. So, she smiled through her sadness, forgave too soon, and avoided talking about the panic attacks that still woke her up at night. Underneath it all, her breath was shallow, her shoulders tight, her grief unspoken. *I must not be healing right,* she thought.

One day, a close friend asked her a transformative question: "What would it feel like to stop fixing yourself?" Something in Mira broke open. Mira realized she hadn't been healing. She had swapped one form of self-abandonment for another: spiritual perfectionism in place of emotional truth. So, she stopped performing. She let herself cry, rage, and walk in silence. She stopped forcing meaning and started feeling. Slowly, she came home to herself by connecting with her pain underneath. Now, her mantra isn't *Let it go*. It's *I can hold what happened and still choose to love myself.*

This is what post-traumatic growth really means. It's about honoring the complexity and pain of what we've lived through and choosing to make something meaningful out of it. For me, that meant facing my deepest fear—loss. Illness and death were constant themes in my family, and aging always felt heavy, almost unsafe. When my mom died, I realized true resilience wasn't about avoiding my pain but showing my inner child that I would always be okay, even when the worst happened. As trauma researcher Janina Fisher notes, healing is not about getting rid of the past; it's about reclaiming the self we had to leave behind to survive it. And as we carry our grief forward, something in us begins to shift. We are no longer who we were before the pain, but we're not defined by the pain either. This is identity transformation.

Next, we'll explore this process of reclamation so that we can retrieve our lost parts, reshape our internal narratives, and reinhabit the fullness of who we are.

PRACTICE
LETTER TO THE SELF WHO ENDURED

There's a version of you that didn't have this wisdom yet. The part of you that walked through fire with instinct, not a map. This practice gives you the chance to speak to them—not with judgment but with love—and let them know they never had to carry it alone.

1. **Choose a Memory.** Bring to mind a moment from your past when you felt broken, scared, unseen, or lost. Let it be one that still feels alive in you.

2. **Write a Letter.** Address yourself at that age or in that moment. You can write from your current self, or even from a future self who's already grown through what you're facing.

3. **Say What Was Needed.** Offer the words you wish you had heard then. Examples: *You were doing your best. You didn't deserve what happened. I'm proud of you for surviving. Here's what I know now . . .*

4. **Let It Be Real.** Don't worry about length or polish. Be honest. Be kind. Write as though you're reaching across time to take your own hand.

You're building a bridge between who you were and who you are becoming. Healing deepens when we reach back with compassion, giving the younger parts of us what they needed but never received. These letters remind us that while we cannot change what happened, we can change how we carry it. Each word is a thread that stitches our past into the present, helping us reclaim pieces of ourselves that were left behind.

RECLAIMING OUR SELVES

Trauma doesn't just leave scars. It reshapes how we see ourselves. It can narrow our world, silence parts of us, or force us into roles we never wanted. Healing asks us to slowly gather those pieces again, to make space for who we've been and who we're still becoming. For Helen, this truth arrived later in life. After being diagnosed with multiple sclerosis in her fifties, her world shrank. Stairs that once felt effortless became mountains and carrying groceries left her trembling. She stopped inviting friends over, too ashamed to ask for help.

One morning, after another night of restless sleep, she noticed an old notebook tucked in the back of a drawer. Almost without thinking, she picked up a pen and began to write. At first her hands shook, but as the words flowed, so did a calm steadiness inside her. The page became a place to speak when words once felt unsafe. She wrote for hours, surprised to find not frustration but release.

She later joined a support group for others living with chronic illness, and for the first time admitted out loud that she was scared and tired of pretending to be fine. No one turned away. Instead, heads nodded, eyes softened. Vulnerability, she realized, wasn't weakness; it was a doorway back to connection. Helen still has hard days, but she no longer sees herself as broken. Illness is part of her story, not the whole of it. Resilience, she learned, isn't about pushing through alone; it's about finding the courage to lean on others.

George's path was a bit different. Raised by strict, emotionally distant parents, he learned early that feelings were distractions. He worked hard, provided for his family, and measured his worth by what he built. When his wife died, the house grew quiet, and yet his regret was even louder than the silence as he constantly thought about decades of unsaid *I love yous* and missed chances for closeness.

In grief groups, George began to do what once felt impossible: speak. At first, his words came slowly, but over time, he shared more, letting others see what he had always kept hidden. With his grandchildren, he practiced presence by listening, telling stories, even letting them see him cry. It felt awkward at first, almost like failure, but over time, it became a new kind of strength. There were no dramatic transformations, no sudden shedding of the past. Just an inner shift that resulted in more openness, more tenderness, and more truth. That was the beginning of George's post-traumatic growth; slow but unmistakably present.

Healing is about giving ourselves permission to be fully who we are, beyond what happened or who we had to be to survive. It's about choosing the story you tell about yourself—not the one written by trauma or survival but the one you want to carry forward.

PRACTICE
THE STORY YOU CHOOSE TO TELL NOW

Life leaves marks. Some are cracks that haven't yet mended, and some are scars that reflect resilience. This practice is about reclaiming your story by choosing what reason you'll give it now. You get to decide what meaning you carry forward.

Part One: Timeline of Growth

1. **Draw Your Timeline.** Open your notebook or journal and draw a horizontal line across the page—this is your life's path.

2. **Mark Key Events.** Identify four to six moments that shifted you: losses, ruptures, transitions, or deep challenges.

3. **Name the Loss.** Beneath each event, write what was lost (safety, innocence, trust, belonging).

4. **Name the Gain.** Above each event, write what was gained, even if it came later (a boundary, truth, strength, new beginning).

5. **Title It.** At the top, write: *The Story I'm Choosing to Tell Now.*

6. **Reflect.** What story does this timeline tell about who you've become? What strengths or wisdom rose from the fracture?

Part Two: Future Story

1. **Imagine Your Future Self.** Picture yourself five years from now living with more freedom, connection, or joy.

2. **Write as If It's Now.** In a few sentences, describe your life as though you are already there. Example: *I wake up feeling grounded. I trust myself to handle what comes. I love and am loved without fear.*

3. **Title Your Story.** Choose a simple phrase that feels true, like *Becoming Real, Rooted,* or *Homecoming.*

4. **Revisit Weekly.** Read your story out loud once a week. Let it remind you that healing isn't about erasing the past—it's about writing the next chapter.

By rewriting your story, you give yourself the power to live forward instead of being pulled backward. You begin to see that every loss carries its lesson, and every scar holds a reminder that you are still here. And once you've named the story you're choosing now, the next step is to meet the version of you who's already living it. That future self—the one who has grown, softened, and come home to themselves—can serve as both compass and companion.

PRACTICE
BECOMING WHO YOU'VE ALWAYS BEEN

Healing is about returning to the truest version of yourself. This practice invites you to connect with your future self—the part of you who has already healed, integrated, and come home to who you really are. Connecting with this version of you helps strengthen trust in your path and reminds you that the wholeness you seek is already within reach.

1. **Find Stillness.** Sit somewhere quiet and close your eyes. Take three slow, deep breaths. Let your body soften.

2. **Visualize.** Imagine yourself three to five years from now. See this version of you whole, grounded, wise. Notice how they move, how they rest, how they speak.

3. **Ask for Guidance.** Ask your future self:

   - What do you know now that I don't yet?
   - What have you let go of?
   - What do you do each day to care for yourself?
   - What message do you have for me right now?

4. **Write It Down.** Open your eyes and capture what came to you in your notebook or journal.

Each time you connect with your future self, you strengthen the bridge between where you are and where you're going. And you don't have to wait for your pain to disappear before you begin again.

You, like all humans, are resilient.[4] Not because pain disappears but because you can learn to live with it differently. Growth and grief can, and often do, exist side by side.[5] Even in times of sorrow, moments of awe, laughter, or gratitude can break through. These aren't signs that you're ignoring your pain. They're signs that you're adapting. Research shows that such moments regulate the nervous system, calm stress hormones, and create room for healing.[6] Every smile, every breath of wonder, every connection is proof: Your system knows how to bend without breaking.

This is the essence of true resilience—not constant ease, but flexibility. It's strengthened in safe, attuned relationships that buffer us against life's storms and help us return to ourselves. And this truth holds whether the wound is personal or collective. Across cultures and centuries, stories of survival, ritual, and community echo what research has found: When we have access to safety, agency, and meaningful connection, we don't just endure. We grow.[7]

Our intrinsic need for support begins in childhood, in the presence of steady caregivers who guide and protect us. When that support is missing, we learn to rely on others in uneven ways—or to go without altogether.

Over time, healing teaches us how to rebuild what was absent. Support may still come from others, but it also begins to grow inside us, becoming an inner resource we can return to again and again.

This is what reparenting teaches us: You are not searching for a better version of yourself; you are uncovering the one who has been here all along. The one who knows what you need. The one who is ready now. No matter how heavy your past, no matter how entrenched your patterns, there is something steady and true in you that can always rise and rebuild.

Healing comes in waves. I know this because I've lived it. I grew up navigating near-constant stress, hiding my needs, believing love had to be earned. Those patterns followed me into adulthood. I became the achiever, the fixer, the one who held it together for everyone else. And yet, through this work, I've learned that awareness changes everything. My old habits haven't vanished, but I see them now. I can pause, breathe, and choose differently.

And still, when stress or change comes, my old wounds get activated. I can find myself slipping back into survival—overwhelmed, too vulnerable to ask for help directly. Instead, I overreact. I bulldoze. I overexplain, trying to justify what is really a simple need: to not feel alone. I notice how much easier it feels to ask for practical help—for someone to run an errand for me or to help cook a meal—than to say what I truly want: *Sit with me in my uncertainty; stay beside me in my pain.* When I don't ask clearly, I push away the very people I long to draw close. And that hurts. It leaves me alone with the story I've carried for decades—that I am too much, that my needs are a burden.

But healing makes room for new experiences. On my forty-third birthday, I spent the day with my dad. Instead of pretending I didn't need him, I let myself be supported by his presence. We went to the batting cages and played mini golf—the same things we enjoyed doing together when I was a kid. Nothing dramatic happened, and yet in those ordinary moments, I felt something shift. I let myself be seen, cared for, and supported without having to perform or prove anything. That's reparenting too—allowing love in where I once would have armored up.

This is what resilience looks like in real life. Not the absence of pain but the shortening of the distance between rupture and repair. My refractory period—the time it takes to come back to clarity—used to stretch for weeks. Now it may be a day, or even a few hours. Sometimes, I catch myself in real time. That's the gift of this work. Not that you never get triggered but that you come home to yourself more quickly and more fully each time.

Reparenting isn't something you finish. It's a practice, imperfect and ongoing. As new seasons of life unfold, new parts of you will surface, each asking for attention and care. Return to these pages when you need them. The reflections, the practices, the check-ins will meet you differently each time, because you'll be different each time. That's the work: not becoming someone new but becoming more fully yourself.

You didn't choose your beginning, but you get to shape what comes next. And what comes next doesn't have to be rushed or grand. Small new choices become big changes. A pause becomes a new pattern. A single honest no becomes the foundation of self-trust. A moment of stillness becomes the doorway to freedom.

This is how you step into the life you were always meant to live: not free from wounds but free from being defined by them. Not untouched by pain but unshakable in the truth of who you are.

You are not starting from scratch. You are continuing something sacred. And the next chapter—your chapter—you get to write with clarity, with choice, and with your whole, authentic, resilient Self. Small changes will lead to big shifts, and you'll keep evolving. And if you really pause to take that in, it's absolutely awe-inspiring.

ACKNOWLEDGMENTS

This book was born from the child in me who longed to feel safe, seen, and free, and from every one of you who has ever carried that same longing. Thank you for walking this path of healing alongside me with such courage, curiosity, and heart.

To Dado, my agent, for your steady belief in me and my voice and for your constant guidance. Your unwavering commitment to this vision and your support through every twist of this wild journey have meant more than words can express.

To the entire team at Flatiron, thank you for holding space for this book to become what it needed to be. Julie, four books in, and your clarity, care, and collaborative spirit continue to shape these pages in ways I'm deeply grateful for.

To Hilary, who helped give language and life to the heart of this work. Your ability to see, articulate, and shape what lives between the lines—with enthusiasm, grace, and perseverance, even through the most demanding parts of this journey—brought this work to its fullest expression.

To my team, whose dedication and commitment allow this work to reach more people than I ever could alone. Thank you for standing beside me through every phase of this process.

To my dad, thank you for asking, listening, and offering support through every stage of this book's creation. To my sister, thank you for showing up in the ways our mom couldn't. To little Suzanne, who, I hope, comes to recognize the strength that has always been within her. And to my friends, your belief in me and my message helps me bring it to life.

To Lolly, who has been there through every chapter—long before the words found the page. Thank you for holding this vision with me, for being the first eyes and most trusted voice behind every book, and for offering your clarity and devotion to this mission. Your insight and humor breathe life into this work and remind me when it's time to close the laptop and touch grass. These pages carry your imprint as much as mine.

This book would not exist without the people and the #SelfHealers community who remind me every day that healing is possible. Every story, message, and moment of vulnerability you've shared has shaped this work. You've shown me that reparenting is not only an individual journey but also a shared act of remembering who we are together. You've turned this work into something beyond what I could have imagined, its influence touching both this generation and ones to come.

To my younger self, and to every reader reconnecting with theirs: May you find compassion where there was once criticism, safety where there was once fear, and belonging where there was once shame. May these pages be a hand on your heart as you return to home to your whole and worthy Self.

NOTES

1. BEYOND ATTACHMENT STYLE

1. Frank C. P. van der Horst, *John Bowlby: From Psychoanalysis to Ethology: Unravelling the Roots of Attachment Theory* (Karnac Books, 2011).
2. A. Schindler, "Attachment and Substance Use Disorders—Theoretical Models, Empirical Evidence, and Implications for Treatment," *Frontiers in Psychiatry* 10 (2019): 727; F. A. Thorberg and M. Lyvers, "Attachment in Relation to Affect Regulation and Interpersonal Functioning Among Substance Use Disorder Inpatients," *Addictive Behaviors* 35(5) (2010): 419–26.
3. H. Ran et al., "Impulsivity Mediates the Association Between Parenting Styles and Self-Harm in Chinese Adolescents," *BMC Public Health* 21(332) (2021).

2. YOUR ORIGIN STORY

1. Markus Heinrichs et al., "Oxytocin, Vasopressin, and Human Social Behavior," *Frontiers in Neuroendocrinology* 30(4) (2009): 548–57; Ruth Feldman, "The Neurobiology of Human Attachments," *Trends in Cognitive Sciences* 21(2) (2017): 80–99.
2. David A. Sbarra and Cindy Hazan, "Coregulation, Dysregulation, Self-Regulation: An Integrative Analysis and Empirical Agenda for Understanding Adult Attachment, Dyadic Processes, and Psychopathology," *Self and Identity* 7(5) (2008): 500–28; Stephen W. Porges, *The Polyvagal Theory: Neurophysiological Foundations of Emotions, Attachment, Communication, and Self-Regulation* (W. W. Norton, 2011).
3. Monique C. Pfaltz et al., "Are You Angry at Me? Negative Interpretations of Neutral Facial Expressions Are Linked to Child Maltreatment but Not to Posttraumatic Stress Disorder," *European Journal of Psychotraumatology* 10(1) (2019): 1682929; K. Lira Yoon and Richard E. Zinbarg, "Interpreting Neutral Faces as Threatening Is a Default Mode for Socially Anxious Individuals," *Journal of Abnormal Psychology* 117(3) (2008): 680–85.
4. Benjamin P. Chapman et al., "Emotion Suppression and Mortality Risk over a 12-Year Follow-Up," *Journal of Psychosomatic Research* 75(4) (2013): 381–85; Claudia M. Elsig, "The Dangers of Suppressing Emotions," CALDA Clinics, January 24, 2022.

5. Michael Lee, "The Neurobiology of Childhood Trauma: Insights into Brain Development," National Child Abuse and Child Injury Association, September 11, 2023.
6. Robert R. Greene et al., "Holocaust Survivors: Three Waves of Resilience Research," *Journal of Evidence-Based Social Work* 9(5) (2012): 481–97.

3. THE TRUTH ABOUT STRESS

1. Bonnie M. Vest et al., "Childhood Trauma, Combat Trauma and Substance Use in National Guard and Reserve Soldiers," *Substance Abuse* 39(4) (2018): 452–60.
2. L. Alan Sroufe et al., *The Development of the Person: The Minnesota Study of Risk and Adaptation from Birth to Adulthood* (Guilford Press, 2005).
3. Suzanne C. Segerstrom and Gregory E. Miller, "Psychological Stress and the Human Immune System: A Meta-Analytic Study of Thirty Years of Inquiry," *Psychological Bulletin* 130(4) (2004): 601–30; Mária S. Kopp and János M. Réthelyi, "Where Psychology Meets Physiology: Chronic Stress and Premature Mortality—the Central-Eastern European Health Paradox," *Brain Research Bulletin* 62(5) (2004): 351–67; Bruce S. McEwen and Elizabeth N. Lasley, *The End of Stress as We Know It* (Joseph Henry Press, 2002).
4. Omer Karin et al., "A New Model for the HPA Axis Explains Dysregulation of Stress Hormones on the Timescale of Weeks," *Molecular Systems Biology* 16(7) (2020): e9510; Scott A. Kinlein et al., "Dysregulated Hypothalamic–Pituitary–Adrenal Axis Function Contributes to Altered Endocrine and Neurobehavioral Responses to Acute Stress," *Frontiers in Behavioral Neuroscience* (2015): 9, 83.
5. Jane A. Foster et al., "Stress and the Gut–Brain Axis: Regulation by the Microbiome," *Neurobiology of Stress* 7 (2017): 124–36.
6. Tracey Bear et al., "The Microbiome–Gut–Brain Axis and Resilience to Developing Anxiety or Depression Under Stress," *Microorganisms* 9(4) (2021): 723.
7. Lucy Serpell et al., "The Role of Self-Compassion and Self-Criticism in Binge Eating Behaviour," *Appetite* 144 (2020): 104470.
8. Bruce S. McEwen, "The Neurobiology of Stress: From Serendipity to Clinical Relevance," *Brain Research* 886(1–2) (2000): 172–89.
9. Nicola Barsotti et al., "Impact of Stress, Immunity, and Signals from Endocrine and Nervous System on Fascia," *Frontiers in Bioscience-Elite* 13(1) (2021): 1–36.
10. David Lesondak and Angeli Maun Akey, *Fascia, Function, and Medical Applications* (CRC Press, 2020).
11. Thomas W. Findley and Robert Schleip, *Fascia: The Tensional Network of the Human Body*, 2nd ed. (Elsevier, 2021).
12. Alison M. Slater et al., "Fascia as a Regulatory System in Health and Disease," *Frontiers in Neurology* 15 (2024):1458385.
13. Slater et al., "Fascia as a Regulatory System."
14. S. Khani and J. A. Tayek, "Cortisol Increases Gluconeogenesis in Humans: Its Role in the Metabolic Syndrome," *Clinical Science (London)* 101(6) (2001):

739–47; Boadie W. Dunlop and Andrea Wong, "The Hypothalamic–Pituitary–Adrenal Axis in PTSD: Pathophysiology and Treatment Interventions," *Progress in Neuro-Psychopharmacology and Biological Psychiatry* 89 (2019): 361–79.
15. Martin Picard and Bruce S. McEwen, "Psychological Stress and Mitochondria: A Systematic Review," *Psychosomatic Medicine* 80(2) (2018): 141–53.
16. Firdaus S. Dhabhar, "Effects of Stress on Immune Function: The Good, the Bad, and the Beautiful," *Immunologic Research* 58(2–3) (2014): 193–210.
17. Andrew H. Miller and Charles L. Raison, "The Role of Inflammation in Depression: From Evolutionary Imperative to Modern Treatment Target," *Nature Reviews Immunology* 16(1) (2016): 22–34; Alain Koyama et al., "The Role of Peripheral Inflammatory Markers in Dementia and Alzheimer's Disease: A Meta-Analysis," *Journals of Gerontology Series A: Biological Sciences and Medical Sciences* 68(4) (2012): 433–40.
18. Steven W. Cole et al., "Social Regulation of Gene Expression in Human Leukocytes," *Genome Biology* 8(9) (2007): R189.
19. Perla Kaliman et al., "Rapid Changes in Histone Deacetylases and Inflammatory Gene Expression in Expert Meditators," *Psychoneuroendocrinology* 40 (2014): 96–107.

4. THE TRACES OF YOUR ANCESTORS

1. Tessa J. Roseboom et al., "Hungry in the Womb: What Are the Consequences? Lessons from the Dutch Famine," *Maturitas* 70(2) (2011): 141–45; Rachel Yehuda et al., "Holocaust Exposure Induced Intergenerational Effects on FKBP5 Methylation," *Biological Psychiatry* 80(5) (2016): 372–80.
2. Walter C. Willett, *Eat, Drink, and Be Healthy: The Harvard Medical School Guide to Healthy Eating* (Free Press, 2001); Jeffrey M. Schwartz, *The Mind and the Brain: Neuroplasticity and the Power of Mental Force* (HarperCollins, 2004).
3. Ole A. Andreassen et al., "New Insights from the Last Decade of Research in Psychiatric Genetics: Discoveries, Challenges and Clinical Implications," *World Psychiatry* 22(1) (2023): 4–24.
4. M. Azim Surani, "Reprogramming of Genome Function Through Epigenetic Inheritance," *Nature* 414(6859) (2001): 122–28.
5. Mario F. Fraga et al., "Epigenetic Differences Arise During the Lifetime of Monozygotic Twins," *Proceedings of the National Academy of Sciences* 102(30) (2005): 10604–9.
6. Jordana T. Bell and Tim D. Spector, "A Twin Approach to Unraveling Epigenetics," *Trends in Genetics* 27(3) (2011): 116–25.
7. Carina Dennis, "Epigenetics and Disease: Altered States," *Nature* 421(6924) (2003): 686–88; Aravinda Chakravarti and Peter Little, "Nature, Nurture, and Human Disease," *Nature* 421(6921) (2003): 412–14; Bruce H. Lipton, *The Biology of Belief: Unleashing the Power of Consciousness, Matter, and Miracles* (Mountain of Love/Elite Books, 2003).

8. Kathleen M. Krol et al., "Epigenetic Dynamics in Infancy and the Impact of Maternal Engagement," *Science Advances* 5(10) (2019): eaay0680.
9. Romain Barrès et al., "Acute Exercise Remodels Promoter Methylation in Human Skeletal Muscle," *Cell Metabolism* 15(3) (2012): 405–11.
10. Alexander K. Murashov et al., "Paternal Western Diet Causes Transgenerational Increase in Food Consumption in *Drosophila* with Parallel Alterations in the Offspring Brain Proteome and microRNAs," *FASEB Journal* 37(6) (2023): e22966.
11. Jeffrey R. Bishop et al., "Methylation of FKBP5 and SLC6A4 in Relation to Treatment Response to Mindfulness-Based Stress Reduction for Posttraumatic Stress Disorder," *Frontiers in Psychiatry* 9 (2018): 418.
12. Bas T. Heijmans et al., "Persistent Epigenetic Differences Associated with Prenatal Exposure to Famine in Humans," *Proceedings of the National Academy of Sciences* 105(44) (2008): 17046–49.

5. THE CULTURE THAT SHAPED YOU

1. C. A. Meissner and J. C. Brigham, "Thirty Years of Investigating the Own-Race Bias in Memory for Faces: A Meta-Analytic Review," *Psychology, Public Policy, and Law* 7(1) (2001): 3–35.
2. LaughPillsComedy, *African Kid Sees White Guy, Thinks He's a Ghost*, #51, video (2017), YouTube.
3. P. Mikulincer and P. R. Shaver, "The Attachment Behavioral System in Adulthood: Activation, Psychodynamics, and Interpersonal Processes," in *Advances in Experimental Social Psychology* vol. 35, ed. M. P. Zanna (Academic Press, 2003), 53–152.
4. J. B. Moseley et al., "A Controlled Trial of Arthroscopic Surgery for Osteoarthritis of the Knee," *New England Journal of Medicine* 347(2) (2002): 81–88.
5. Shawn Achor, *Success: You Have the Power to Lead with Positivity*, n.d., shawnachor.com/project/success-you-have-the-power-to-lead-with-positivity.
6. Andrew F. Leuchter et al., "Changes in Brain Function of Depressed Subjects During Treatment with Placebo," *American Journal of Psychiatry* 159(1) (2002): 122–29.

7. THE SHADOW OF SHAME

1. J. Momeñe et al., "Childhood Trauma and Body Dissatisfaction Among Young Adult Women: The Mediating Role of Self-Criticism," *Current Psychology* 42 (2023): 24837–44.
2. Richard J. Davidson and Bruce S. McEwen, "Social Influences on Neuroplasticity: Stress and Interventions to Promote Well-Being," *Nature Neuroscience* 15(5) (2012): 689–95.
3. Daniel J. Siegel, *The Developing Mind: How Relationships and the Brain Interact to Shape Who We Are*, 2nd ed. (Guilford Press, 2012).

4. Nora D. Volkow and Joanna S. Fowler, "Addiction, a Disease of Compulsion and Drive: Involvement of the Orbitofrontal Cortex," *Cerebral Cortex* 10(3) (2000): 318–25; Barry Everitt and Trevor W. Robbins, "Neural Systems of Reinforcement for Drug Addiction: From Actions to Habits to Compulsion," *Nature Neuroscience* 8(11) (2005): 1481–89.
5. Nora D. Volkow et al., "The Neuroscience of Drug Reward and Addiction," *Physiological Reviews* 99(4) (2019): 2115–40; see A. Thomas McLellan et al., "Drug Dependence, a Chronic Medical Illness: Implications for Treatment, Insurance, and Outcomes Evaluation," *Journal of the American Medical Association* 284(13) (2000): 1689–95.
6. George F. Koob and Michel Le Moal, "Addiction and the Brain Antireward System," *Annual Review of Psychology* 59 (2008): 29–53.

8. THE TOTAL HEALING TOOL

1. Jonathan R. L. Schwartz and Thomas Roth, "Neurophysiology of Sleep and Wakefulness: Basic Science and Clinical Implications," *Current Neuropharmacology* 6(4) (2008): 367–78.
2. Britta K. Hölzel et al., "Mindfulness Practice Leads to Increases in Regional Brain Gray Matter Density," *Psychiatry Research: Neuroimaging* 191(1) (2011): 36–43.
3. James J. Gross and Oliver P. John, "Individual Differences in Two Emotion Regulation Processes: Implications for Affect, Relationships, and Well-Being," *Journal of Personality and Social Psychology* 85(2) (2003): 348–62.
4. Stuart Brown, *Play: How It Shapes the Brain, Opens the Imagination, and Invigorates the Soul* (Avery, 2009).

9. BECOMING WHOLE

1. Mele Taumoepeau and Ted Ruffman, "Stepping Stones to Others' Minds: Maternal Talk Relates to Child Mental State Language and Emotion Understanding at 15, 24, and 33 Months," *Child Development* 79(2): (2008): 284–302.
2. Robyn Fivush, "The Development of Autobiographical Memory," *Annual Review of Psychology* 62 (2011): 559–82.
3. Rachel R. Romeo et al., "Beyond the 30-Million-Word Gap: Children's Conversational Exposure Is Associated with Language-Related Brain Function," *Psychological Science* 29(5) (2018): 700–10.
4. Ruth Feldman, "Parent–Infant Synchrony: Biological Foundations and Developmental Outcomes," *Current Directions in Psychological Science* 16(6) (2007): 340–45.
5. Bessel A. van der Kolk, "The Neurobiology of Childhood Trauma and Abuse," *Child and Adolescent Psychiatric Clinics of North America* 12(2) (2003): 293–317.
6. Steve W. Cole et al., "Social Regulation of Gene Expression in Human Leukocytes," *Genome Biology* 8(9) (2005): R189.

10. RESILIENCE

1. Steven M. Southwick and Dennis S. Charney, *Resilience: The Science of Mastering Life's Greatest Challenges* (Cambridge University Press, 2012).
2. Richard G. Tedeschi and Lawrence G. Calhoun, "Posttraumatic Growth," in *Encyclopedia of Mental Health*, 2nd ed., ed. Howard S. Friedman, vol. 3 (Elsevier, 2016), 318–22.
3. Adriana Feder et al., "Psychobiology and Molecular Genetics of Resilience," *Nature Reviews Neuroscience* 10(6) (2009): 446–57.
4. George A. Bonanno, "Loss, Trauma, and Human Resilience: Have We Underestimated the Human Capacity to Thrive After Extremely Aversive Events?," *American Psychologist* 59(1) (2004): 20–28.
5. Vicki S. Helgeson et al., "A Meta-Analytic Review of Benefit Finding and Growth," *Journal of Consulting and Clinical Psychology* 74(5) (2006): 797–816.
6. Michele M. Tugade and Barbara L. Fredrickson, "Resilient Individuals Use Positive Emotions to Bounce Back from Negative Emotional Experiences," *Journal of Personality and Social Psychology* 86(2) (2004): 320–33.
7. World Health Organization, *Building Back Better: Sustainable Mental Health Care After Emergencies* (World Health Organization, 2013).

INDEX

abandonment/distance. *See also* insecure attachment
  parental, 21–22, 24, 32, 42, 44–45, 143, 162, 168, 175–76, 183, *185*, 195, 205, 306, 308, 334
  schema, 22–23
  self-, 65, 201, 212, 226, 249, 260, 307, 309, 314, 332
  wounds, 175–76, *185*
abuse, 117, 162–63, 168, 214
  sexual, 102, 166, 169, 196, 216
  shame from, 191–92, 194, 196
  trauma, 26, 69, 102, 216, 298
ACE questionnaire, 26–27, 120
addiction, 38, 40, 102
  attachment pattern's tie to, 23–26, 212–14
  connection's tie to, 212–14
  shame's tie to, 190, 205, *206*, 207, 209–16
  to stress, 99–101
  types of, 214–16
adrenaline, 96–97, 157, 159–60, 164, 214–15, 293
Adverse Childhood Experiences (ACE) study, 26–27, 120
agency, 75, 148, 169, 304, 337
  and boundaries, 59–61, 181–82, 183
  empathy and, 66, 67–73, 84, 89

  restoring, 218, 228, 281, 289, 309, 314
Age of Genetics, 115
aggression, 69, 203, 287
Ainsworth, Mary, 20
Alexander, Bruce, 213
allostatic load, 98
The American Journal of Play, 272
amygdala, 44, 52, 61, 123, 157, 169, 213, 272, 325
ancestral influences
  on emotional development, 9, 111, 112–29
  on growth post-adversity, 327–29
  practices exploring, 118–19, 126–28
  resilience and, 118–19, 124–26, 298, 327–28
  stress/trauma related to, 112–29, 132, 154, 327–29
anxiety, 192, *206*, 207, 213, 292, 299, 309. *See also* stress
  attachment insecurity and, 20–25, 37–45, 94, 306
  coping strategies and, 2–13
  emotional wounds and, 161, 168, 175, 179, *185*
  epigenetics and, 113, 115, 122–25

anxiety *(continued)*
  stress as root of, 94–96, 103, 105, 108
  trauma's tie to, 31, 121–25
anxious attachment, 21–22, 25–26. *See also* insecure attachment
  integration and, 290, 293
Attachment and Loss trilogy (Bowlby), 20
attachment style(s). *See also* insecure attachment; secure attachment
  addiction's tie to, 23–26, 212–14
  ancestral influences on, 121–22, 124
  beliefs influenced by, 132, 134, 142–46, 154
  ego's tie to, 301–13
  insecure, 17–18, 21–45, 94, 102, 113, 123, 143–44, 179–80, 194, 249, 290, 293, 298–301
  integration and, 289–91, 293–94
  mental health's tie to, 115
  practices exploring, 27–31, 42–43
  secure, 21, 24, 34–35, 50, 94, 143, 272, 290, 301, 320–21
  our shadow's tie to, 314–18
  shame's tie to, 23–25, 29, 32, 176, 191–200, 212–14
  wounds, 19–45, 210, 289–300
attachment theory, 19–22
authenticity, 31, 39, 70, 122, 177
  cultivation of, 43, 73, 74–81, 89, 218, 240, 247–48, 251, 260–70, 282, 291, 301–3, 306, 310, 312, 316, 339
  practices for, 262–70
  shame and, 75–77, 188, 196–204, 216

authoritarian parents, 39, 183–84, *185*, 237–38
autonomic nervous system, 104, 158
autonomy, 39, 47, 89, *185*
  boundaries and, 58–66, 181–82, 237–39, 309
  practices supporting, 62–66, 240–48
avoidance, 18, 37, 43, 121–22, 163–64, 180–82, 188, 202–3, 215–16, 226, 249, 254, 289, 306–8, 313, 324, 326, 331–32
  and avoidant attachment, 21–22, 25–26, 32, 52, 63, 72, 143, 161–62, 193, 198, 200–201, 211–12, 249–51, 293, 298–99
  of conflict, 7, 10, 35, 37–38, 41, 161, 179, 222
  and humiliation wounds, 177–78, *185*, 264
awe, cultivation of, 6, 84–87, 227, 270–71, 273–75, 277–78, 337

Barker, David, 116–17
Barrett, Lisa Feldman, 136
belief systems
  attachment's relation to, 132, 134, 142–46, 154
  brain's role in, 136–40
  confirmation bias in, 145–46
  cultural, 131–49, 154
  ego's, 304–5
  family's influence on, 130, 132–36, 138–44, 146–47
  "normalcy" and, 139, 140–41
  physical impact of, 147–48, 154
  practices exploring, 135–36, 139–40, 146–47
belonging. *See* connection/belonging

biology. *See also* brain; nervous system; physical health
ancestral experiences in our, 112–29
brain lateralization and, 286–91
emotional development and, 26–27, 47–89, 93–111, 112–29, 136–38, 142–48, 153–69, 204–5, 209–16
GBA network and, 98–99
HPA network and, 97–98
negativity bias in, 153–55
physical stress reactions and, 103–11, 123
resilience and, 321–22, 325–27
survival as focus in, 52–53, 153–55, 158–72
The Biology of Belief (Lipton), 117
boundaries, 142, 162, 194–95
brain's rewiring and, 224, 226
emotional development and, 35–36, 38, 41, 61–66, 173, 175, 179, 181–82, 184, *185*, 226, 237–48, 249–51
exploration of, 58–66, 237–48
integration work on, 287–88, 309–10
parental immaturity and, 35–36, 38, 41
resilience and, 321, 335
shadow personalities and, 314–15, 317
types of, 239
Bowlby, John, 19–22
brain. *See also* rewiring of nervous system
belief systems and, 136–40, 148
emotional development/regulation by, 7–8, 19–22, 27, 35, 43–45, 51–53, 61–62, 69–70, 77, 84, 124, 134–40, 144–45, 148, 154–57, 212–13, 221–29, 234, 255, 286–90, 296–300, 321, 325–28, 330
GBA network and, 98–99
habit loop in, 222–23
HPA network and, 97–98
integration process and, 286–91, 296, 298–99
lateralization, 286–91
meaning-making and, 325–28
negativity bias in, 153–55
neuroplasticity in, 44–45, 121, 124, 195, 222, 224, 226, 272, 320–21
reward system of, 213, 216, 222–23, 234
stress's impact on, 93, 95–99, 106–7, 109, 111, 154–72
survival as focus of, 51–53, 153–55, 158–69, 330
brain-body map, 223
brain-derived neurotrophic factor (BDNF), 321
BRCA gene mutation, 115
Broaden-and-Build theory, 321–22

Calhoun, Lawrence, 322–23
cancer, 26, 115–16, 168
Center for Attachment Research, 23
Centers for Disease Control and Prevention (CDC), 26–27
Children's Time Out program, 2
cognitive behavioral therapy (CBT), 125
coherence, 285–86, 289–90, 294, 298–99, 325
compulsive habits, 50, 53, 100, *185*, 209–13

connection/belonging, 5–13
  addiction's tie to, 210, 212–16
  ancestral influences on, 112,
    121–27
  attachment style's impact on,
    17–45, 172–87, *185*
  authenticity's tie to, 74–81, 200,
    202, 216, 218, 226–27, 229–32,
    235–36, 238–41
  autonomy's balance with, 46–66,
    240–45, 248
  culture's role in, 130–49
  to Earth elements, 95
  emotional attunement's tie to,
    67–73, 94, 132–33, 248–59,
    290
  in emotional development, 19–45,
    46–62, 66–89, 172–77, 180,
    183–84, *185*, 222–32, 235–41,
    248–55, 258–80, 290, 337
  emotional wounds and, 8–9,
    172–87, *185*
  integration work on, 261, 283–303,
    306–8, 313–15
  practices supporting, 85–86
  to purpose, 81–89
  reparenting work on, 222–32,
    235–41, 248–55, 258–80
  resilience's tie to, 250–51, 320–24,
    328, 330, 334–37
  shame's tie to, 190–96, 201–6, 210,
    214–18
  social, 94, 95, 109, 116, 124,
    213–14
  stress/trauma and, 94–101, 109,
    298–300
  survival states and, 158–72, 289
  transcendence and, 85, 88–89, 218,
    228, 270–81

controlling behavior, 8, 36–37, 39,
  159, 173, 183, 191, 203, 309
cortisol, 52, 93, 95–98, 106, 108–9,
  113, 157, 160, 234, 321, 328
creativity, 6, 20, 73, 76, 79–85, 88–89,
  227, 237, 250–51, 260–70, 291,
  321–22, 327–28
  play as portal to, 272–73
  stifling of, 195, 314, 316
  stress's impact on, 97–98, 158
criticism
  by inner critic, 55, 184, 187,
    189–91, 193, *197*, 202, 207, 210,
    226–27, 285, 310, 312, 315, 317,
    331
  parental, 24, 37, 44, 64, 71, 75, 102,
    143–44, 168, 176–78, *185*, 188,
    191, 197, 305–6, 308
  shame's connection to, 204–5, 207,
    216–17
  survival responses and, 156, 160,
    168
cultural neuroscience, 327–28
culture
  belief systems in, 131–49, 154
  brain's responses to, 136–40
  and cultural gaslighting, 330
  early life impacts of, 141–42
  "normal" defined by, 139,
    140–41
  parental resources in, 33–34, 40
  practices exploring, 135–36,
    139–40, 146–47
  safety and, 131–34, 137–38,
    141–47
  as shaping factor, 9, 33–35, 37, 41,
    43, 80, 95, 100, 102, 121, 122,
    129, 130–49, 190–91, 221, 272,
    327–30

curiosity
  boundaries as support for, 58–59, 61, 64
  cultivation of, 85, 272–82, 323
  listening/exploring with, 8, 18, 49, 75, 119, 134, 169, 189, 229, 250, 255, 257–58, 272–75, 285, 287–88, 303, 311–13, 317–18
  natural, 5–6, 12, 39, 58, 61–62, 64, 70, 77, 83–85, 229, 261, 268, 272

Default Mode Network (DMN), 84, 136, 325
defensiveness, 35, 168–69, 173, 203, 205, 293, 310–11
deflection, 25, 201–2
depression, 22, 25–26, 148, *206*, 207, 250, 272, 306
  genetic tie to, 113, 115–16, 120
  stress and, 95, 104, 108
diabetes, 26, 113, 115, 125
diet. *See* nutrition/diet
discipline, 39, 81, 141, 143
  positive internal, 59–61, 182, 237–40
disconnected parents, 37, 54, 175–76, *185*, 192, 196. *See also* connection/belonging
The Disconnector ego, 307–8
disorganized attachment, 21–22, 24, 290. *See also* insecure attachment
dissociation, 50, 163, 204, 292, 331
distrust wounds, 174–75, *185*
DNA, 112–13, 115, 117, 119, 120, 125
dopamine, 70, 96, 98, 213, 216, 223, 272
DSM (Diagnostic and Statistical Manual of Mental Disorders), 116
Dutch Hunger Winter, 112, 125, 298

Eastern traditions, 142, 286, 322
eating, as coping strategy, 10, 22, 99, 103, 106–7, 138, 164
  and addiction, 212–16
Eger, Edith, 84–85
ego
  identity's tie to, 271, 300–313
  reactivity, 302–4
  selves, 304–9, 312–13
  working with, 310–13
emotional attunement, 47, 50–53, 57, 59, 93–94, 96, 120, 132–33, 141, *185*, 300, 337. *See also* emotions
  and attachment styles, 20–45
  in developmental sphere, 66, 67–70, 248–60, 290
  practices supporting, 253
  reparenting for, 248–60
  and shame, 192–96, 212–16
emotional development. *See also* attachment style(s); integration of selves; reparenting; Individual Development Model
  ancestral factors in, 9, 111, 112–29, 132, 154, 298–99, 327–29
  attachment's impact on, 17–45
  belief system's tie to, 131–40, 148
  boundary dynamics in, 35–36, 38, 41, 61–66, 173, 175, 179, 181–82, 184, *185*, 226, 237–48, 249–51
  connection's tie to, 19–45, 46–62, 66–89, 172–77, 180, 183–84, *185*, 226, 248–59, 337
  cultural factors in, 130–49
  early theories on, 47–48

emotional development *(continued)*
  emotional wounds stemming from, 3–13, 148–49, 153–57, 167, 172–87, *185*
  Individual Development Model of, 49–89
  integration as tool for, 283–318
  reparenting as tool for, 221–82
  resilience supporting, 319–39
  safety as factor in, 46–81, 86–87, 89, 94, 154–57, 159, 168–69, 172–86, 223–38, 241–71, 281–82
  of shame, 188–218
  stress's impact on, 93–111
  survival responses impacting, 158–72
emotional flooding, 169
emotional immaturity, 34–35, 248–59. *See also* attachment style(s)
  parental patterns associated with, 36–39
  parentification tied to, 39–42, 102, 178–80
emotional maturity, 248–59
emotional memories, 20, 156, 223, 301
emotional parentification, 40–41, 102, 178–80, 194
emotional wounds, 3–13, 148–49, 153–57, 167. *See also* emotional development; shame; wounds, inner-child
  addiction's tie to, 209–16
  practices exploring, 186
  shame as, 187, 190–96
  types of, 172–84, *185*
emotions. *See also* emotional attunement; emotional development
  immune system's tie to, 108–9
  paralysis of, 41
  regulation of, 11, 19–23, 34–38, 41, 50–52, 77, 94–97, 101, 106, 112–13, 115–16, 119, 121, 124–25, 132–33, 143, 148, 158, 176, *185*, 204, 207–9, 212–16, 226, 234, 248–51, 272, 298, 301, 325–26, 328
  suppression of, 74–81
empathy, 35, 52, 158, 191, 307
  agency's connection to, 66, 67–73, 84, 89
  cultivation of, 218, 226–28, 248–59, 281, 304, 328
epigenetics
  methylation patterns and, 117, 125
  physical health's tie to, 112–16, 119–21, 123, 147
  prenatal development and, 112–13, 116, 120, 125
  resilience and, 124–26
  stress responses and, 112–29, 154, 327
Epigenetics, 125
Erikson, Erik, 47–48
escapism, 331–33
exercise, 93, 107, 125, 208, 294
  as coping tool, 10, 142, 202, 215
expectations, 36, 41, 43, 46, 52, 74–75, 78–81, 95, 129, 134, 141–46, 196, 251, 309
exploration
  using boundaries, 58–66, 237–48
  practices supporting, 62–66, 258–59
  of purpose, 81–89
  safety in, 57–66, 81–89, 237–48, 258–59

exposure, unwanted, 178, 196–201, 205, 306–7, 311
The Externalizer ego, 307
external validation, 74, 144, 179, 193, 212–13, 271, 302
  addiction to, 195, 215
eye movement desensitization, 125

faint/flop response state, 158, 164–67
family environment
  ancestral influences on, 112–29
  attachment's tie to, 17–45
  belief systems influenced by, 130, 132–36, 138–44, 146–47
  emotional development and, 1–13, 46–89, 148–49, 153–57, 160–64, 168–69, 172–86, *185*, 188, 190–207, *206*, 210–16, 218, 282–83, 285, 289–318
  stories told in, 297–300
  stress/trauma and, 94, 96, 100–103, 297–300, 305, 306
fascia, 103–5, 123
father hunger, 212
fawn response state, 158, 162–63, 165–67, 240, 289
fight response state, 96–97, 100, 104, 158, 159–60, 163, 165–67, 289
Fisher, Janina, 332
flight response state, 96–97, 100, 104, 158, 160–62, 163, 165–67, 289
flop/faint response state, 158, 164–67, 289
forgiveness, 257–58
Frankl, Viktor, 85
Fredrickson, Barbara, 321
freeze response state, 53, 100–101, 104, 158, 163–64, 165–67, 196, 240, 289

Freud, Sigmund, 157
fulfillment, 4, 82–84, 164
functional freeze response, 100–101, 163–64

GABA, 96, 98
gambling addiction, 212–14
GBA. *See* gut-brain axis
gender variables, 135, 191, 261
genetics, 112–29, 147, 154, 320, 327. *See also* epigenetics
glimmers, 171–72
Gottman, John, 169
growth, post-traumatic
  ancestral ties to, 327–29
  assessment of, 323–25
  barriers to, 330–31
  escape masked as, 331–33
  meaning-making for, 84–85, 320, 322, 324–27, 330, 332, 335, 337
  resilience's tie to, 84–85, 319–37
guilt *vs.* shame, 196–97, *197*
gut, 106, 123
  microbiome, 48, 98–99
gut-brain axis (GBA), 98–99

habit loops, 222–25
The Happiness Advantage (Achor), 148
heart, 50, 93, 104, 234, 273, 321
  disease, 26, 95, 115–16, 125
Hebb's law, 222
helicopter parents, 38–39, 182–83, *185*
hippocampus, 97–98, 157, 325
hoarding, 122, 212, 215
the Holocaust, 84–85

hormones. *See also* stress; *specific hormones*
  GBA network and, 98–99
  HPA network and, 97–98
  stress, 93, 96, 106, 108, 148, 157, 273, 328, 337
HPA. *See* hypothalamic-pituitary-adrenal axis
Human Genome Project, 115
humiliation wounds, 177–78, *185*, 264
hyperarousal, 100, 163, 205
hypo-arousal, 100–101, 205
hypothalamic-pituitary-adrenal (HPA) axis, 97–98
hypothalamus, 61, 97

identity, 297–98, 319, 325, 328
  cultural narratives and, 130–49
  ego's tie to, 271, 300–313
  our shadow's tie to, 314–18
  transformation, 324, 333
imagination, 6, 56, 83, 87
  cultivation of, 260–70, 273, 279
immune system, 48, 52, 75, 98, 108–9, 119, 121, 147–48, 321
Individual Development Model, 9. *See also specific spheres*
  Sphere One of, 49–57, 228–29, 230–37, 281–82
  Sphere Two of, 57–66, 228, 237–48, 281–82
  Sphere Three of, 67–73, 228, 248–60, 281–82
  Sphere Four of, 74–81, 228, 259, 260–70, 281–82
  Sphere Five of, 81–89, 228, 270–82
individuation, 58–66, 218, 228, 281
inflammation, 95, 98, 108–9, 119, 148

injustice wounds, 183–84, *185*
insecure attachment, 94, 113, 123, 143–44, 301
  anxious form of, 21–22, 25–26, 290, 293
  avoidant form of, 21–22, 25–26, 32, 52, 63, 72, 143, 161–62, 193, 198, 200–201, 211–12, 249–51, 293, 298–99
  disorganized form of, 21–22, 24, 290
  due to parental immaturity, 34–39
  due to parental imperfection, 31–34, 298–300
  parentification resulting from, 17–18, 39–42, 102, 178–80, 194
instrumental parentification, 40–41
integration of selves, 8–13, 193–94, 261, 282–84, 336
  and ego/identity, 301–13
  and family stories, 297–300
  narrative coherence in, 286–88, 294, 298–99, 325
  narrative reframing for, 289–92, 297–300, 306, 333
  practices supporting, 287–88, 291–92, 294–97, 303–4, 311–13, 317–18
  and shadow self, 314–18
  via somatic work, 289, 292–97, 304
  trauma-based, 289–97, 320, 322–27, 330–32, 334–35
  wounds and, 289–91, 322
Internal Family Systems (IFS), 193–94
interoception, 229

Jung, Carl, 285, 314

Levine, Peter, 227, 290, 293
limbic system, 51, 61, 69, 156
Lipton, Bruce H., 117, 138
loneliness, 95–96, 109, 210, 214, 306
The Loner ego, 308

major depressive disorder, 104, 148
meaning, 5, 58, 61, 81–83, 88–89, 118, 163, 246, 249, 259–62, 271, 273–75. *See also* purpose
   culture's influence on, 130–31, 134, 138–40
   integration's focus on, 286–87, 290–91
   neurobiology of, 84, 325–27
   post-traumatic need for, 84–85, 320, 322, 324–27, 330, 332, 335, 337
meditation, 108–9, 114, 251, 326, 331
mental health/illness, 38, 40, 147, 157, 190
   attachment style and, 22–27, 115
   GBA network and, 98–99
   genetic role of, 113, 115–16, 120
   HPA network and, 97–98
   immune system's tie to, 108–9
   shame's impact on, 204–9
   stress as factor in, 93–111
   survival responses and, 159–72
   treatments for, 115–16
methylation, 117, 125
mindfulness-based stress reduction (MBSR), 125
Minuchin, Salvador, 40
mirror neurons, 69–70
mother hunger, 212
movement practices, 94, 116, 127, 170–71, 208, 216

developmental, 224, 229, 232, 236–37, 247–48, 250, 258–59, 269–70, 280–81, 292
somatic, 294–97

negativity bias, 153–55
nervous system. *See also* rewiring of nervous system
   addiction and, 213–16
   ancestral influences on, 112–29
   attachment styles and, 19–20, 23–26, 34–35, 44–45, 290, 293, 299–300, 301
   belief formation and, 132–33, 138, 141–43, 146–48
   co-regulation of, 19, 22, 34–35, 96, 132–33, 141, 155, 172, 213, 216, 251, 290, 321
   ego and, 301–2
   emotional attunement and, 61, 69–70
   emotional wounds and, 7, 11, 149, 154–55, 157–75, 178, 186
   integration work on, 286–87, 289–318
   reparenting our, 221–37, 241, 248–51, 254–55, 258–60, 264, 269, 272, 276–78, 282
   resilience and, 296, 320–23, 325–28, 330, 337
   shame and, 195, 200, 204–9, *206*, 217
   stress's impact on, 7, 11, 46–57, 61, 77, 84, 89, 93–111, 112–29, 166–67, 330
   stress states of, 159–72, 289
   substance use's tie to, 23–26
   survival responses by, 7–11, 50–53, 96–97, 100, 104, 134, 138,

nervous system *(continued)*
  survival responses by *(continued)*
      153–55, 158–72, 186, 196, 200, 289, 291–94, 325, 330, 338
neuroception, 154
neuroplasticity, 121, 124, 224, 272, 320–21
  relational, 44–45
"normalcy," concept of, 139, 140–41
nurturance, 227, 283
nutrition/diet, 116–17, 120, 123, 228–29, 235
  stress's relation to, 94, 98–99, 106–7

obesity, 113, 120, 125
OCD, 53. *See also* compulsive habits
operant conditioning, 47
overcompensation, 202, 302, 304
over-permissive parents, 38, 181–82, *185*
over-responsibility wounds, 173–74, 178–80, *185*
oxidative stress, 107–8
OxyContin, 25
oxytocin, 50, 52, 70, 84, 124, 227

pain, 302, 305–8
  addiction's tie to, 210–16
  physical, 10, 94, 97, 103–4, 109, 123, 141–42, 144, 148, 164, 203, 213, 215
  resilience's tie to, 321–39
panic, 2–3, 49–50, 53, 100, 114, 161, 168, 176, 332. *See also* anxiety
parasympathetic nervous system, 84, 97, 159, 287
parentification of children, 17–18, 39–42, 102, 178–80, 194

parents. *See also* attachment style(s); family environment
  attachment styles of, 17–45
  belief systems influenced by, 130, 132–36, 138–44, 146–47
  emotional maturity of, 34–39
  imperfections inherited by, 31–34
  parental patterns of, 36–39
  parentification of children by, 17–18, 39–42, 102, 178–80, 194
  resources/support for, 33–34, 40
peer-like parents, 38, 178–80, *185*
people-pleasing, 7, 10, 41, 94, 135, *185*, 188, 191, 201, 207, 285, 302, 311
The Perfectionist ego, 305
phantom trauma, 122–24
physical health, 95. *See also* biology; *specific diseases*
  addiction and, 212–16
  attachment insecurity's tie to, 22–27, 33–34
  awe's impact on, 273
  belief's impact on, 147–48, 154
  and brain-body map, 223
  caring for, 228–37
  fascia and, 103–5, 123
  GBA network and, 98–99
  genetic influences on, 112–16, 119–21, 123
  gut and, 48, 98–99, 106, 123
  HPA network and, 97–98
  immune system and, 48, 52, 75, 98, 108–9, 119, 121, 147–48, 321
  lying's effect on, 260
  nutrition and, 94, 98–99, 106–7, 116–17, 120, 123, 228–29, 235
  shame's embodiment in, 204–9

stress's tie to, 103–11, 123, 260
survival responses and, 154–55, 158–72
Western *vs.* Eastern views on, 142
Piaget, Jean, 47
pituitary gland, 97–98
placebo effect, 147–48
playfulness, 2, 6, 8, 20, 39, 58, 62, 315
reclaiming, 81–84, 139, 259, 268–69, 271, 272–79, 317, 321, 338
Polyvagal Theory, 158, 167, 171
Porges, Stephen, 132, 154, 158
Post-Traumatic Growth (PTG), 322. *See also* growth, post-traumatic
Inventory (PTGI), 323–25
powerless wounds, 182–83, *185*
prefrontal cortex, 44, 51, 69, 77, 96–98, 148, 156, 169, 213, 272, 325–26
prenatal stress, 112–13, 116, 120, 125
projection, 201–2, 315, 317
psoas muscle, 104–5
psychotherapy, 22, 45, 116, 125, 162, 323, 326
PTSD, 114, 125. *See also* trauma
purpose, 58, 195, 316, 321, 326
awe's tie to, 84–85
connecting to, 81–89, 260–62, 270–74, 278–79
fulfillment's role in, 82–84
practices for, 85–89, 278–79, 317–18

radical acceptance, 322
Rat Park study, 213
reactive parents, 35–37, 41, 174–75, *185*, 249
rebellion, 39, 75, 133, 284
The Rebel ego and, 309

The Rebel ego, 309
rebellion wounds, 173, 181–82, *185*
rejection wounds, 176–77, *185*, 307
shame's tie to, 188–89, 195, 200, 203–4, 217
reparenting, 9, 26, 27–31, 33, 46, 94, 124, 128, 218, 338–39. *See also specific developmental spheres*
daily practices for, 224–25, 276, 281
across developmental spheres, 228–81
five core practices supporting, 226–27
habit loops and, 222–25
rewiring of system in, 221–82
repetition compulsion, 157
reprocessing (EMDR), 125
resilience, 159, 169, 182, 318
activation-recovery cycle building, 97
ancestry and, 118–19, 124–26, 327–29
attachment styles and, 20, 31, 38, 45, 321
emotional, 69–70, 85, 96, 195, 209, 229, 234, 250–51, 272, 277, 294–95, 337
families and, 132, 141, 290, 298–99
meaning-making for, 84–85, 320, 322, 324–27, 330, 332, 335, 337
post-traumatic growth as, 319–37
practices supporting, 328–29, 333, 335–37
reclaiming selves through, 334–39
as root system, 320–22
stress's impact on, 89, 93–111, 234, 293–96

rest, 46–47, 53, 55–57, 80, 95, 103, 107, 109, 129, 133, 179–80, 189, 193–94, 227–30, 280, 285–88, 291, 305, 321–22, 337. *See also* stillness
  practices supporting, 55–56, 231, 234, 236
reticular activating system (RAS), 145
rewiring of nervous system, 11, 43–45, 65, 69, 101, 124–25, 155, 195, 213, 286, 291–92, 295. *See also* reparenting
  during growth, 325–28
  via habit loops, 222–25
  through reparenting, 221–82
rituals, 122, 140, 224–25, 228, 275
  cultural, 130, 138–39, 212, 327–29, 337

safe and social state, 159
safety, 5–13, 283–85
  attachment styles and, 20–21, 24–45
  authenticity and, 75–81
  culture's shaping of, 131–34, 137–38, 141–47
  in emotional development, 46–81, 86–87, 89, 94, 154–57, 159, 168–69, 172–86, 223–38, 241–71, 281–82
  empathy's tie to, 69–70, 73
  in exploration, 57–66, 81–89, 237–48, 258–59
  integration work and, 286, 289–317
  negativity bias and, 153–55
  practices supporting, 54–57
  repair cycle of, 194–95
  reparenting work and, 218, 221–38, 241–52, 255–71, 281–82
  resilience and, 320–25, 328–34, 337
  shame and, 188, 190, 194–95, 200–206, 211–17
  stress responses and, 94, 96–97, 99–107, 109–11, 113–15, 121–29
  survival responses and, 154–55, 158–72
The Scapegoat ego, 305–6
scarcity wounds, 180–81, *185*
Schema Therapy, 22
schizophrenia, 24, 25–26, 113
Schwartz, Richard, 193
scratch therapy, 233
secrecy, 39, 114, 190–91, 198, 203, 297–99
secure attachment, 24, 50, 94, 290, 301, 320–21. *See also* insecure attachment
  activities aiding, 34–35, 272
  description of, 21, 143
secure bases, 50
self-awareness, 61, 209, 249–50, 303
The Self-Blamer ego, 308–9
self-care, 46–47, 73, 228–29
  practices/movement for, 224–25, 230–37
self-esteem, 179, 195, 298
self-expression, 39, 74–76, 81, 178, 199, 260–70, 272, 301
self-harm, 37, 203–4, 215
The Self-Saboteur ego, 306–7
Sentinelese people, 131, 137
serotonin, 95, 98
sexuality, 200, 212, 215, 315
shadow selves, 314–18

shame, 7, 10, 20, 102, 122, 168, 178, 183, *185*, 186, 221, 226, 258, 282, 284–87, 299–309, 311–12, 314–17, 329, 331, 334
   abuse/assault-based, 191–92, 194, 196
   addiction's tie to, 190, 209–16
   attachment insecurity and, 23–25, 29, 32, 176, 191–200, 212–14
   authenticity and, 75–77, 188, 196–204, 216
   autonomy and, 47, 59, 71, 73, 237
   connection's tie to, 190–96, 201–6, 210, 214–18
   cultural basis of, 133–35, 138, 141, 144
   cycle of, 205–9, *206*
   disconnection's role in, 192–94
   emotional wounds and, 187, 190–96
   fear of being seen and, 196–201, 205
   function of, 190–92
   vs. guilt, 196–97, *197*
   physical embodiment of, 204–9
   practices addressing, 189–90, 207–12, 216–17
   responses to, 191, 200–204
   toxic, 191–92
shopping addiction, 205, 212, 214
Siegel, Dan, 100, 290
Skinner, B. F., 47
sleep, 34, 46, 49, 95, 100, 106, 108–9, 116, 141, 163, 229, 234, 320, 334
social connection, 94, 95, 109, 116, 124, 213–14
The Soldier ego, 306

somatic work, 105, 114, 116, 123, 148, 216, 323
   for ancestral release, 127–29
   for healing and attachment repair, 293–94
   for integrating past wounds, 289, 292–97, 304
   via Somatic Activation and Flow Movement, 294–97
   via Somatic Experiencing, 293–94
somatosensory cortex, 223
Sphere One of development, 281–82
   body care in, 229, 235–37
   movement for, 236–37
   practices supporting, 54–57, 230–35
   safety/security's exploration in, 49–57, 228–37
Sphere Two of development, 228, 281–82
   disciplined exploration as focus of, 57–66, 237–48
   movement for, 247–48
   practices supporting, 62–66, 240–47
Sphere Three of development, 228, 281–82
   emotional attunement's exploration in, 67–73, 248–60
   movement for, 258–59
   practices supporting, 70–73, 251–58
Sphere Four of development, 228, 259, 281–82
   movement for, 269–70
   practices supporting, 78–81, 262–69
   self-expression's exploration in, 74–81, 260–70

Sphere Five of development, 228
movement for, 280–81
practices supporting, 85–89, 274–80
purpose beyond selves explored in, 81–89, 270–82
transcendence focus in, 85, 88–89, 270–81
wonder/awe cultivation and, 84–87, 270–75, 277
spirituality, 83–85, 320, 324, 331–33
spontaneity, 6, 82, 272–82
status-oriented parents, 37, 176–77, *185*
Steele, Howard, 23
Steele, Miriam, 23
"Still Face" experiment, 51
stillness, 5, 55–56, 84, 100, 164, 170–71, 248, 271, 275–76, 287–88, 306, 319, 339.
See also rest
stomach, 10, 48, 106–7, 245, 260, 317
and digestion, 97–99, 103–4, 123, 158
storytelling/stories, 140–41, 146–47, 153, 227, 268, 289–90, 297–300, 326, 328, 334–36
Strange Situation studies, 20
stress, 138, 204, 213, 215.
See also panic; trauma
activation-recovery cycle of, 96–97
addiction to, 99–101
ancestral factors in, 112–29, 154, 327–29
beneficial, 93
biological system of, 97–101
chronic, 48, 61, 77, 89, 97–98, 103–11, 166, 251, 338
cycles, 96–97
energy and, 107–8
GBA and, 98–99

HPA and, 97–98
immune system impacted by, 48, 52, 75, 98, 108–9, 196
nervous system impacted by, 7, 11, 46–57, 61, 77, 84, 89, 93–111, 112–29, 166–67, 330
nutrition's impact on, 98–99, 106–7
oxidative, 107–8
physical impact of, 103–11, 123
practices addressing, 94, 101–3, 105–6, 110, 148, 170–71, 272–73
prenatal, 112–13, 116, 120, 125
stress states in, 159–72, 289
substance use, 10, 23–26, 103, 147, 164, 198, 205, 212–15
survival responses, 7–11, 50–53, 96–97, 100, 104, 134, 139, 158, 186, 196, 200, 325, 330, 338
being stuck in, 167–72
integration process for, 289, 292–94
misunderstanding, 166–67
negativity bias in, 153–55
practices exploring, 165–66, 170–72, 291–94
stress states associated with, 159–67, 289

Tedeschi, Richard, 322–23
Tiger Parents, 37
toxic positivity, 330
transcendence, 218, 228, 270–73
post-suffering, 85
practices supporting, 88–89, 274–81
trauma, 9, 77, 84–85, 104, 134, 207, 286
from abuse, 26, 69, 102, 168–69, 216, 298
ancestral, 113, 116, 118, 121–25, 132, 154, 327

Index

attachment styles and, 20, 22–27, 31, 34, 38, 40, 69, 94, 96
  family, 297–300, 305, 306
  growth post-, 319–37
  integration of, 289–97, 320, 322–27, 330–32, 334–35
  and nervous system, 94, 156–57, 166–67, 289, 292, 294
  phantom, 122–24
  transgenerational, 121–24, 131–32, 154, 327–29
  treatments for, 125, 234, 272, 320
Tronick, Edward, 51
truth
  as developmental need, 237–39, 260–67
  in storytelling, 198, 203, 298–300, 326, 331–33

uninvolved parents, 38, 180–81, *185*

vagus nerve, 97, 106, 123, 158, 204, 234, 273
van der Kolk, Bessel, 156, 299
vasovagal syncope, 164–65
ventral vagal pathways, 159

wholeness, 1, 5, 6, 238, 261
  ego's tie to, 301–13
  family stories and, 297–300
  integration as tool for, 282, 285–318, 336
  practices supporting, 291–92, 294–97
  reconnecting to, 85–89, 172, 271–72, 283–318, 336
  resilience as need for, 84–85, 319–39
  our shadow's tie to, 313–18

window of tolerance (for stress), 100–101, 169, 250–51
withdrawal, 21, 40, 51, 94, 141, 154, 161–62, 175–76, 179–80, 191, 195, *197*, 201, 205, 222, 302, 308, 311, 317, 326
  substance, 213
wonder, cultivation of, 6, 8, 84, 87–88, 270–75, 277, 337
wounds, inner-child. *See also* attachment style(s); emotional wounds
  attachment, 19–45, 210, 289–300
  cultural, 142, 144
  emotional, 3–13, 148–49, 153–57, 167, 172–87, *185*
  glimmers supporting, 171–72
  integration of, 282, 283, 285, 289–300
  practices exploring, 165–66, 170–72, 186
  reparenting process for, 221–82
  resilience as tool for, 319–39
  shame's tie to, 7, 10, 20, 23–25, 29, 32, 59, 71, 73, 75–77, 102, 122, 133–35, 138, 141, 168, 176, 178, 183, *185*, 186–87, 188–218, *197*, *206*, 221, 226, 237, 258, 282, 284–87, 299–309, 311–12, 314–17, 329, 331, 334
  survival responses/states and, 158–72, 289
  transgenerational, 121–22, 131–32, 154, 327–29
  types of, 172–87, *185*

yin and yang, 286–88
Yoga Nidra practice, 234
Young, Jeffrey, 22

ABOUT THE AUTHOR

Dr Nicole LePera is the *New York Times* bestselling author of *How to Do the Work* and *How to Be the Love You Seek*, as well as the workbook *How to Meet Your Self*. She was trained in clinical psychology at Cornell University and the New School for Social Research and studied at the Institute for Modern Psychoanalysis of Philadelphia. She is a holistic psychologist whose work addresses the connections among the mind, body, and soul, incorporating overall lifestyle and psychological wellness practices. She is the creator of the SelfHealers Circle, a membership platform where people from around the world join together in community to take healing into their own hands.